BELL'S SCOTTISH CLIMBS

BELL'S SCOTTISH CLIMBS

by

J. H. B. BELL

Selected and introduced by
Hamish Brown
with a Foreword by Patricia Bell

LONDON
VICTOR GOLLANCZ LTD
1988

First published in Great Britain 1988
by Victor Gollancz Ltd,
14 Henrietta Street, London WC2E 8QJ

First published in Gollancz Paperbacks 1988

Originally published in *A Progress in Mountaineering*
(Oliver & Boyd) 1950

British Library Cataloguing in Publication Data
Bell, J. H. B.
   Bell's Scottish climbs.
   1. Mountaineering—Scotland   2. Scotland
   —Description and travel—1981–
   I. Title   II. Brown, Hamish M.
   796.5'22   GV199.44.G72527

   ISBN 0-575-04308-3
   ISBN 0-575-04212-5 pbk

Typeset in Great Britain by Centracet
and printed in Finland by Werner Söderström Oy

CONTENTS

ILLUSTRATIONS

Carn Dearg, Ben Nevis (*photo R. N. Rutherford*)

Summit Cornice, Braeriach (*photo W. S. Thomson*)

Tower Gap, Ben Nevis, summer (*photo Dr W. Inglis Clark*) and winter (*photo R. M. McIntyre*)

The Cioch, Sron na Ciche, Skye (*photo J. H. B. Bell*)

Black Spout Pinnacle, Lochnagar (*photo W. S. Thomson*)

Sgoran Dubh showing C. M. Allan, J. H. B. Bell, D. Myles (*photo Dr D. Myles*)

Buttress of Coire Mhic Fhearchair, Beinn Eighe (*photo Rev. A. E. Robertson*)

The Long Climb, Ben Nevis. Mrs Bell and the author on the Great Slab (*photo J. E. McEwen*)

Glover's Chimney, Ben Nevis (*photo J. E. McEwen*)

The Chasm, Buachaille Etive Mor (*photo J. D. B. Wilson*)

Map and Diagrams

FOREWORD
by Patricia Bell

MY HUSBAND'S BOOK, *A Progress in Mountaineering*, has been out of print for many years, and I am very grateful to Gollancz for republishing the part of it relating to his Scottish climbs. The book was originally commissioned and published by Oliver & Boyd who wanted a book to put into the hands of aspiring young mountaineers to help them technically and inspire them to go from our Scottish Mountains to the greater ranges of the world. He therefore included what he considered as typical Scottish Climbs, and showed how, to begin with, one could learn so much from them. He did not include his best climbs hoping to use them in another book.

He never climbed with a Guide, and was one of the very few in the S.M.C. from 1921 onwards to climb unguided.

He was sad to see so much in the way of ironmongery creeping into climbing. I only knew him to use a piton once, on the Eagle Ridge of Lochnagar. I sometimes wonder whether some of those warriors these days who are doing wonderful severe routes could do some of his routes without these props. He thought nothing of running out one hundred feet of rope on a severe climb, without pitons or running belays between him and his second. He belonged to the generations of climbers who knew that the leader must never fall off, and he never had an accident. Climbing with him, I always had a feeling of absolute security. Although he enjoyed climbing in Vibrams, he considered nailed boots were much safer in Scotland in the winter, and on wet rock. Of course on really severe rock he preferred to abandon his boots and climb in stocking soles. He kept me busy re-footing his stockings—I remember especially, after a day on Craig an Dubh Loch, when I dropped his rucksack with his boots in it, and he descended a gully to the bottom in stocking soles!

His love of the mountains went far beyond the satisfaction of interesting climbs well done, and he enjoyed his "Munro bagging" which he started counting from his sixtieth birthday, saying firmly that hill walking was a form of climbing. He was within twelve tops of completing them when old age caught up with him. For many years he was Honorary President of the Grampian Club, and applauded their dedication to the Munros.

Jim was five foot seven, slightly built and very tough. He had immense stamina, and was a great contrast to his friend Colin Allan, who he used to say was built like a gorilla. Colin would climb anything he could get his hands on, and his boots might wave vaguely in the air (probably lacking some nails) as he hauled himself up. Unfortunately Colin went to South Africa before the war, and was lost to the climbing world.

Jim climbed with younger people before the war and, as editor of the *S.M.C. Journal*, gave others much good advice and encouragement. He continued to climb long after most of his contemporaries had stopped or died. His last rock climb was from Belalp when he was seventy-four, and his last Munro, Sgurr Fhuaran in 1972; but he continued to walk on his beloved Lomonds of Fife and the forests of Auchtermuchty.

His climbing was the most important thing in his life, a great refreshment from his working life. He climbed for fun and as a joy, and never competitively. For him every climb, even if not a first ascent, was an exploration.

His last Munros in 1972 came after a very wet week in Skye, where our activities had been confined to the lower ground. We crossed the Kylrhea Ferry and reached the car park on Mam Ratagan in the late afternoon. We cooked a meal there, and as we sat eating it the clouds rolled away leaving a bit of mist on the Five Sisters of Kintail and, stretched over the mountains, was the most amazing rainbow. The bow was repeated four times inside the bow, and the secondary bow with the colours reversed was outside. We slept there that night and next day descended to Glen Shiel, and set off up Sgurr na Carnach followed by Sgurr Fhuaran. We were slow and tired when we reached its summit at 7 p.m. As the September day drew to its close we reached the glen and started on the long walk back to the car. Finally we gave up the struggle and found a fairly dry seat among the bog-myrtle where we shivered away the night. Then we had an unexpected bonus—a magnificent display of the Merry Dancers (Northern Lights). A fitting climax to a grand climbing career.

Mummery, his great climbing hero, summarized much of Jim's feeling for the mountains—The True Mountaineer.*

* From *My Climbs in the Alps and the Caucasus* by A. F. Mummery

"The true mountaineer is a wanderer, . . . Equally whether he succeeds or fails, he delights in the fun and jollity of the struggle. The gaunt, base slabs, the square precipitous steps in the ridge, and the black bulging ice of the gully, are the very breath of life to his being. I do not pretend to be able to analyse this feeling, still less be able to make it clear to unbelievers. It must be felt to be understood, but it is potent to happiness and sends the blood tingling through the veins destroying every trace of cynicism and striking at the very roots of pessimistic philosophy."

Auchtermuchty   P.B.
1987

INTRODUCTION

by Hamish Brown

WITH A PARTY of school kids I once arrived at the hostel at Achnashellach to find Gerry, the owner, rather worried. His concern was over the non-return of an old couple who had gone off that morning to tackle the distant Munros of Bidean a' Choire Sheasgaich and Lurg Mhor. While assessing the situation I asked if he had their names. "Jim and Pat Bell," Gerry said. "They seemed to be quite experienced." My reaction was to suppress a laugh. "Aye, they're experienced—and probably indestructible. I wouldn't do anything about them till midday tomorrow. We might meet them, anyway, as those Munros are our objective too."

We had our long day (to claim the school's "last Munro"), met nobody but, on return, found Jim and Pat sunning themselves on the garden seat. "Och, we just ran out of time so we found a good howff and slept in it. Nae problem. We had some chocolate and a wife's a grand help in keeping you warm."

Bell at this time was in his seventies. He had decided sixty was the right age at which to start the salvationist game of Munro-bagging, ignoring the hundreds of Munros he had done before then. One of the boys in our gang had been on a pre-war Bell route on Ben Nevis and found it almost beyond belief that this could be the same J. H. B. Bell. "But, Hamish, he's history"—which is really quite a good summing-up of a remarkable climber who, as this lad had discovered, was a legend during his own life. Sadly he died before completing his Munros (Pat has done so) but he took the line "You've got to give the mountains a bit of a chance." Bell had enjoyed the mountains for a long lifetime and was a walking contradiction of the comment, "there are plenty old climbers, plenty bold climbers but few old *and* bold climbers". It was a great privilege to have met him on that occasion.

Charlie Gorrie, a fellow teacher at Braehead School, had known Jimmy Bell for many years and it was through him that we were first introduced. The kids found Bell fascinating and I've a memory of us stopping the school bus *en route* to Glencoe to call in on the Bells, then living in Clackmannan. An individualistic (if not eccentric) couple, they produced a vast pot of soup for the gang. One kid described it later as "coloured water and raw vegetables". The resigned-polite behaviour as the kids munched their soup had Charlie and me desperately trying not to catch each other's eye. "Jimmy always could be guaranteed to enliven things," Charlie commented as we drove on, and he recounted the story of the first ascent of the North Post on Creag Mheagaidh in June 1936, a day of sweltering heat that saw the party reach the lochan below the cliffs dressed in boots only.

Jim Bell, Iain Ogilvie, Colin Allan and Charlie Gorrie made the team and the day was almost given over to the lochan rather than the hill (Bell was an enthusiastic swimmer), but eventually, in various states of dress or undress, they ambled up to the crags and Bell led up the first pitch. This proved quite difficult in gym shoes, and Iain, seconding, yelled up to Bell that he'd better have a decent belay. "Of course I've got a good —— —— belay," Bell retorted. "Safe as houses." Iain struggled up and finally landed on the stance, a minute ledge; and there was Jim Bell busy pulling on his tatty breeches, the rope held between his teeth.

Creag Mheagaidh was just the sort of place Bell would have been attracted to. The Posts are serious winter routes of over 400 metres, while in summer they present frightening, steep, mica schist. Bell was to observe that the rock of these crags formed "a fertile subsoil for lichens and other vegetation, and they abound in undercut faces and ledges which thin out and peter away into nothingness". Wedderburn, one of Bell's partners, who sadly did not survive the war, put it more bluntly, "the faces would be easier if turned upside down". Bell, like Patey a couple of generations later, was a great explorer. Neither, in his time, could be matched for his delight in wandering up places which more timid venturers quietly passed by.

The Centre Post was climbed by Bell and Allan in March 1937, and "Bugs" McKeith, in his original Guide, was content to reckon it "one of the most impressive routes on the mountain", while an earlier winter climb, Staghorn Gully (1934), is still a popular route. Creag Mheagaidh is most famous as a winter climbing ground. It has been plastered with routes by many fine climbers (Patey, Brown, Robertson, McKeith, Harper, Marshall, Haston, MacInnes to mention a few), yet

Bell's routes of fifty years ago still hold their place. Indeed, "he's history."

Bell's reputation is enshrined in many memories and sayings, the most famous perhaps being his, "Any fool can climb good rock, but it takes craft and cunning to get up vegetatious schist and granite." This comment arose on a journey to Lochnagar and the first ascent of Parallel Buttress with W. H. Murray who describes the day in *Mountaineering in Scotland* (1947), a book which, with Bell's *Progress* (1950), was to be a great influence on all aspirant climbers for many years.

W. H. Murray, in *Undiscovered Scotland* (1951), quotes his own diary of October 1938 about an ascent of Elephant Gully on the Brack. The party was Dr J. H. B. Bell, Dunn, MacAlpine, Garrick and Murray. "A foul and dismal day. Elephant Gully lies across Glen Croe from the Cobbler and splits a great crag 600 feet below the summit. A gully 300 feet high with vegetation enough to feed all the elephants that ever were. . . . After reaching the summit I was so wet and the wind was so numbing that I persuaded Bell to climb with me down the gully again, where at least we had some shelter. We finally left Bell in Glen Croe in torrential rain, and the last we saw of him he was dancing about on the main road naked, preparatory to a bathe in the river."

It is interesting to see the youthful Bill Murray respectfully entering "Dr" J. H. B. Bell in his diary and, more than once, in his first book there are references to Bell which reflect lessons learnt from the master. A second Bell chapter in *Mountaineering in Scotland* tells of an ascent of Tower Ridge in winter. Read them again after you've finished this book. Read too, if the Alps have called, the Alpine chapters of *A Progress in Mountaineering* and also Harry Calvert's biography of Frank Smythe, *Smythe's Mountains*, for its insights on the major escapades these two unpretentious climbers shared. Smythe wrote the original Foreword to *A Progress in Mountaineering* and some of it is worth quoting:

"We first met at Wastdale and began our climbing on the British hills. This is one of Dr Bell's tenets . . . there is no better preliminary training than the hills of Scotland, the Lakes and Wales. . . . Mark well what Dr Bell writes about the importance of small beginnings . . .

"I should like to cap his story of our Jungfrau traverse with another. We had spent an expensive night at the Jungfraujoch Hotel, for prices in Switzerland are directly proportional to the height, and the Jungfraujoch is the highest in Switzerland. As we left I heard Bell muttering about the magnitude of the bill. The path cut across steep snow slopes . . . we came on a stout Teuton, edging sideways with shut eyes, moaning piteously 'Schwindel! Furchtbarer schwindel!' Quick as a flash Bell turned to him and said, 'Ay, man, you're right. It was a swindle, a —— swindle!' "

To me the pungent humour and forthright speech are an abiding memory, but these were a reflection of his irrepressible zest for life, on and off the hills. He was thorough and authoritative. For an unrivalled twenty-four years (1936–1959) he was editor of the *Scottish Mountaineering Club Journal*. Naismith, founder of the club, was alive in 1936, Patey in 1959 was telling of a wee trip to Rakaposhi. Bell was the natural successor to men like Naismith, Collie, Ling and others in his commanding knowledge of Scotland whole, rather than of any one area. He made first ascents from Goatfell to Ben Hope and from Skye to Lochnagar. Torridon, Applecross, Sgoran Dubh, Creag Mheagaidh, Creag an Dubh Loch all received visits, while in Glen Coe, on Ben Nevis or the Cairngorms the classic routes are many: Spillikin Route, Diamond Buttress, Eagle Buttress, Green Gully (now credited to Raeburn in 1906!), the Centre Post, the Long Climb, these still receive regular ascents.

Dr Bell packed in this remarkable record with very limited leisure time. Being a busy industrial chemist (D.Sc., Edinburgh 1932), he was often not free at weekends till midday on the Saturday. His twenty-three visits to the Alps were seldom of more than two weeks' duration. He also made two visits to Russia, climbing with a one-time student friend and visiting the Caucasus—travelling out with loads of equipment, unavailable in Russia in those days. Notes of these and other hard climbs were saved for a sequel to *Progress* and can only be found in journals of the period.

His interest in political theory, philosophy and music were pursued with equal vigour. He was widely read, and liked nothing better than a good-going argument on any topic. I can recall him once so craftily orchestrating his points that his opponent, equally loquacious, ended advocating the opposite argument to the one he'd held at the start. Jim would puff at his old clay pipe and relish every moment of his social life. (He grew his own tobacco and also made unusual wines.) His language was of the "robust" variety, in broad Fife dialect, so he could appear rather awesome on a first meeting but, as Bill Murray put it, "I never met a tougher character, nor a kinder man." He did not enjoy formal social occasions, like Dinners, and could not be persuaded to become S.M.C. President. He enjoyed the more relaxed atmosphere of the Grampian Club.

James Horst Brunnerman Bell was born in 1896, his father being a minister at Auchtermuchty. His mother was of German extraction. It was from this Fife village that Jim, as a teenager, found his way to the hills and to which he and his wife retired. Auchtermuchty looks across to the Lomond Hills but the young Bell was soon cycling further afield, perhaps to climb Schiehallion as a day trip or, at sixteen, cycling from Newtonmore to climb Ben Nevis. Later came visits to Wales and the Lakes and the discovery of Glen Coe. He and his sister Ilse left their names in the box in Ossian's Cave in 1920. His rather solitary apprenticeship he always regarded as an invaluable experience. In 1921 he was fortunate enough to fall in with Frank Smythe (recently invalided out of the R.A.F.), who became a firm friend. They were climbing in the Alps a year later and Bell had joined the S.M.C. In 1924 Smythe and Bell made the fourth traverse of the Cuillin ridge and they shared leads for some of the hardest routes of the period as well as recording the first of his seventy new routes, a contribution that only ended in 1950 with a climb on A' Mhaighdean with his wife Pat. In between were first ascents of diverse character and standard. Like Patey, years later, Bell was content just to be there, generous and open, for whatever any mountain or cliff had to offer. His ranging round Scotland and his long *S.M.C. Journal* editorial work brought him in contact with many young climbers. He and Graham Macphee sowed seed in a period which had been largely fallow since the days of Collie and Raeburn. He met and influenced most of the rising "tigers" (Mackenzie, Murray, and company) and was ever ready to climb with novices. A good clutch of his new routes were done with women: V. Roy, N. Forsyth, and Pat, with whom he spent several of his last seasons exploring Wester Ross.

Bell was not a stylist, but a keen eye, suppleness, craft, and cunning learnt of long experience, allowed a singularly direct approach, as logical and concise as anything else he did. "Vigour of mind pairing with vigour of body," in Bill Murray's words. He was prepared to tackle rocks and conditions which few others would consider. In the wet he would climb in stocking soles. He never had an accident and one can only wonder how some of today's heroes would fare given the gear and lack of protection which were normal then. Bell's fertile imagination would have been fascinated by our new techniques and equipment. He tried out hollow steel tubing on ice (see p. 226) and did not hesitate to bang in a peg on Lochnagar in 1939. Bell used crampons long before most people, but winter-climbing was not a special interest—the rocks then just happened to have snow and ice on them!

The *S.M.C. Journal* of 1976 has an unprecedented ten pages of obituary material which reflect both what Bell had done and what he was. A final anecdote from Alex Small: "Often in the company of Sandy Wedderburn we would, after attending a concert, compress ourselves into the redoubtable Austin Seven and head out for Glencoe, Jim driving with his legs wrapped in a rug against the cold and invariably taking his logically direct route over the Anniesland roundabout, discoursing the while— Marx, dialectical materialism, Engels, Russell, Mozart, civil rights, Cambridge and more supporting proof of his theory that there had to be three concurrent factors to induce a major accident. Kingshouse would appear out of the dark and stiffly we entered."

A Progress in Mountaineering was not Bell's first book. In 1940 Batsford published the popular survey, *British Hills and Mountains* (Bell, Bozman & Blakeborough), to which Bell contributed the Scottish section. The *S.M.C. Journal* has scores of his notes over the years and his lengthy editorship of that journal was a literary feat in its own right. Bell's *Progress* (as it was affectionately called) became a sort of mountaineer's "Pilgrim's Progress" to those of us who were young tyros in those years. Right up to the time of the new gear and techniques the book remained a unique combination of practical instruction and personal inspiration. If Murray occasionally led us into the clouds, Bell kept our feet firmly on the ground. The authoritative 1957 history *Mountaineering in Britain* by R. W. Clark and E. C. Pyatt notes, "The writings of Bell and Murray have been a persistent and all-pervading influence" and, of Bell, that "as early as 1924 there had appeared one name which was to play one of the most important parts in Scottish mountaineering during the succeeding quarter of a century." His position had not changed in the subsequent quarter of a century but his book had become a scarce and treasured collectors' item.

Bell's writing is concise yet packed with good things. Being 424 pages long, however, *Progress* stood poorly in the line of classics deserving re-issue. By dropping most of the dated (but fascinating) technical sections and keeping to the Scottish portions, Gollancz have been able to give us what many would regard as "the best of Bell". Personally I find the Alpine chapters the most exciting so, if enough of us say so, perhaps Gollancz will give us a follow-up volume. What I am sure of is that, with this book read, Bell will join your pantheon of "special" people (he would hoot at the word "hero")—and you will want another swig at his literary bottle. This Bell is the best of malts.

Kinghorn   H. B.
1987

BELL'S SCOTTISH CLIMBS

I

GLENCOE

I FIRST SAW Glencoe in June 1919, when on a walking tour with a friend of my student days. We left our bicycles at Bridge of Orchy station to be forwarded to Tulloch by rail. Then we proceeded on foot along the old road by beautiful Loch Tulla and the Blackmount. Tom Lumsden was not a mountaineer, but he had a keen appreciation of the grand things of nature and delighted in hill walks over rough country. His clear and active mind derived contentment and fresh interest from the Scottish Highlands, although he was essentially a thinker in science and sociology. It was one of my regrets that I could never persuade him to take to rock climbing. Mountaineering has owed a great deal to men of his type, such as Forbes, Tyndall and many others.

We were fascinated by the noble outline of Buachaille Etive Mor, as we came down the long stretch of rough road past Black Rock cottage to Kingshouse, and even more as we continued past the Study and down the gorge of Glencoe, with the evening sunshine lighting up the Three Sisters and the cone of Stob Coire nan Lochan which, from that point of view, conceals Bidean nam Bian and dominates the wild grandeur of Glencoe. We slept at Clachaig that night, and next day, in the company of D. H. Menzies, who had just returned from climbing in the Cuillin, traversed the three high tops of Bidean. It was a perfect introduction to the mountains of Glencoe, and I have never forgotten it.

In the years which have followed I have spent numberless week-ends on these mountains. Their charm has never palled, either in summer or winter. It might be some rock-climbing problem on Buachaille Etive, some snow and ice expedition up the gullies or ridges of Bidean, some days that were failures owing to storm and rain, or simply to an ill-planned piece of exploration: yet every occasion contributed something of interest, enjoyment and permanent value. There were delightful summer camps in Glen Etive, the best of them when we used sleeping sacks without tents, or even a wet night in sleeping

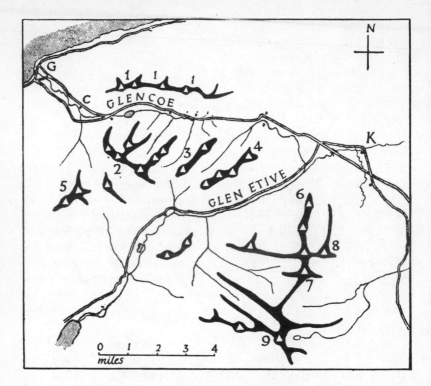

GLENCOE AND BLACKMOUNT

	PEAKS	Height in feet
1,1,1	Aonach Eagach Ridge	3167
2	Bidean nam Bian	3766
	Ridge to N.W. goes over Stob Coire nam Beith	
	Ridge to N.E. over Stob Coire nan Lochan, and forks left to Aonach Dubh and right to Gearr Aonach	
	The easterly ridge goes N.E. over Beinn Fhada	
3	Buachaille Etive Beag ridge	3,129
4	Buachaille Etive Mor ridge (climbs on N.E. peak) . .	3,345
5	Sgor na h-Ulaidh	3,258
6	Sron na Creise	2,952
7	Clachlet	3,602
8	Meall a' Bhuiridh	3,636
9	Stob Ghabhar	3,565
K	Kingshouse Inn	
C	Clachaig Inn	
G	Glencoe Village and Hotel	

sacks under one of the bridges of the new Glencoe road in the gorge: there were delightful swimming pools in the Etive, in Loch Etive, in the gorge of Glencoe where the river is always cold and clear on the hottest day of summer, or in the little loch below Clachaig by the side of the old road. And there were amusing convivial gatherings in the old Clachaig Inn before it was modernized and made attractive to the touring motorist, and many more in Kingshouse under successive landlords. All these are delightful memories of the companionship and free-masonry of the mountains.

There were not so many climbers in Glencoe in the old days, especially in the winter months. The new road, completed round about 1931, conferred many benefits on the week-end climber, but I cannot help thinking that it has also taken some good things away, indefinable though these may be. At least in the depths of a snowy winter, nature reasserts her empire for a time, and one is content to reach the summits of Buachaille and Bidean by the simplest, time-honoured ways.

The Glencoe area, now owned by the National Trust for Scotland, is by far the most accessible for Scottish climbing of reasonable length, variety and difficulty. It is not to be compared with the Cuillin or Ben Nevis, but it is a very good second. Its mountains, Bidean nam Bian (3,766 ft), Buachaille Etive Mor (3,345 ft), and the Aonach Eagach ridge north of Glencoe (3,167 ft), all carry a good deal of snow in winter, especially in their northern and north-eastern declivities. Glencoe has the distinction of possessing the two longest and finest British gully climbs—the Chasm of Buachaille Etive Mor and the Clachaig Gully of Sgurr nam Fiannaidh, both far superior to the Waterpipe Gully in the Cuillin. Best known to English climbers are, no doubt, the Crowberry Ridge of Buachaille, the Church Door Buttress of Bidean and the moist rift of Ossian's Cave, high above Loch Achtriochtan.

Especially during the last quarter of a century, the merits of Glencoe as a first-class centre, both for rock-climbing and difficult winter climbing on snow and ice, have become much more widely appreciated. In this chapter we shall indicate where the easier and safer rock climbs are to be found, a matter which is often neglected or cursorily handled in guide books which are written by experts for experts. As to the more difficult expeditions, one or two will be described which, in the author's opinion, are typical of the best which Glencoe has to offer, from the point of view of mountaineering value rather than exceptional difficulty.

Structure and Geology

The geology of the Glencoe mountains is of great interest and has much to do with their excellent climbing possibilities. Here there is a great modification, in quite a small area, of the general character of the Highland rocks, away from the usual, metamorphic, ancient schists, owing to the intrusion of subsequent igneous rocks. In Glencoe there were many successive lava flows during the Old Red Sandstone period. They were of two types: andesites which flowed freely, and subsequently the more viscous rhyolites which formed thicker beds and which now afford excellent climbing rock. This rock occurs, not only in Glencoe on the upper tiers of cliff on the west face of Stob Coire nan Lochan and on Stob Coire nam Beith, but also on Buachaille Etive Mor where it forms the best climbing rock of the district. The latest lavas are typified in the hornblende-andesite found near the summit of Bidean nam Bian. Simple mountaineers call it trap rock when they climb the Church Door Buttress of Bidean or some of the cliffs on the north-east face of Stob Coire nan Lochan.

Geologists speak of the Cauldron Subsidence of Glencoe. It is no longer a subsidence, as the rocks within the area have been more resistant to the erosive action of time than the surrounding masses. Hence they, nowadays, stand up as mountains. The area is bounded by an oval-shaped geological fault, about eight miles long by five across. Inside are the volcanic lavas, as well as some agglomerate or consolidated volcanic ash: outside are the old schistose rocks. Along the fault line is a granite intrusion, pushed up in a molten state by the subsiding core. The granite is still found on An t-Sron.

It is well, however, to remember that the present-day contours of the mountains have been developed long since the time when the foundation rocks were laid. In the tertiary period, long afterwards, there was probably a river running from Ardgour, in the west, across the present site of Loch Linnhe through Glencoe and eastwards to Rannoch Moor. It is likely that the glen was carved out by this river, although the drainage is now divided by the watershed west of Altnafeadh. In the more recent, quaternary age there has been much glacial erosion, as elsewhere in Scotland, leaving moraines and rock-basin lakes like Loch Achtriochtan.

Even although the contours have been so vastly altered since the Old Red Sandstone age, it is worth while for climbers to consider that the igneous rocks then extruded now form the actual core of the Glencoe peaks and the cliffs on which they climb. The excellence of the rock depends on the composition, texture and system of joints developed while the original lavas cooled. As the forces of erosion must also be guided by the original characteristics of the rocks it follows that the present-day outlines of the mountains are, to a large extent, determined by these ancient volcanic upheavals.

Easy Ways and Easy Rock Climbs

The Glencoe area provides excellent opportunities for climbing of all grades of difficulty, both in summer and winter conditions. The mountains and the types of rock are sufficiently variegated. Climbing is available on ridges, gullies, chimneys and faces. There is ample opportunity in winter for testing one's ability on all kinds of snow and ice, though not so good as on Ben Nevis, where the snow and ice persist later into the spring, owing to the greater height of the mountain.

Before doing any difficult rock climbing or any serious winter climbing it is well to be familiar with the appearance and layout of the prominent ridges, crags, gullies and corries in snowless conditions. This can usually be combined with some easy rock climbing. In fact, it ought to be. The first thing is to learn the easy ways off the mountain, in case bad weather or nightfall should overtake the party.

There are two useful, easy lines of descent from Buachaille Etive Mor. A descent to Glen Etive is started by following the ridge southwards from the cairn on Stob Dearg until it begins to bend steeply down to the right towards the next saddle. An easy scree slope runs down towards Glen Etive for a long way, but one must avoid a steep section near the bottom, either by the corrie on the left (the shortest way to the road) or, still easier, by the right. For the descent to the Glencoe road one turns right off the top ridge, making for the top of the easy shoulder opposite Altnafeadh. A more direct route towards Altnafeadh would be down the Great Gully, which offers only moderate difficulty in summer, but may be very difficult in winter. This route is not so easy as the other.

Next, one should memorize the main features of the crags facing north and east. The key landmark is that conspicuous pinnacle, the Crowberry Tower, just north of and below the summit. It stands out best from the Glencoe road about halfway from Kingshouse to Altnafeadh. The Tower crowns the steep mass of rock known as the Crowberry Ridge. Most eastern

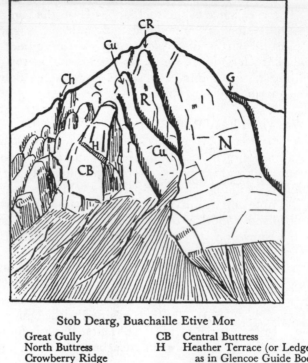

Stob Dearg, Buachaille Etive Mor

G	Great Gully	CB	Central Buttress
N	North Buttress	H	Heather Terrace (or Ledge,
CR	Crowberry Ridge		as in Glencoe Guide Book)
R	Rannoch Wall	CC	Collie's Route
CuCu	Curved Ridge	Ch	Chasm

climbing routes converge on the Crowberry Tower. It is well to recognize it from Glen Etive also. With the help of a sketch diagram of the climbs they can all be picked out by their position relative to the Crowberry Ridge. Towards Glencoe there are in succession the long, deep Crowberry Gully, the broad, impressive North Buttress and the Great Gully. There are now quite a number of routes beyond this. In the opposite direction from Crowberry Ridge we have the Easy Gully flanked on its left by Curved Ridge, the easiest continuous rock climb on the mountain which, once climbed, can be later used as a practice route for descent. Proceeding, we come to D Gully and D Gully Buttress, which merges on its left with a very steep, narrowing face on a broad base, traversed at mid-height by a heather terrace running steeply up to the left. This is Central Buttress which affords some good, difficult routes on the sunny side of the mountain. The main landmark on the Glen Etive face is farther south. It is a long, steep cleft, splitting the face for a height of about 1,800 feet and known as the Chasm. Any easy descent must be well to the south of the Chasm.

We may now come to close quarters with the mountain. The Curved Ridge is the best objective. The line of approach should be chosen so as to avoid any tier of rocks or steep slabs. This is not difficult, but it is advisable to locate any prominent landmarks, so that a retreat, if necessary, may be executed safely and easily. There is a little steep section at the base of Curved Ridge which is taken on the Crowberry Ridge side. This approach will give one an idea of where to start a climb on the Crowberry Ridge on another occasion, and also how to cross Crowberry Gully, if bound for North Buttress. The Curved Ridge is very steep in parts, but has good holds and belays. Its upper end is just below Crowberry Tower, and the way to the summit lies short of the Tower Gap and to the left. It is easy to find and to follow. It is a very good idea to use the Curved Ridge as a line of descent. It teaches the party how to use the rope properly without wasting too much time. Only on the steep bits should it be necessary to belay each member of the party and move one at a time.

The next climb chosen might well be North Buttress. It is a broad buttress, and several routes are possible. One must get on to it low enough, before the Crowberry Gully becomes too deep. A good route goes up a sort of ridge near the edge overlooking that gully, but the most interesting way is nearer the middle of the buttress, involving some very steep rock and good practice in short clefts and chimneys. The rock is sound and there are adequate belays.

In cold weather, when northerly winds prevail, the Glen Etive face of the mountain is more attractive. The original rock-climbing route on the mountain, Collie's Route, first done in the year 1894 by Professor Norman Collie, is interesting and fairly easy. First identify the Central Buttress, of which the lower rocks are conspicuous on the left, by reason of a vertical, streaky-looking cliff of alternately bleached and blackened rock. It is often called the Waterslide, though it is not usually wet. To its left is a sort of stepped ridge, a series of rocky buttresses one on top of the other, rather like a giant staircase. Collie's Route started on the left of the lowest buttress and then followed the crest of the ridge. It is an excellent route of moderate difficulty, but a start can also be made on the right. Choose the easiest way on the lower crag, or serious difficulty may be encountered.

There is much broken rock between Collie's Route and the Chasm. The North Wall of the Chasm gives some good sections on moderate rock, with grass and heather in between. Higher up, one can work back towards the upper part of Collie's Route. As this face of the mountain is less definite it offers good opportunities for easy route selection. The novice may also feel attracted to Sron na Creise on the opposite side of Glen Etive. On the side facing Kingshouse one can enjoy 250 feet or more of pleasant climbing on two buttresses and in two gullies, but there is some unsound rock. The Sron offers good gully climbing in snow conditions. There is one other part of the Buachaille which offers good practice. These rocks are situated opposite Altnafeadh at the western end of the mountain, and one can start at a fairly low level. They are convenient to Lagangarbh Hut. The easy ways can be picked out on the spot. They are not easy to describe in detail.

Now for Glencoe proper. One of my earliest rock climbs was the traverse of the Aonach Eagach Ridge which walls in Glencoe on the north side. The entertaining section is narrow and short, but it is good practice to try everything as it comes, including the *gendarmes* which block the ridge at the narrowest part. They can be passed on easy ground, if necessary. One impulse must be sternly repressed—to seek a way down to Glencoe before all the difficulties are well past. This applies particularly if one is going eastward, when it is necessary to get past Am Bodach, in order to make sure of an easy descent to the Glen above the Study. I ought to know something about this ridge, as E. A. M. Wedderburn and I traversed it by night, by the light of the harvest moon in September 1937. The moon chose to obscure itself behind some dense clouds as we were approaching the narrow section, so we sat down and smoked a contemplative pipe. It was a delightful excursion. As a snow expedition it can be very difficult. There is not much good rock climbing on the north side of Glencoe.

On the south side is Bidean nam Bian (3,766 ft), the highest peak of Argyllshire, with its cluster of subordinate peaks and ridges. Before doing any rock climbing one should traverse these ridges. Starting from Clachaig, the route should be over An t'Sron (2,750 ft), Stob Coire nam Beith (3,621 ft), Bidean and then a choice between the eastern or northern ridges. Each has its merits. The shorter expedition crosses over Stob Coire nan Lochan (3,657 ft), then downwards by a long ridge to Aonach Dubh (2,849 ft), which overlooks Loch Achtriochtan.

The best descent is from the col before reaching Aonach Dubh, by the easy Dinner Time Buttress, between two gullies, into lower Coire Beith. There is a little rock to avoid, here and there.

If one goes east from Bidean the route is longer, over Stob Coire Sgreamhach (3,497 ft), and then sharp left over the very long ridge of Ben Fhada (3,120 ft), the northerly nose of which overhangs the gorge of Glencoe. It should be mentioned that between Stob Coire Sgreamhach and Ben Fhada there is a col with a sharp drop just above it. This is best avoided by descending the slope on the east side before coming to the rocky descent. It is best to leave the crest and descend the easy, eastern slopes before reaching the Nose, to the boggy glen of the Larig Eilde. A descent can also be made to the valley on the left, but this should be done much earlier. Most climbers call this the Lost Valley, as its lower end is blocked by a huge, V-shaped accumulation of boulders which conceal and isolate this charming little valley most effectively. A beautiful meadow, with a huge boulder eminently suited for practice climbing, makes it an ideal spot for camping. There are a few, deep caves amongst the boulders, which are perfectly dry, even in wet weather. The final descent to the Coe is on the left side of a deep, tree-clad gorge. It is best to go well down-stream from the gorge until the river becomes broad and shallow.

If the ridge-walk just described is taken in the opposite direction some excellent rock scrambling can be enjoyed by going straight up the nose of Ben Fhada above the gorge of the Coe. There is a choice of routes of varying difficulty. It is a good place for practice, and also for judgment in selection of route, so that one may not land into difficulties. There should be no fear of that, however, as everything is in full view from below. The middle one of the Three Sisters, Gearr Aonach, consists of an upper and a lower cliff of good, red rock. This is also suitable for a climb of moderate difficulty, and was, in fact, climbed by Naismith's party in Easter 1898, and again descended by a parallel route. It is worth while to repeat their climb.

On the face of the westerly Sister, Aonach Dubh, is a curious fissure, like a narrow, lofty portal into the interior of the mountain, called Ossian's Cave. The poet is unlikely to have visited the place at all, but it was climbed by Nichol Marquis, a shepherd, in the early nineteenth century. It is easy to ascend a long, steep, inclined grassy ridge to the left of it, and then to work across a watercourse to another inclined terrace, leading up to the right below the cliff on which the Cave is situated. The final 100 feet, Ossian's Ladder, is not so easy. The rock holds are masked by vegetation, often very wet, and the descent can be awkward and difficult, as there are no good belays for a rope. The Cave is an impressive eyrie, with a steep, stony floor, and very uncomfortable. It does not go far back, and is usually wet. It contains a metal box for visitors' cards. It is not to be recommended as an expedition, as accidents have occurred. Parties have been stuck there for the night and rescue parties called for. By following the terrace below the Cave for a considerable distance to the right it is quite easy to work one's way through the broken, upper crags on to the summit of Aonach Dubh.

Better rock for moderate climbing is available on the buttress to the right of Dinner Time Buttress, overlooking Coire Beith, but not on the lowest tier of rock. There is some very good rock on the middle and upper tiers, the approach being by the gully to the right of Dinner Time Buttress. There are many interesting possibilities and a few, good routes a good deal farther to the right on these same tiers of rock. In fact, one would never expect from below to find a huge amphitheatre of steep crags in that quarter. Most of the climbing, as well as the approaches, are difficult.

The best place of all for good, moderate rock climbing is on the northern face of Stob Coire nam Beith, the grand, pyramidal, rocky peak which fills the skyline above Coire Beith, as seen from the foot of Loch Achtriochtan. It is a large face of rock and demands some study, but the diagram will help. First identify the long Arch Gully near the left edge of the continuous rocks. The Arch is not easy to see unless one is close under it. The two buttresses on either side of Arch Gully give good, longish, moderate rock climbs. The Crack Climb, to the right of these, is excellent, but a good deal more difficult. My earliest climb on these cliffs was No. 4 Buttress (long before the numerical nomenclature was adopted). I had a novice with me, and the buttress gave us an excellent, easy climb. The buttress is on the right of the Deep-cut Chimney. After the first stretch to the right one follows the crest to the left, and the route can be considerably varied. The upper rocks of the Stob turn out to be quite easy, and all the rock is very sound. The Arch Gully is moderately difficult up to the base of the final obstacle, a severe triple chimney, over a hundred feet high, which was first

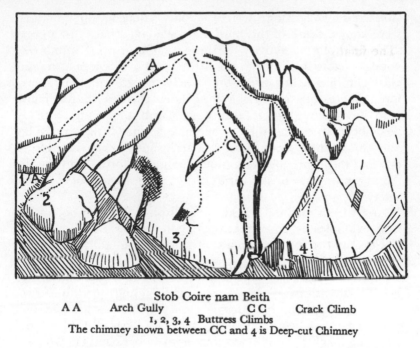

Stob Coire nam Beith
A A   Arch Gully   C C   Crack Climb
1, 2, 3, 4 Buttress Climbs
The chimney shown between CC and 4 is Deep-cut Chimney

climbed by Colin Allan and myself in November 1933. The
pioneers, led by Mr G. D. Abraham, avoided this pitch by
climbing out of the gully on the right-hand side, and so gaining
the upper rocks fairly easily.

The eastern side of Stob Coire nan Lochan offers one
moderate, classic rock climb. This is the middle, north-eastern
buttress, called Raeburn's Buttress. It could be taken as a
sequel to a climb on Aonach Dubh. One starts up to the right,
from the bottom of the deep gully between the central and
southern buttresses. This is stepped trap rock with one or two
small chimneys. Above this one is faced with the steep upper
wall, one part of which is rather difficult, where one has to
traverse left along a thin flake and climb on to a shelf above,
with very little in the way of holds. The climb finishes easily
enough. Raeburn's Buttress makes an excellent and very difficult climb under snow conditions.

More difficult Rock Climbs
A few years ago it would have been little exaggeration to say
that the Crowberry Ridge of Buachaille Etive Mor, the Church
Door Buttress of Bidean nam Bian and the traverse of the

Aonach Eagach Ridge were the only Glencoe climbs which were known south of the Border. Nowadays, thanks to a great spurt of exploring activity on the part of a growing number of younger Scottish climbers, the attractions of Glencoe as a first-class climbing centre are more widely recognized. It is, therefore, unnecessary to describe these older, classical routes. Those who have proved their ability to climb the routes already described can extend their experience to the Crowberry Ridge and the Church Door Buttress, and should even be able to descend the former in its original or simplest form (omitting the Abraham traverse or the variation by Speirs) with comparative safety.

Apart from medium length face climbs, of which one of the best examples is Agag's Groove, Glencoe is outstanding in possessing two of the longest and grandest gully climbs in Britain. The Chasm of Buachaille Etive Mor is described in a separate chapter. Clachaig Gully, at the foot of Glencoe, has been dealt with by W. H. Murray, the leading spirit in its first ascent in 1938, in his *Mountaineering in Scotland*. These two gullies, strongly contrasted in character, are of fairly equal climbing height, about 1,500 feet or so. Most climbers who are familiar with both of them would, I think, consider that the Chasm is the harder and more variegated climb. The rock scenery is very grand and the rock remarkably sound, but the existence of more frequent avenues of escape offends some climbing purists. The standard of climbing increases in severity as one ascends.

Clachaig Gully has been a challenge to rock climbers since Norman Collie led the first party to the attack in 1894. Until the successful ascent by Messrs W. H. Murray, A. M. Mac-Alpine, W. G. Marskell and J. K. W. Dunn in May 1938, all previous parties appear to have been stopped by what is now known as the Great Cave Pitch. The pioneers climbed this by a severe route, involving a very difficult traverse, on small holds, on a vertical cliff, high above the pool at the foot of a waterfall. In 1940 I climbed it with John Wilson and Douglas Laidlaw, and we found that, by climbing somewhat higher up steep slabs on the right, the traverse to a grassy niche, from which it was easy to reach the lip of the fall and the top of the pitch, could be made much easier and safer. The hardest pitch of the gully is Jericho Wall, some distance higher. The only severe part is, however, near the bottom. The rock on the upper part is not all sound, and the leader should go fairly high to a good belay and stance. Accidents have occurred when this has not been done. John Wilson, my wife and I revisited the gully on 27 October 1946, a day of hard frost, when the ascent occupied us for six hours. We were of opinion that the Chasm provided more and better climbing, as there were long stretches of very moderate difficulty in the upper part of Clachaig Gully. The latter is, however, an excellent, hard climb, the difficulties commencing about 700 feet above the level of the road. In early summer the profusion of trees, shrubs and ferns in the lower part make it an attractive expedition of an unusual type, but the actual climbing is mostly on very sound rock. The gully carries much less snow in winter than the Chasm, and is usually somewhat drier than the latter. Escape routes are neither frequent nor easy.

Two other gullies should be mentioned. Crowberry Gully on Buachaille Etive is only formidable as a winter route, but offers a good climb of sustained interest in summer. The hardest gully on Buachaille is a narrow rift between North Buttress and Cunciform Buttress, the latter offering a very difficult climb as well, especially if the exit is effected by the upper chimney. The crux of Raven's Gully, which was first led by John B. Nimlin in June 1937, occurs at the fourth pitch. It is in the form of an overhung cave with smooth, vertical sides, and is usually regarded as a problem in combined tactics for a party of three, one of whom belays the others from a recess at the back of the cave. Nimlin, however, accepted no such assistance. I have not tackled the pitch myself, but have seen two very good climbers fall off it, on separate occasions, when I was securing them at the back of the cave. The gully has many good pitches, but none to compare with this in severity.

Shadbolt's Chimney, near Ossian's Cave, on the face of Aonach Dubh, is almost the only classical route which has maintained its place, when judged by modern standards of difficulty. It was climbed in June 1908 by A. C. McLaren and L. G. Shadbolt. The lower section is a smooth, strenuous, orthodox chimney. The middle is a steep face with thin ledges and small holds leading to the crux, which is a short, severe chimney with a welcome belay at the foot. When I climbed it in 1927 I was much impressed by the steepness and difficulty of the face, but very little other climbing seems to have been done there by the modern school.

Colin Allan and I had several happy hunting grounds on the rocks of Bidean nam Bian and its subordinate ridges. We enjoyed several excellent climbs in the Amphitheatre, high up on the western face of Aonach Dubh, and at least one good day on the lower, north-east nose of the same peak. In 1931 we made a direct route up the centre of Diamond Buttress, which faces Church Door Buttress across Central Gully, beneath the summit of Bidean nam Bian. The lower rocks of this 550-foot cliff are somewhat loose, but the interest of the climb continues until within fifty feet of the top, including the ascent of a prominent pinnacle, which is severe. On the upper section there are too many easy ways of escape to one side or the other, but the nature of the rock, hornblende andesite, does not favour continuity of difficulty. We never had any success on the rocks below Aonach Eagach.

The modern school of difficult climbing in Glencoe has shown a tendency to concentrate on the Rannoch Wall and the walls of the North Buttress of Buachaille Etive. Many of these newer climbs are severe in standard and on very sound rock, but there have also been discoveries in several other places.

II

RANNOCH AND GLENCOE IN WINTER

SOME OF THE best winter climbing on the Scottish mountains is available in the Rannoch, Blackmount, and especially the Glencoe areas, often as early as December and always in the early spring. After a heavy snowfall there is often very good weather, most convenient of all if the roads are clear and the snow has become hard and icy on the mountains. There is climbing of all grades of difficulty—easy mountains such as Clachlet and Stob Ghabhar, grand, long ridges such as those of Bidean nam Bian and the Buachailles Mor and Beag, but also difficult gullies and even face climbs on rocks which, although easy in summer, are now transformed into complicated problems of a high Alpine standard of difficulty.

Let us begin with basic mountaineering, getting to the top of the mountain by an obvious, natural route and, if possible, traversing several peaks in the day's expedition. A grand range for this purpose is the arc of hills bordering Rannoch Moor on the south-eastern side. On 6 February 1937, I motored to Bridge of Orchy, climbing Ben Ledi on the way. Four of us gathered there and spent the night at the hospitable cottage of Mrs Morrison, close to the railway station. Sunday dawned clear and cold, with cirrus clouds above and some stratus in the valleys. We left early by car for Achallader farm. Our objective was Ben Creachan (3,540 ft), a few miles to the north-east. After leaving the railway line, where it passes through the lovely old pine wood of Crannach, we struck upwards across the moor. At first the way led through the thinning forest, with alluring glimpses of the sun-kissed summit line of Ben Achallader. Then we, too, were in sunshine, which was so hot that we stripped to the waist. High up on the slope we arrived at a frozen loch below the upper crags. The surface was a curious mixture of contorted waves of snow and ice. It seemed compact, and we crossed it on foot, although two of us crashed in at the last step before landing on the far bank. There we split into two parties, each choosing our own gully for the ascent.

The climbing was not difficult, though we had a few steps to

cut on an awkward, rocky traverse below the narrow part. Near
the top we were again forced to cut steps, as the final slope was
icy, leading up to a small cornice, which we climbed at one
point where it was vertical but not under-cut. As we stepped on
to the ridge the view was magnificent to the east, down the
valley of Glen Lyon to the gleaming snow-caps of the chain of
Ben Lawers. We turned to the left to the summit of Ben
Creachan. Visibility was perfect in all directions. Creachan is
an outpost above the south-eastern corner of Rannoch Moor.
The desolation of this huge expanse was beautifully variegated
by its many sheets of water and the encircling snowy mountains.
We looked down upon Lochs Lyon, Rannoch, Ericht, Laidon,
Ba and Tulla. Bidean nam Bian was somewhat hidden by the
Buachaille, and the peaks of Mamore Forest set off the com-
manding outline of Ben Nevis. To the south-west were the
peaks of Ben Cruachan.

The rest of that day was good, hard ridge walking. The wind
was easterly and most invigorating. It was a day when it was
good to be alive. Life pulsed within, at every step over these
crisp, icy ridges. We passed easily over Meall Buidhe, climbed
up to twin-topped Ben Achallader (3,404 ft), and then swept
downwards to a low saddle, only to climb again steeply to the
summit of Beinn an Dothaidh (3,283 ft). By this time the wind
was much colder and clouds were rising in the west. Far to the
south we could see the serrated outlines of the peaks of Arran
in the Firth of Clyde. Old friends, such as Ben Vorlich, Ben
More and Stobinian, Cruach Ardrain and Ben Lomond came
into view as we progressed along the ridge. The ever-changing
prospect of the surrounding hills and valleys is, indeed, the
major charm of ridge walking.

We were now racing down to the last gap before the final
1,000-foot slog to the last summit of the day, Ben Doran
(3,524 ft). Fighting against time as we were, it was hard, hard
work. We only reached it long after sunset, with the snow
whirling about us in the icy blasts of the east wind. In the haste
of our exertions we had taken no notice of the changes in the
mountain scene about us. All was now a patchwork of deathly
cold hues of grey and livid blue, with one last coppery vestige
of departed day over Ben Cruachan. We hurried back to the
saddle and were down the short, rocky funnel and on to the
moor before night swallowed us up. Our last flounderings over
the ridges of heather and peat were directed by one bright light
which emanated from the kitchen of Mrs Morrison. Arriving

about a quarter past six we were soon enjoying a huge meal before a comfortable fireside. Next day I went over our route on the map and found that we had traversed fourteen miles and climbed 5,800 feet during the eight and a half hours of our outing. If the Scottish mountains grant even one occasional day so delightful and invigorating, the rest of life becomes eminently worth while.

To those who visit these hills, but are more interested in improving their technique in snow and ice gullies, I would recall another day in December 1938 when I climbed from Bridge of Orchy with W. H. Murray. We walked to the beginning of Crannach Wood and made for the northern corrie of Achallader, where we climbed the mountain by hard frozen snow slopes and a rocky gully crowned by a steep cornice. Having traversed Achallader we enjoyed a fast descent to the recesses of the north-western corrie of Ben Dothaidh and ascended the latter mountain by the narrow, steep gully which finishes just to the right of the main summit. This gave us some excellent step cutting in the upper part, and much variation is possible. If there is plenty of snow it is possible to glissade from the top of Dothaidh for about three-quarters of the way down to the railway, using one of several shallow gullies of no great steepness. This expedition took us about eight hours.

Now let us take a shorter day, from Kingshouse Inn. Again in severe mid-winter conditions, John Wilson and I crossed the moor to the foot of Sron na Creise (2,952 ft), which we ascended by one of its steep gullies. This gave us a good spell of step-cutting in snow-ice, finishing very steeply with a short, difficult eight-foot pitch in a rock chimney, where wedging tactics were necessary in order to get above a chockstone. Then we emerged into brilliant sunshine on the ridge and strode along briskly towards the higher tops. A few streamers of cloud played hide and seek among the peaks of Cruachan to the southward. Only the higher mountains protruded through the level sea of wavy cumulus cloud on that perfect January day. We went on to the summit of Clachlet (3,602 ft) and then returned, dipped to a saddle on a ridge and gained the highest top, Meall a'Bhuiridh (3,636 ft) before returning to Kingshouse in the late afternoon.

Looking southwards towards Stob Ghabhar from the Clachlet, I recalled one of my earliest snow expeditions in 1923 when a party of us walked up Coire Ba and enjoyed a good climb on the northern buttress of Sron a'Giubhas, a northern outlier of Stob Ghabhar. The main attraction of Stob Ghabhar is, how-

ever, a short but exceedingly steep, rocky gully, close under the
summit on the north face, known to climbers as the Upper
Couloir. It is only about 200 feet in height, but comprises two
difficult pitches, the upper of which is often very icy. In 1923
we found it too difficult for us and retreated by the way we had
come. In 1927 it was the scene of an accident which just missed
being a very serious affair. Two parties were on the climb at the
same time. The second man of the upper party had just warned
the leader, who was precariously poised on ice steps near the
top of the upper pitch, that he was not securely placed and
could not hold him if he fell. The second party was watching
the proceedings from a lower stance. At that moment the leader
of the first party slipped, with the result that they both went
hurtling down the icy snow slopes. As the Couloir is very
narrow they cannoned into and detached the other party as
they shot past. Two axes were torn from their moorings in the
snow and the third, having to take all the strain, broke in two.
Fortunately, all the victims came to rest in soft snow before
reaching the edge of a lower line of cliffs. Most of the men
suffered sprains and bruises, but only one casualty had to be
carried down to the road through the long hours of a miserable,
wet and stormy night.

It was, of course, quite wrong for two parties to be on such a
climb at the same time. The primary fault, however, was the
lack of a secure belay for the second whilst the leader negotiated
the severe ice pitch. Even although a longer run-out of rope
would be necessary the invariable rule must be to have a secure
belay in such a situation. It is difficult to comment fairly on the
breaking of an ice-axe. The shaft may have been faulty, but it
is all too probable that the tightening rope exerted its leverage
on the axe at some distance above the snow level. In snow and
ice climbing the rope should be laid round the axe shaft at
ground level, and kept there.

On New Year's Day, 1936, I climbed the Couloir with
A. McClure. We found the first pitch fairly easy. The upper
pitch promised better prospects on the right, but when McClure
tried that route he found dry, incoherent snow lying on thinly
glazed rock. So the next attempt was made up an icicle-fringed
wall in the left corner. I remember getting good holds at crucial
points behind thick icicles. The upper part of the pitch was very
slow work, as every foot- and hand-hold had to be chipped in
hard ice. There is one comforting feature about this Couloir. If
conditions are hard and icy at the crux one is almost certain to

meet with a straightforward slope of perfetly secure, hard snow above the vertical section. Short as it is, the Upper Couloir of Stob Ghabhar must always be treated with respect.

Other straightforward winter expeditions are the traverse of the parallel ranges of the Buachailles of Etive and the traverse, in varied combinations, of the peaks of Bidean nam Bian. So far as my own experience goes I have usually aimed at combining such an expedition with a preliminary ascent, by a route involving some degree of technical difficulty, to the main ridge or one of the peaks. That is not so easy in the short days of December or January, but, in March and April, several hours of good and interesting climbing can be followed by some delightful ridge walking in the later afternoon and early evening. There is no more delightful finish or rounding off to an interesting climb.

On several occasions Colin Allan and I have finished a climb with a snow bath on the summit plateau of Stob Coire nam Beith (3,621 ft), a fitting sequel to our labours in an ice gully or on a rocky face, for there are many practicable winter routes on the rocks of Stob Coire nam Beith, which, though easy in summer, are interesting and difficult when sheathed in snow and ice. To the critical but uninitiated reader a snow bath under such conditions may appear to be an extreme of asceticism or bravado, according to his attitude of admiration or cynicism. In fact, it is neither the one nor the other. It is far less of a shock to roll about in deep, powdery snow on a calm, sunny afternoon than to dive into ice-cold water, and enormously less than the revolting chill of the domestic cold bath, which rudely shatters the peaceful rhythm of the nervous system after a warm and comfortable sleep. In any case, whoever indulges in a snow bath on a mountain crest will continue his progress along the ridges with renewed zest and vigour.

Another easy but rather long winter expedition is the traverse of the twin ridges of the Buachailles Mor and Beag. When Allan and I did so on a day of hard frost in early April we started off with the ascent of the North Buttress of Stob Dearg of the Buachaille Etive Mor. From the southern summit of the ridge, Stob na Broige (3,120 ft), we should normally have glissaded nearly all the way to the Larig Gartain (1,600 ft), between the ridges of Mor and Beag. The snow slopes were so icy that we were compelled to use a more cautious mode of descent, proceeding step by step and hooking in the snow-ice above us with the picks of our axes. A standing glissade would almost certainly have got out of control, tossed us on our backs and battered us about all the way to the saddle. We adopted the same tactics for the descent from Stob nan Cabar, our last peak for the day, at the northerly end of the Buachaille Beag.

According to the text-books one should usually be able to check a slip on snow-ice (or even ice, in the opinion of some optimists!) by holding the pick of the axe down against the surface with the whole weight of the body. This may be so at the very start of the slide. It is only necessary to reflect that the braking force must be steadily applied, that the results will vary inversely with the square of the speed and that irregularities of the surface must give rise to side thrusts which are likely to defeat our best efforts to maintain the pick in the braking position. The divergence between static rule and dynamic experience should beget a wise degree of caution when glissading on snow-ice.

When traversing the Bidean ridges there are several places where splendid, safe glissading is usually feasible into the corries, but one must be assured of a clear run-out of gentle snow slope at the lower end of the glissade. Standing glissades are preferable to sitting, for control is easier and visibility better. It is best to choose the line by a previous inspection from below. Glissades into Coire Beith are usually feasible from the top of Stob Coire nan Lochan, from the col between it and Bidean nam Bian or from the col between Stob Coire nam Beith and An t'Sron. They are not advisable from the Glencoe ends of ridges running down to the Three Sisters. There are also one or two good lines to the head of Coire nan Lochan and to the head of the Hidden Valley between Stob Coire nan Lochan and Beinn Fhada, but there are bands of cliff at various places, and one ought to be sure of one's ground.

More difficult Climbs

The Aonach Eagach ridge, bounding Glencoe on the north, is the best long traverse of the district under hard winter conditions. It is excellent practice for Alpine work. I have been on it in early April when conditions were all that could be desired. Sandy Wedderburn and I ascended the long gully which sweeps down from the ridge to Glencoe and is bounded on the east side by that impressive, rocky nose called "The Chancellor". After a little rock-work near the foot the gully provided a long, uneventful plug up a steep, hard snow slope. The view from the crest of the ridge through the jaws of the Chancellor gully provides a grand setting for Bidean ridges when they are plastered with snow and ice. To the north-west were the jagged, golden outlines of the Cuillin ridges of Skye. Ben Nevis towered over the Mamores and the Aonachs.

The narrow part of the ridge exacted great care and a fair amount of step-cutting, for there were cornices above the cliffs, now on one side and now on the other. W. M. McKenzie has described conditions when there has been a double cornice at one part. It would then be necessary to traverse along the steep slopes below the cornice, sometimes a long and difficult task. Even with a single cornice one should keep very well away from the edge. This, again, is good experience for Alpine work. Except at the narrow section we had no serious difficulty, and it is unlikely that any sections of hard ice will be found in a normal Scottish winter. Such a ridge gives excellent practice for a roped party to move continuously, unless at positions of difficulty where the rope must be secured over an ice-axe and the party move one at a time.

Now for a good gully climb. On 15 March 1936, Allan and I were joined by John Dow and R. L. Beveridge, who wished to ascend the long, steep gully between the Central (Raeburn's) and South Buttresses of Stob Coire nan Lochan, at the head of the corrie between Aonach Dubh and Gearr Aonach. After an early lunch we started up this 500-foot gully. The first pitch was well smothered in snow. It demanded step-cutting of a relatively simple type. Soon we came to the real crux, a formidable wall of ice which was not far short of vertical. This statement has no real, physical significance. It simply means that a climber, whose balance is reasonably good, would be unable to climb such a pitch without cutting both handholds and footholds in the ice, and that he would feel, most of the time, as if he were perched on a steeplejack's ladder, hanging a little backward from his hands. This does not actually imply verticality, as ice steps are both narrow and slippery. But the position is both difficult and tiring to hold for any length of time. Allan did most of the leading. I followed and improved the steps.

He started from under the vertical wall of rock on the left and worked his way up in a rising line, linking up a series of narrow ice pockets and ledges towards the equally perpendicular right wall, and finally reaching the top of a steep, rocky shelf, dripping with icicles. For about 150 feet the difficulty was continuous. It was a grand lead and a strenuous piece of work, as we all recognized when it came to our turn to follow. Then we struck an excellent, steep slope of hard snow-ice at a uniform gradient, which was only varied by one or two minor ice pitches. We made good progress in spite of the hard labour of cutting steps; and the small cornice at the top gave us very little trouble, as it thinned away at one corner into a low wall. I am told that there has been, of recent years, a considerable rock-fall in the gully, so that its climbing qualities are modified. W. H. Murray informed me that, in the early part of the year 1947, the ascent was very severe and icy. W. H. Tilman, the Himalayan climber and explorer who accompanied him, was much impressed by the strenuous and severe nature of Scottish winter climbing.

The quality of such a climb must depend on the type of weather during a period, measured sometimes in terms of weeks rather than days, before the ascent takes place. The Central Gully of Bidean nam Bian is perfectly easy in summer, but Colin Allan and I enjoyed a hard, icy ascent in December. In early January we could make nothing of the South-Central Gully of Stob Coire nan Lochan, on account of much new and powdery snow which was not consolidated to the ice-crusted rock underneath. The Curved Ridge of Buachaille Etive, though an easy route for descent in summer, can be an exceedingly hard climb under severe, winter conditions. Exceptionally heavy snowfalls may often fill up pitches in gullies, leaving steep, uniform slopes of snow, which, after thawing and re-freezing, are excellent for climbing. A much lesser snowfall, followed by a short thaw and a prolonged frost, can convert a gully floor into a thin ribbon of ice. This happened in March 1947 to the Great Gully of Buachaille Etive, which is not normally a hard winter climb. Herein lies the charm and adventure of winter climbing. It is not repetitive work: guide book directions are only of minor value: the work demands initiative and intelligent forethought.

Again and again I have come to realize the benefit of my Scottish winter experience, which cannot be gained by a few casual visits to the hills at Easter time, for climbing in the Alps in summer; especially after bad weather, when ridges and faces, normally easy, are plastered with new snow or icy crust. Naturally, the conditions are very different. Alpine bad weather is usually succeeded by days of brilliant sunshine, and the new snow is quickly stripped from the rocks. In a Scottish winter or early spring the sun has little power, especially on northerly faces.

It may now be of interest to describe two face climbs, chosen because they are by no means difficult in summer conditions. In April 1939, in company with Alex Small and Miss J. McNeill I climbed Raeburn's Buttress on Stob Coire nan Lochan. The day was not particularly cold, but snow was plentiful and great quantities had to be cleared off the ledges in order to make secure stances, so that it took us about an hour to climb sixty or seventy feet; for this was a stepped face of rounded trap rock with very few belays. Having ascended by a loose, open chimney we were faced by an oblique upward traverse where the condition of the snow, betwixt frost and thaw, was somewhat unsound, with a tendency to slide. Avalanches were unlikely owing to the rough, bouldery nature of the underlying rock, but it was well to be careful. Then we got on to a hog-back ridge where it would have been possible to retreat into the north-central gully, which is always an easy way of ascent. The mist thickened as we approached the steep, upper wall of the buttress. When Raeburn's party first climbed the buttress in April 1907 there was no snow at this stage. I had climbed it myself with Colin Allan in 1935 under good conditions, but now I had grave doubts about the short, difficult section at the foot of the wall.

We passed a rock pinnacle by a series of steep ledges and gained a neck behind it. Then came the crux—a mantelshelf on the wall which overhung slightly but seemed to be free of ice. The solution was a low traverse of several yards to the left, an ascent behind a small flake and a strenuous pull up a corner to the ledge above. One more pull landed me on a good ledge with a satisfactory belay, but I was fortunate in the absence of ice on the crucial handholds, and I should never have attempted the move without previous experience of the landing under snow-free conditions. Difficult winter climbing can always be aided by knowledge of the mountain under summer conditions. That was the last difficulty, and we attained the summit ridge by six p.m., enjoyed a splendid glissade down the slopes into Coire Beith and reached the Glencoe road in less than an hour. Raeburn's Buttress must be a very tough proposition in real icy conditions earlier in the year.

My other example concerns the oldest climbing route on the Buachaille, climbed by Dr Collie's party in March 1894. Like many other routes on Scottish mountains it is an old and superior vintage which is best tasted and savoured in very *dry* winter conditions. On 31 December 1944, Ian Charleson and I

were fortunate in getting a lift by car to the head of the Glen
Etive road. The car was due to return to Crianlarich later in
the day, and we were allowed from eleven a.m. until four p.m.
to try our luck on the mountain. That was a short allowance of
time, so that we had practically no halts, eating our sandwiches
at any odd moment. The moor was frostbound and as hard as
iron. It was a perfect winter day with bright sunshine and a
light northerly air. The rock ledges were iced up to a considerable degree, and dry powder snow overlay the whole upper
cone of the mountain.

My first, rather venturesome intention was the ascent of
Central Buttress. It did not take us long to reach the base of the
rocks at its southern end. Charleson started to lead the first
pitch of the route which I had pioneered in 1934. When he was
about thirty feet up I asked for his opinion on our prospects.
The answer was just what I ought to have expected, "Rocks
about 75 per cent iced higher up, but I think I can go on." As
this part was, in summer, of a very moderate standard of
difficulty I could easily guess what the really steep section of
the climb would be like. Our prospects on Central Buttress
were negligible, so we decided to retreat and try something
easier. To the left of the sheer cliff was a snowy gully leading to
a little saddle which gave access to Collie's route. We decided
that here lay our only chance of reaching the summit of the
Buachaille.

From the saddle we ascended as directly as possible, using
short traverses where this was necessary for avoiding the
difficulties. This whole face is characterized by short, steep
walls of rock separated by narrow, heather-covered ledges. The
heather was most useful, as the dry powder snow which lay
upon it protected the rock underneath from icing up. We kept
no count of time. All I remember is that we never relaxed our
progress. The pitches were never long ones, but some were
sufficiently testing for all that. Uncertainty as to the outcome
persisted until we were a little way above the level of the upper
end of Heather Terrace on Central Buttress. The genial sunshine made all this clearing of snow from ledges and crawling
over mantelshelves on our stomachs both endurable and entertaining. At length we reached a good horizontal terrace,
bounded on the left by a vertical drop into a steep, narrow,
curving, snow-filled gully.

The character of the climbing became safer and easier. We
kept up the broken rock ridge with the gully on our left until we

arrived at the base of an upper snow-field. We now looked
upwards to the right across a snowy col to the Crowberry
Tower, and to the left towards another skyline of snow. This
snow-field is not directly underneath the summit rocks; above
it lies another, descending from a saddle high up on the left and
running down to the right to converge on the snow-field below
the Crowberry Tower Gap. It was now close on three p.m. and,
judging from summer experience with an allowance for winter
conditions, we expected to reach the summit in about twenty
minutes. We soon found our mistake, for we had to slash out
steps practically all the way.

The snow structure varied a good deal. In places there was a
polished, icy crust covering dry powder snow, a few inches in
depth, which again covered a much harder, icy surface of old
snow, thawed and re-frozen. This was the Scottish counterpart
of what is known as wind-slab in the Alps: a very dangerous
snow structure on steep slopes, as it tends to break up into
cakes which readily avalanche. Probably it is more compact
and stable in Scotland, but we took no risks where we found it,
securing ourselves with the axes to the firm layer underneath.
We cut straight up, and then to the right, to a little col which
we crossed to the upper snow-field. Then we contoured to the
left, cut straight up the slope to the skyline at the top, traversed
beneath some rocks until we found an easy place to climb up
between them, and finally reached the top of the mountain at
four p.m.

The view was clear and splendid, except to the west where
haze obscured the peaks of Rum and Skye. Nevis, the Mamores
and the Aonachs were brilliant in sunshine. Lochs Rannoch,
Laidon and Ba were a wonderful translucent green, with the
least hint of yellow. Bidean nan Bian looked a great mountain,
majestic and aloof. It was typical, perfect winter colouring. We
were very late and started to descend almost at once. On the
convex summit ridge, frozen to the hardness of concrete and
gleaming with icy plates, the going was difficult. At last we
turned leftwards on to the easy boulder and scree slopes towards
Glen Etive. The boulders were still ice-glazed and the snow
crust broke under our weight at every step. Still, we raced down
the familiar slopes and reached the glen road about five p.m.
with about a mile and a half to walk, expecting that we should
be soundly rated by our friends for being an hour and a half
behind our trysted time. However, it turned out that they, too,
were over an hour late, so that we were justified in pushing the
attack to a finish and securing a perfect winter climb.

In this varied chapter on winter climbing in the Glencoe area no attempt has been made to describe the most difficult expeditions of all; for the main purpose is rather to show the contrast between summer and winter climbing and to point out the likeliest routes and conditions for building up technique on varied types of problem. The hardest winter climbs of Glencoe have been well described elsewhere, for most of them have been carried out by a comparatively small group of Glasgow enthusiasts during the years since 1935. These men were content to face expeditions of anything up to twelve hours' duration and longer. Once they were benighted in December, half-way up the Garrick Shelf Route on the Crowberry Ridge, but they returned to the assault on another occasion and succeeded.

The two most graphic accounts are from the pen of Mr W. H. Murray, in articles which first appeared in the *Scottish Mountaineering Club Journal* and have subsequently formed the core of *Mountaineering in Scotland*, the first book which deals adequately with modern Scottish climbing, particularly under severe, winter conditions. A general account of difficult winter climbing in the Glencoe area has also appeared in the 1947 issue of the *S.M.C.J.* from the pen of W. M. Mackenzie, who was one of the same, small group. These hard expeditions are only for parties in good physical condition, with a long record of Scottish snow and ice expeditions behind them. For such men, who know each other's capacity, the risks, such as they are, can be taken with a large margin of safety, even when the weather changes for the worse. Other parties must examine themselves and count the cost before embarking on the venture; but the rewards are great, especially if a man has the ambition to proceed to the greater Alpine expeditions. Such a man, writes A. F. Mummery, "gains a knowledge of himself, a love of all that is most beautiful in nature, and an outlet such as no other sport affords for the stirring energies of youth; gains for which no price is, perhaps, too high."

III

BEN CRUACHAN IN SNOW

MANY PEOPLE IMAGINE that hills can be climbed with enjoyment only in summer. They have heard of those tough eccentrics who go there in the depth of winter, lose themselves, it is to be hoped without fatal results, but, in any case, oblige rescue parties of police, shepherds and gamekeepers to go and look for them amidst snow drifts as high as a house. All this makes good reading in the newspapers and invites indignant comment from the armchairs by the fireside. The truth is that anyone who had enjoyed a perfect day on the snow-clad Scottish hills in winter has discovered a new experience, the exhilaration of which can hardly be matched by any mountain ascent at midsummer.

On 3 January 1936, three of us left Taynuilt in order to climb Ben Cruachan by an unusual approach from Glen Noe on its northern side. It was a day of bright sun, blue sky, hard frost and clear visibility. We were ferried across the mouth of the river Awe, and then followed a long and delightful track winding through the woods, high above Loch Etive. Far away, at the head of the loch, was the snow-capped dome of Ben Starav (3,541 ft), gleaming in the morning sun. Just before the track left the margin of the loch I went in for my New Year swim from a grassy peninsula. Yes, it was cold, but invigorating. Only the mile or two at the head of the loch was actually frozen over! A grassy track now led us up Glen Noe, with a cheerful stream, interspersed with waterfalls, on our left. We walked on steadily until we had rounded the lower slopes of a bulky, grassy shoulder on our right, and we could look up a side glen and view the summit ridge of Ben Cruachan.

From the top of the Taynuilt, or westmost peak of Cruachan, a faint streamer marked the shadow line of the summit-cone cast upon the slight haze on its northern side. A steep, snowy ridge descended directly towards us. Nothing was hidden; the ridge was certainly steep and possibly iced in its upper portion. The only question was whether we had time to traverse the mountain before nightfall. In the early annals of the Scottish Mountaineering Club there is a record of a party of good men, well equipped with ice-axes and rope, who took eight hours to ascend this very ridge when the conditions were very icy. We were no better than our forerunners, but also there would never be a more perfect day for the job.

The approach to the ridge was easy, and so was the lower part of it. As we rose the snow became very much harder and the ice-axes were brought into use. At first it was only a question of steadying ourselves as we kicked steps in the frozen surface. Then that became impossible and we had to cut a slash through the hard crust, using the adze blade of the axe. Still, we made good progress. To the north the view became more extensive and splendid. Loch Etive was of a sombre green colour with a curious, mottled sheen several miles to the north where the loch was frozen over. To the east, the main summit of Cruachan was edged with a bright, fiery band of sunshine, amazingly remote and beautiful, rather like a picture of Siniol-chun in the Himalaya with its translucent upper ridges of clear ice. Straight ahead, our own peak was wrapped in cloud.

As we ascended, the going became slower and more difficult. The icy patches became much more frequent, and steps had to be hewed out more laboriously with heavy blows from the pick of the axe. The ridge was broken up with ice-encrusted rocks and boulders, every one beautifully cased in long, feathery, frost crystals. The course became tortuous among these outcrops, as we sought the easiest route towards our objective. There was little time to lose, so we pressed on as fast as we could. In that clear, exhilarating atmosphere it was good to be alive and we made light of the labour of step-cutting, warmed as we were by the exercise, but fanned and kept to it by the cold northerly breeze. For a long time the summit hardly seemed to come any nearer, but we scarcely noticed the passage of time. It is on such days that the steady rhythm of healthy muscular action promotes a calm serenity and enjoyment which are almost the greatest gains of mountaineering. It is not only a matter of bodily contentment; the mind is ever active on the problems of balance and route selection, whilst all the senses co-operate in absorbing the grandeur of the surroundings, the colours of mountain, snow and cloud, the crunch and tinkle of the passage over snow, ice and rock.

Then the cloud cap retreated before us and we suddenly found that we were close to the final peak. To the west the horizon fell away to the Sound of Mull and the islands. As we approached the top the last remains of cloud flamed up, a glorious crimson, in the gap between ourselves and the highest summit. We emerged into the last of the sunshine, close to the summit cairn of the Taynuilt peak, just before four p.m., and stayed to feast our eyes on the most perfect winter sunset of my experience.

The sun itself was surrounded by a coloured corona, quite a local phenomenon, for, with a shift of position of twenty yards, it almost vanished. At the cairn it did not exist: twenty yards to the east it was a complete ring of brilliant colours with the violet on the outside. The cause must have been a thin mist of very fine spicules of ice whirled up from the snow-fields by the wind flurries. As the sun set, the colouring became more impressive than ever. Along the northern horizon the colours ranged from a gorgeous heliotrope through a liquid green to a pure, dark blue. These winter colours must be seen in order to be believed. Summer cannot vie with them in purity and intensity. I remember, on another New Year, looking eastward from the summit of Ben More at sunset. The whole length of Loch Tay, as well as the windings of the river Dochart, were a pure, luminous green surmounted by the russet lower slopes and the lovely pink of the snow-fields of Ben Lawers.

Here the summit panorama was more varied and impressive. Beyond the head of Loch Etive were the cloud-capped tops of Bidean nam Bian, highest mountain of Argyll, only Ben Starav remaining clear. To the east, beyond the Drochaid Glas peak of Cruachan, was the snowy pyramid of Ben Lui. Far to the south were the hills of Cowal, with the serrated outlines of the Arran peaks on the right. Loch Awe was spread out beneath us as a dark, sinuous band. In the west lay Mull, with snow-streaked Ben More, surrounded by the fiery line of the Atlantic, which also enclosed the distant peaks of Rum, far to the north-west. Such brilliant colouring and visibility are characteristic of the West Highlands of Scotland in fine, frosty, winter weather. It is the combination of pure colour, snowy mountains, loch and ocean which affords views which are unequalled for sheer beauty amidst ranges of much higher mountains, such as the Alps. There, the scale of the mountains and their abrupt grandeur and savagery of outline are far more awe-inspiring, but there are no expanses of water in the picture, nor does the dry climate lend itself so readily to the atmospheric perspective which enhances the appreciation of distance and the delicate gradations of colour.

My friend, Dr Myles, had already left the summit and it was

time for McClure and myself to follow, racing down the easy western slopes. The snow was good and we enjoyed one or two excellent standing glissades, until we finished on the rim of the deep gorge of a stream, unfortunately on the wrong side. In the gathering twilight we reached the main road at the west end of the Pass of Brander, near Bridge of Awe. We made light of the three miles of walking to Taynuilt, well contented with our day and with the prospect of a good dinner. One cannot always remain on the heights; the inner man will not be put off with *the baseless fabric of this vision*, even if the memory of such days lives on through the years.

IV

THE CENTRAL BUTTRESS OF BUACHAILLE ETIVE MOR

IT WAS ONLY after the opening of the new Glencoe road, about the year 1932, that rock climbing activity in the area became really popular and parties began to frequent the crags of Buachaille Etive Mor at most week-ends in summer, and gradually in winter as well. Many of the new-comers were tough in fibre, and they usually camped, even in winter time.

The "bad" old days were very pleasant, however. Then one had the mountains to oneself and conditions at Kingshouse Inn were still primitive. From one's bedroom one could smell the bacon frying through a hole in the floor, which was better than a breakfast gong. In another it was said to be necessary to put up an umbrella in bed if the weather was wet, which was very often the case. Rock climbing on the Buachaille was little more advanced than in the days of the pioneers at the beginning of the century. The difficulty was not in making a new route on the crags, but in doing so with discrimination, owing to the lavish display of attractive alternatives. Many visits may be necessary for the working out of the best route on a crag, and a number of climbers may make their several contributions to one good discovery before it is perfected.

The rocks of the Buachaille, like most British crags, have the defect of facing northwards for the most part, receiving little sunshine to dry them after rainy weather. For winter climbing this is an advantage, as the frost helps to consolidate the snow, but in summer one prefers dry rocks and welcomes a little sunshine for the harder problems.

The Buachaille has also a south-easterly face, but the crags tend to be less continuous and are broken up into shorter sections. The actual climbing starts at a lower level and the separate sections can be linked up into a very long expedition, finishing close to the top of the mountain (3,343 ft), and capable of yielding no less than 2,000 feet of climbing when taken all together. Herein lies the attractiveness of Central Buttress for a long summer day's climbing. The original route on the Buttress was climbed in 1898. The difficulties were not great by modern standards. The Buttress is split into an upper and a lower section by a long rake, called Heather Terrace, sloping steeply upwards from right to left. The pioneers used this rake for linking up an approach on the north side with an easy scramble for a finish from the higher southern end of the Terrace. Practically nothing more was done on this face for about thirty years.

In July 1929 Alexander Harrison and I enjoyed an excellent climb on the northern face of the Buttress, crossing the foot of Heather Terrace. We solved the final difficulties by ascending two consecutive chimneys, one of which I was only able to climb by using the shoulder of my friend as an essential foothold. We were fortunate in being able to finish the climb by nightfall, for we had begun about six p.m. This upper section, some years later, was made much more direct by W. H. Murray and his party. In the summer of 1931 Colin Allan and I prospected the cliff a good deal further to the left, hoping to make a direct route up the rocky wall to the upper end of Heather Terrace.

On the extreme left is a smooth, almost vertical wall of alternately bleached and blackened rock, sometimes termed the Waterslide, although very little water ever comes down it unless the weather is really wet. No one had ever climbed this wall directly to the top end of Heather Terrace, for the upper half is perfectly smooth and holdless. Of course, it is never safe to make a sweeping negative assertion in rock climbing. Modern climbers are not all averse to driving spikes into cracks and doing a certain amount of steeplejacking, and I may be wrong in thinking that it cannot be climbed by orthodox methods.

On a cold, windy day in November 1931 Allan and I started as near the foot of the alleged Waterslide as we thought feasible, climbed straight up for nearly 200 feet to a prominent little semi-detached pinnacle on the face and found that we could not proceed much farther in a direct, upward line. On that day we solved the problem by traversing along a ledge to the right and gaining Heather Terrace by a short, exposed chimney where the only available holds were lumps of frozen turf. Allan gave a great lead in the second half of the climb up a severe wall about ninety feet high. On wet, cold rock, for it was raining by that time, his performance was outstanding. The middle thirty feet caused me some anxiety but little enjoyment as I followed him. We both considered that we had not exhausted the possibilities of Central Buttress, but we tacitly postponed all further proceedings until a warm summer day.

On a perfect, sunny day in July 1934 we had our opportunity. The party consisted of Colin Allan, Miss M. B. Stewart and myself. This time we confirmed the fact that we could not climb directly up the wall above our little pinnacle, but that a rising traverse to the left was quite feasible on small ledges until we reached a small recess in the cliff. The next short pitch was delightfully steep and exposed, but there was a secure anchorage above. The rest of the climb was very steep, but no more than "difficult" according to modern rock-climbing standards. We finished at the upper end of Heather Terrace.

Colin and I, on a later occasion, were able to make a number of lesser variations on this route, but they make little difference to its character as a climb. The face is very steep but intersected by many cracks and ledges. The rock is very sound, and the combination of good rock with small holds, steepness, some degree of exposure and sunshine makes for delightful rock climbing. We lunched on the Terrace in a mood of self-satisfied, lazy contentment. But there was something of a different nature awaiting us before we managed to finish the climb. The upper cliff consisted of two tiers of rock, one above the other. The lower one was obviously easy, but the final wall of sixty to eighty feet was suspiciously smooth and steep.

After lunch, when we turned round again to face the rocks, that upper tier appeared to be not only vertical but somewhat undercut. Colin Allan, not being susceptible to such optical illusions, was eager to take the lead. We soon climbed to the base of the steep wall and I belayed his rope round a little spike of rock. After thirty feet or so his progress became very slow. He had started obliquely upwards to the left but was now almost above me, moving very carefully and exhibiting almost the whole of the soles of his boots to my upward gaze. Then he commenced to move upwards to the right, making for a sharp edge of rock. With a supreme effort he grasped it with both hands, kicked about with his feet and pulled himself up. Then he took a prolonged rest on his perch, without answering any of my anxious inquiries as to his present comfort or future prospects.

Evidently the next move was likely to be critical, so I was eventually summoned to join him. I have never climbed anything more strenuous. We called it Spillikin Pitch on account of a small thin flake of rock, sticking loosely in a crevice of a steep slab on the left. The Spillikin was irrelevant to the climb, as it was quite useless and off the best line. From Spillikin Slab I

could find practically no holds on the last ten feet to the safe
ledge, and I was grateful for the tension of the rope.

Colin now wished to climb a holdless, vertical, open corner
of rock on his right, what rock climbers, whose terminology is
often inexact and always limited, call an open chimney, about
fifteen feet high. In order to do so he wished to stand on my
shoulders. From my cramped position on the ledge the problem
could only be solved after I had tied myself to a spike of rock at
shoulder level, for Allan is no light weight. As he mounted up,
the rope strained to meet the outward thrust, but Colin found a
hold and climbed the pitch.

I had insisted on Allan removing his boots for the final
move, so the next procedure was the hoisting of all the boots
and sacks to the upper stance. Midge had been sunning herself
all this time and passing occasional flippant remarks. It was
now her turn to move up, which she did very neatly and
quickly. On the last ten feet I gave her the benefit of a tight
rope, but never an actual pull when she was moving. Clearly
there must be enough holds for the negotiation of the pitch
without strenuous arm pulling, granted sufficient balance and
confidence. I was not to find the solution for several years.
When it came to my turn to climb the last part I could not, of
course, reach the essential hold in the open chimney, but I
ascended the wall directly. There, the holds were just sufficient,
so long as one knew where to find the crucial handhold for the
right hand. As I was on a rope from above I could afford to
take a chance and grab the unseen hold. At future visits I knew
where it was and led the pitch unaided.

Spillikin Pitch has always interested me for the way in which
it served as a test of climbing technique and a striking illustration that, in rock climbing, the battle is not always to the
strong. Allan found the pitch very severe and exhausting in
1934. In May 1935, along with Sandy Wedderburn, Allan failed
to lead it at all. In July 1936, climbing with me, he again led
it and I had a hard struggle as his second. In May 1945,
I climbed Central Buttress with Ian Charleson as second.
Commonsense, after such a lapse of time and the lack of
climbing during the war years, should have prompted me to
avoid the pitch, as there was an easy alternative way from
Heather Terrace. Perhaps it was Ian's way of looking at it and
saying that it did not seem so steep after all!

In any case I started up in stocking soles, going deliberately
and slowly. I found two intermediate resting places. The

Spillikin had disappeared, but I found another little flake of rock above the slab which I used as a temporary anchor for my rope, as, though not quite immovable, it was safe for a direct pull from below. I was feeling a bit stretched and tried to think out my moves as far as the safe ledge or mantelshelf. Could I get higher before attempting the irreversible movement of swinging across to the right and grasping the edge of rock? There was a footscrape and a small, steadying fingerhold. I was soon high enough to see and almost to feel the necessary movement beforehand. I swung across; my right hand grasped the edge: my left followed immediately, stretching over far enough to gain a positive, pulling hold. I was up, slightly out of breath but with plenty of energy to spare. I was there again on 14 April 1946, with my wife and my friend, John Wilson. The same tactics were again successful. My wife came up very neatly and enjoyed the pitch. John came up and said it was a horrible place!

After Spillikin, the remainder of the climbing is fairly easy to the cairn on the summit of Central Buttress. For those who have a practical interest in C.B. but would prefer an easier alternative above Heather Terrace, I can recommend another route which is very steep, with good, small holds and an exhilarating sense of exposure. This route was worked out by W. M. McKenzie in 1937. It starts from Heather Terrace about fifty yards to the right of our luncheon spot, by a steep ledge inclining upward to the left. Whoever can lead the route below Heather Terrace with ease and confidence should be able to lead this upper continuation to the top of the Buttress.

At the beginning of this account I alluded to the possibility of enjoying as much as 2,000 feet of rock climbing on the Buachaille. From the top of Central Buttress it is an easy, undulating scramble over D-Gully Buttress and Curved Ridge to the foot of Rannoch Wall. This is the eastern rampart of the famous Crowberry Ridge and a happy hunting ground for the modern rock gymnast. There are many routes on its apparently vertical precipice. There are also complicated traverses along intersecting ledges, so that one could spend a long day without repeating oneself. The best and most popular route is, however, by a conspicuous natural feature of the cliff, a long, steep groove, just round the lower corner from the orthodox classical route up the Crowberry Ridge.

This route, Agag's Groove, was first climbed in May 1936 by J. F. Hamilton, A. Anderson and A. C. D. Small, a group of members of the Junior Mountaineering Club of Scotland. It was an amusing day, for a competing party of the same energetic fellowship arrived at the rocks just a little too late. The easy rocks of the Curved Ridge made a perfect gallery (or dress circle) for the competitors, and it was a fine day. The venture was successful, and the name of the climb recalls the delicacy and exposure at the crucial pitch, which Hamish Hamilton led in stocking soles.

In April 1946 my wife demanded some more climbing after Central Buttress, so we ascended Agag's Groove, while John Wilson acted as photographer from several stances on the Curved Ridge. Until we got near the crux we moved fast, as the Groove, though very steep, has just sufficient good holds and stances on sound rock. At about 250 feet above the bottom there seems to be a bulging wall. The satisfying holds continue until one is just below the crux. This is quite short, but it is practically vertical. There is, however, no single movement which could not be reversed by a competent climber, without any undue effort, provided that he uses the holds properly. It is a very difficult pitch, but, on account of its shortness and directness, is much less formidable than the ascent of Spillikin. My wife was exactly of this opinion, and came up very easily. All difficulty is not ended at the crux, above which there still remains about 100 feet of good, steep climbing on small holds, before one finishes on the easy, intermediate part of Crowberry Ridge. It is this combination of sound, steep rock with sufficient holds and considerable exposure which has made Agag's Groove one of the most popular climbs in Glencoe. It is one of the best of modern Scottish rock-climbing discoveries.

There is another, less worthy reason for its popularity. There are perfect photographic stances on the Curved Ridge, from which the camera can depict the performers as veritable flies moving on a slightly roughened, vertical wall. The views are half profile and include the eastern edge of the Crowberry Ridge at its steepest as a presumptive vertical line for comparison. What luxury and satisfaction to look at the photographs and show them to one's friends!

We continued up the Ridge and over the Crowberry Tower, the rope being no longer necessary. A short, difficult drop took us to the Crowberry Gap and some easy scrambling to the summit of Buachaille Etive Mor. We were content to descend the mountain by easy scree slopes to Glen Etive with its perfect bathing pool, which can be refreshing and pleasant after a dry spell in hot weather at the end of April.

V

THE CHASM OF BUACHAILLE ETIVE MOR

ON THE SOUTH-EAST side of Stob Dearg of Buachaille Etive Mor broken rocks and scree descend for about 500 feet beneath the summit in a sort of wide funnel, below which the mountain face is cleft by a great, vertical rift between precipitous cliffs for about 1,500 feet or more, ending on the gently sloping moorland not very far above the road in Glen Etive, about a mile and a half below its junction with the main road west of Kingshouse.

The early age of British rock climbing specialized in the ascent of gullies, and its most exciting problems were encountered where the gullies were bridged by huge boulders with caves underneath them. Such difficulties were usually accentuated by a stream of water coming over the chockstone and clothing the rocky walls with spongy, green moss, circumstances in which the older pioneers appeared to put forth their best efforts and find keen enjoyment. The Chasm of the Buachaille was bound to attract attention in the early days of Scottish rock climbing, and its history is, in fact, a long one.

In July 1898 J. H. Bell (a past president of the S.M.C., but not related to the author) and J. Maclay were forced to retreat after a hard struggle, from below a 100-foot waterfall pouring down over a seemingly impregnable, vertical cliff. This point is now recognized to be less than half-way up the Chasm. In June 1903 the ablest Scottish climber of his time, Harold Raeburn, accompanied by Dr and Mrs Inglis Clark, entered the Chasm above this difficulty. They found a good deal of old snow and, at one place, traversed about fifty feet through a snow tunnel. Time was against them, for Raeburn had to catch an evening train at Tyndrum. They escaped on to the south wall at a point where two severe pitches still remained to be tackled, above which was the culminating difficulty, now known as the Devil's Cauldron. Their climb ended on the Lady's Pinnacle, about 200 feet high, situated on the south wall. Dr Clark considered that this was the most prolonged piece of difficult climbing in his British experience.

Raeburn, however, returned to the assault in April 1906,

accompanied by W. N. Ling. Although it should have been obvious that the Chasm would be most likely to yield its last secrets as a pure rock climb, uncomplicated by snow or water, and preferably after a long, dry period, the pioneers of those days were in the habit of doing their Scottish climbing in the early part of the year and spending their summer vacations in the Alps. Climbing the Chasm was thus rendered much more difficult by the presence of masses of old snow which had partly melted away from the side walls of the gully, the rocks of which were often exceedingly smooth and water-worn. If the weather was fine and the sun was hot, copious streams of descending water added to the difficulties.

Raeburn and Ling put up a very good show. At certain places stocking-sole technique was necessary. At others the snow was of some assistance, as it piled up against the walls and lessened the effective height of the pitches. Raeburn reported that this applied to most of the pitches which were climbed in 1903. Finally, they too were driven out on to the south wall at a point where the last pitch, "a black, slimy slit of smooth rock, down which gurgled enough water in gallons per minute, to furnish an ample supply to a fair sized town", loomed high above them.

The next attempt resulted in a successful ascent of all but the direct route up the back of the Devil's Cauldron. A reconnaissance on the previous day solved the problem of the 100-foot pitch which had frustrated the party of 1898, and a fixed rope was left hanging down the pitch. The ascent was started at six-fifteen a.m. (from the foot of the first pitch) on 13 April 1920 by R. F. Stobart and Mr and Mrs N. E. Odell. There was plenty of snow and running water. The mist closed down on the party after second breakfast at half-past ten. Combined tactics were necessary at a pitch where smooth, waterworn, vertical walls converged at middle height and permitted the necessary bridging tactics. At the back of the Devil's Cauldron the waterfall hung suspended as a 100-foot curtain of great icicles, but the party was able, by a second use of combined tactics, to climb a vertical chimney on the south wall. So ended the Chasm and its difficulties at five-twenty p.m.

The first direct ascent of the back of the Devil's Cauldron was effected on 30 August 1931 by J. G. Robinson and I. G. Jack. They took four hours to reach its floor and another three to climb the pitch. This triumph was the climax to a number of attempts by a small band of enthusiasts.

Colin Allan and I had no part in the exploration of the

Chasm. Our first visit, entirely unplanned, was in May 1932. It was not a complete success, as we were defeated by a considerable flow of water at the middle section of the Cauldron, but we returned to the Chasm, year after year, as a sort of standard climb which never failed to yield a grand day of strenuous rock work in magnificent surroundings. If we could climb Buachaille by the Chasm, run down to the Etive and enjoy a swim in its long pool and feel no fatigue, we concluded that we were in reasonably good training.

We spent a pleasant evening at Kingshouse, but left our friends after eleven p.m. in order to pass the night in our own way. About midnight we were seated on the pier at Lochetivehead, watching the full moon rise over the shoulder of Ben Starav. We sat for so long, absorbing the peace and beauty of that perfect night, that a half-formed impulse to climb the mountain died away of itself. About four miles back on the way to Dalness we found a little wood where we spread our sleeping sacks on a carpet of pine needles and went to sleep. There is nothing more delightful than such a bivouac in a cool, spring night. A few midges awoke us between four and five a.m., but they were only a handful of skirmishers, and not the hordes of summer-time. Our day commenced with a swim in a cold, deep pool of the river Etive. Then came plenty of breakfast—kippers toasted over a wood fire, boiled eggs, pork pies, bread, cheese, marmalade and tea. We paid tribute to dietetics and vitamins with a final course of oranges. Nowadays, even were it possible, I should doubt the value of such a preparation for a day's climbing. Then, the procedure was normal, and most enjoyable too.

A few introductory pitches loosened our muscles before the walls of the gully closed in about us. A triple pitch loomed ahead, with three huge chockstones in succession, each surmounting a cave. The ascent was effected on the right wall. This is almost the only vegetatious pitch in the Chasm, but even here there are good rock holds where required. We made one pitch of it and traversed back on to the floor of the gully above the waterfall. The next long pitch was up a slabby wall of red rock, on the left, with an awkward traverse to the right at the top of the difficulty, where the holds were not in-cut. The leader should have adequate length of rope for this pitch. In wet conditions it can be very wet at the bottom.

Little need be said of the successive difficulties which we encountered below the 100-foot waterfall pitch which had defeated the earliest explorers. They are all interesting and varied, but Colin Allan and I, in successive visits, became so familiar with them that we did not use the rope at all on this lower section. This is a confession rather than an example to be followed. Some of the pitches are exposed and difficult. If we took guests with us we always roped them up. The reputed sixth pitch is a test of the dryness of the Chasm. It is a straight-forward staircase with the usual waterfall pouring down. In wet weather it means a certain drenching on the stair on the left. We discovered an alternative through-route by a cave on the right, but this is mossy, slimy and difficult and unlikely to be drier. If the sixth pitch is dry one has a reasonable expectation of being able to climb the rest of the Chasm. The last pitch below the Cross Roads is a delightful, airy problem on a nearly vertical rib on the left, followed by a lofty traverse back to the bed of the gully above a waterfall.

Now we arrived at the Cross Roads, where a transverse, eroded dyke forms two gullies, to left and right. It was a good place for lunch. Any party that has had enough difficulty or enough climbing for the day can escape here on either side, the more interesting being the right or north side, with a pleasant descent from the crest of the north wall, involving some good practice scrambling. Allan and I contemplated the waterfall. The only possible route was obvious enough, by a near-vertical, shallow cleft on the right-hand buttress of the fall. The first thirty feet to a little pinnacle, with stance and belay, were easy. Then the holds became small and more widely spaced. At a return visit in 1945 I found some loose rock in this upper section, but there are still sufficient sound holds. It is an exposed pitch with small but adequate holds, technically excel-lent if one goes about it with care and deliberation. At the top there is a perfect stance and belay. Although it is possible to continue up this wall, the better way is to make a short, difficult traverse into the gully bed, cross this and go up the other wall for a few feet to a narrow ledge which goes almost as far as the lip of the next waterfall. The handholds are few and wide apart. The ledge peters out towards the finish and the rock is very smooth and rounded. Delicate balance and a long arm span are necessary if one is to be successful in negotiating the Piano Pitch, as it has been named. Careful selection of holds and study of the direction of stresses are essential to make each movement safe, especially for a short man. Brute force and rush tactics may land one in the pool beneath the waterfall. I have seen two seconds who have slipped in at the last move. It is only eight or ten feet down to the water. Those who slipped were, of course, lowered into the pool!

After some inclined, water-worn slabs, which are not too easy, we came to a narrow rift with smooth walls, about sixty feet high. About twenty feet up on the left was a rounded bulge projecting from the wall, and just above this point the walls converged to their narrowest aperture, about three feet or so. The stream came down in a fall at the innermost part of the rift. This pitch may, unfortunately, be avoided by climbing out of the gully on the left. The back of the rift is somewhat undercut, which would make it altogether impossible to climb up there by orthodox chimney tactics. I have never tried, as it must be a very wet proceeding. It is not a cave pitch, and the neat solution of the problem makes use of the bulge of rock on the wall. Combined tactics were used by the Stobart-Odell party in 1920. I think that Colin Allan was the first man to climb the pitch unaided by the direct method. He climbed it in boots, which makes the performance all the more creditable on smooth, rounded, waterworn rock, taking into consideration the corresponding qualities of Allan's boots, which seldom had many nails at all!

I led up to the bulge by bridging movements with feet on one wall and hands on the other. There is a good stance at the bulge, hardly enough room for two people, but no belay. Colin pushed up past me, wedged between the walls, reached across to a handhold on the opposite (north) wall and pulled himself over and up with both arms. He was strong enough to do it in that way and I respected his performance. Somehow, I failed to get the knack, so that I had to accept a good pull on the rope. This failure made me think on ways and means of making up for my relative lack of stature and arm strength.

The solution is applicable to many other, difficult, cross-stepping traverses on severe rock climbs. The guiding rule is to spare no effort in order to get high enough, and somewhat above the holds which one is aiming for. One should also study the holds for one or two moves ahead. Accurate co-ordination of eye and limb replaces brute force and hard pulling. In 1933, when climbing the Chasm with G. C. Williams, I led the Converging Walls Pitch and found that I had a good reserve of energy. The landing on the north wall is still on rounded rock ledges, but is perfectly secure. If you lead the pitch and have doubts of the ability of your second it is a good idea to make him take off his boots and proceed in stocking-soles. There is a belay on the north wall some distance above. On one occasion Colin was taking a lady climber up to the first bulge, when the latter had the misfortune to slip. Colin was obviously enjoying himself as the lady executed a few pendulum swings below him on the rope. Then he simply took in the rope, pulling her up as if he were landing a fish. He was a good man to climb with.

As in first-class drama, there is now a breathing space. The Chasm is walled in on both sides to a height of over 100 feet. Numerous pitches succeed one another, all in the line of the watercourse where there should now be only a trickle of water. At one point there is an easy exit on to the south wall. A somewhat difficult, short cave pitch lies below the great hall of the Devil's Cauldron. There is an undercut handhold near the top on the right wall of the cave and a good hold above.

The Devil's Cauldron is a savage and magnificent place, the north wall of 200 feet being vertical and unclimbable. The impressive wall on the south side is cleft by a narrow vertical chimney. At first sight the wet repulsive slit at the back of this narrow enclosure appears to be utterly unclimbable, so that it is small wonder that the earlier parties never attempted to do so. Unless after dry weather in summer, and preferably no earlier than June, as there is often snow in the Chasm till well on into May, one should not attempt the direct route up the back of the Cauldron.

The weather had deteriorated when Allan and I got thus far. I was deputed to lead the first fifty or sixty feet to a small platform underneath a narrow undercut chimney which was the crux of the climb. Although reasonably dry at the start, the last ten feet below the platform sprayed me fairly effectively. Colin joined me on the stance and I belayed him for his attempt on the crucial chimney. Conditions were altogether against him. Like all strong men he delighted in forcing himself up and pulling with both hands, keeping far too close inside the chimney and so becoming the butt for a vigorous stream of water from above, which poured over his head, down his neck and down his sleeves. He failed to gain a foothold on the north wall, but was wise enough to retreat in good order. I was so overawed by the sight of my friend in the guise of a mermaid that I called out for a complete withdrawal while we were still not too chilled to grasp the rocks. On the floor of the Cauldron I took off all my clothes, wrung them out and put them on again. It was worth doing. We traversed out of the Chasm by the south wall, but we had enjoyed a good day's climbing.

The next time I visited the Chasm was in the company of
G. C. Williams on 9 July 1933. There was only a trickle of
water at the back of the Cauldron. I had a hard struggle with
the crucial chimney, and retained a wholesome respect for the
place. Above it I found a little rock arch where Williams
belayed me for the final, straight section of the pitch. From
below, this appears to be far worse than what goes before. The
side walls are vertical and the water comes trickling down over
mossy slabs which seem to be almost as steep. The reality is
much more comforting. The technique is orthodox backing-up,
such as is used for most chimneys, and the exposure, with a
sensational drop to the rocky floor of the Cauldron, need not
worry any confident expert. With feet pressed against the wall
in front and palms of the hands at my hips pressed against the
wall behind, I progressed upwards, a few inches at a time, with
very little effort and almost as much comfort as if I had been
seated in an armchair with my feet against the sides of the
fireplace. At intervals I could rest across the gap and take a
bird's-eye-view of the countenance of my second. Fortunately,
the holds improve below the upper overhanging chockstone,
which is the last difficulty.

In the first edition of the *Central Highlands Guide* the exit pitch
from the Cauldron is given as 175 feet high. The earlier
explorers thought it must be 200 feet at least. Debunking is
a sordid occupation, but I have measured the height with a
reliable surveying aneroid with a 4-inch dial, and the result was
between 105 and 110 feet. Climbers are but human: they would
not indulge in such an irrational sport without a lively imagination, singularly sensitive to the impress of difficulty and the
self-satisfaction of victory. Even the crux is not so difficult and
strenuous as I have suggested. In August 1945 I led an English
climbing friend up the Chasm. The Converging Walls Pitch
pleased him, but it was only at the Cauldron that he became
visibly impressed. Then it dawned upon me that, after a lapse
of twelve years, which had taken my own age very close to the
half-century, I might not be able to lead the crux at all. I
discounted the effect of those years in better co-ordinated
movements and economy of effort. By keeping as far out of the
chimney as possible and resting frequently I was able to gain
the critical foothold on the north wall without any undue effort.
It is true that the other wall shrinks away to nothing at a
certain height and that the position feels and appears to be
highly precarious, but exposure is not the same thing as danger.
August 1945 was, however, a dry month in the West Highlands.

It is seldom that conditions are good enough for a comfortably dry ascent of the back of the Cauldron. On all other occasions but the two already mentioned Allan and I were obliged to climb out of the Cauldron by the chimney on the south wall. In 1920 the Stobart-Odell party used combined tactics for climbing this severe chimney. About 1938 or so, E. R. Zenthon climbed it alone, and W. H. Murray has also climbed it. Our problem was to find a safe way up the south wall for more ordinary climbers in conditions when the back of the Cauldron was too wet. We found the best solution at our second attempt, using the chimney only for the first twenty feet or so. The second can then safeguard the leader over a severe traverse out of the chimney, by an exposed corner and along a smooth, narrow ledge on the south wall. The movement is as difficult as anything on the direct route, but it is safe and dry. The leader can then climb straight up to an excellent stance and belay, from which he can safeguard his second. The final ascent to the top of the wall is by a moderate, upper chimney. The climb finishes on the top of the Lady's Pinnacle, which was first reached by Harold Raeburn, Dr and Mrs Inglis Clark in 1903. So history tends to repeat itself, but there is no easy ascent of the Devil's Cauldron and the Chasm keeps its best pitches for the end.

VI

BEN NEVIS: ROCK

Introduction

AMONG SCOTTISH MOUNTAINS, especially from the climber's point of view, Ben Nevis holds as much pre-eminence as does Mont Blanc above the other peaks of the Alps. Indeed, the parallel is remarkably apt. Both are great, dome-shaped mountains, with a relatively easy way up one side and very steep and formidable rocks on the other. Ben Nevis, owing to its greater height than most other Scottish hills, carries more snow in winter and spring, so that its steep, north-eastern aspect offers the most nearly Alpine type of climbing which can be enjoyed in Britain. At the same time the magnitude of its north-eastern cliffs and the excellent quality of the rock afford the longest and most difficult Scottish rock climbs in summer. No parallel should be overdone, but it is perhaps admissible, as has already been suggested and printed, to adapt the lines from Byron's "Manfred" to Ben Nevis, although originally composed in honour of the great Alpine mountain:

> Ben Nevis is monarch of mountains,
> They crowned him long ago,
> On a throne of rocks, in a robe of clouds,
> With a diadem of snow.

The meteorological records accumulated during the twenty years from 1883 until 1904 at the old Observatory on the summit of Ben Nevis make very interesting reading. They are described by W. T. Kilgour in *Twenty Years on Ben Nevis*. Temperature records show that the overall mean was 31.4°F. over the entire period, so that, if the same rate of temperature fall continued to hold good with increase in height, 1°F. per 275 feet of ascent above sea level, a permanent snow cap and a small glacier would certainly be in existence if the mountain were a thousand feet higher. The figures for the annual snowfall at the summit are considerable. In any one year the maximum depth at the summit is usually attained between mid-March and mid-April, although maxima for the year have been recorded as late as the end of May. The greatest recorded depth amounted to twelve feet in each of the years 1884 and 1885, but it appears that the figure has been much less of recent years. Rainfall is also very great and amounted to an average of 157 inches over the twenty years, the rainfall at Fort William being very much less. There are, on the average, only 104 fair days per annum on the summit of the Ben.

In spite of this dismal picture climbers can take heart, for the months of April, May and June are very much drier than the others. It also follows that the best conditions for snow and ice climbing are normally prevalent during March and April, although first-class climbs are available much earlier and are sometimes possible in May. Indeed, the north-eastern gullies are very seldom clear of snow until much later, and, in most years, small snow patches do not melt completely before the late autumn supplies a fresh covering. The accumulation of snow and ice is usually enormous at the end of winter, the tops of the cliffs and gullies being decorated with huge cornices, which have been estimated to reach a thickness of from fifteen to twenty-five feet.

All kinds of snow conditions may be encountered when climbing gullies, ridges and buttresses, so that the quality, difficulty and duration of the climbs are such as to tax the powers of the toughest experts, and to compare very favourably with some of the great Alpine climbs. The geographical situation of the Ben, coupled with the mutations of its Atlantic type of weather, result in great precipitation combined with frequent changes of wind and temperature, and a consequent partial thawing and refreezing which produces the toughest quality of snow-ice on ridges and gullies. The flattish summit dome acts as a catchment area for snow, and the prevalent westerly winds blow a great deal of it over the edge of the cliffs, thus helping to pile up enormous amounts on sheltered ledges and in the gullies.

No one who has visited the valley of the Allt a' Mhuilinn, between Ben Nevis and its easterly neighbour, Carn Mor Dearg, on a fine day in early spring is likely to forget the splendour of the Nevis cliffs in their gleaming panoply of snow and ice. Finer still is the summit view from Carn Mor Dearg, especially if one can see it in early morning or late afternoon.

Ben Nevis could hardly offer such excellent snow and ice climbing if it did not possess a rugged outline with long, steep ridges and gullies. In addition, the quality of the rock is so good that it provides sound routes of all degrees of difficulty for the rock climber. The frontage of cliff, from the saddle between Ben Nevis and Carn Mor Dearg to the north-westerly cliffs on Carn Dearg, is nearly two miles, and there are parts of the cliff as much as 2,000 feet in height. It will assist the reader at this stage to look at the diagram of the ridges and gullies of the north-east face of the Ben (see p.72).

Most prominent in a good, distant view from the road over the moor between Spean Bridge and Loch Lochy, or from road and railway about two or three miles east of Fort William, is the steep edge of the North-East Buttress, but most picturesque from the Mhuilinn Glen is the long, graceful sweep of the Tower Ridge, with a great 700-foot pyramid of rock as its base, named the Douglas Boulder after the best known editor of the *Scottish Mountaineering Club Journal* during the classical period of climbing exploration on the Ben. Below the base of the Boulder, at 2,000-feet elevation, is the Charles Inglis Clark Memorial Hut of the Scottish Mountaineering Club. The C.I.C. Hut was presented to the Club by Dr W. Inglis Clark, one of the most noted of these early explorers and photographers, in memory of his only son, also a keen mountaineer, who was killed in the 1914–18 War. The Hut was opened in 1929.

Ben Nevis is a curiously isolated mountain. Glen Nevis, which bounds it on the west and south, is a very deep valley, only rising to 400 feet above sea level at the exit of the Nevis gorge, seven miles from Fort William and due south of the summit of the Ben. The saddle between Ben Nevis and Carn Mor Dearg at the head of the Mhuilinn valley is 3,475 feet above sea level, and the foot of the Douglas Boulder is little over 2,000 feet in altitude. It is also of interest to note the contrast between the steep, prominent and rugged grey cliffs of the Ben and the reddish, uniform scree slopes of Carn Mor Dearg, so that one is prepared to find that the Ben is just as unique from the geological as from the mountaineering point of view.

It is, in fact, the central core of a series of lava flows, due to volcanic outbursts in that early epoch when the Old Red Sandstone was deposited elsewhere. Not all the intruded igneous rock is good for climbing, for Carn Mor Dearg itself consists of a granite intrusion which has nevertheless weathered away into scree slopes. The easy path up the western flank of Ben Nevis crosses part of this "Inner Granite" of the Carn Mor Dearg formation below the site of the old half-way Hut. The core of Ben Nevis formed an area which collapsed into the molten "Inner Granite", with faulting and injection of dykes round about itself. The result was generally a rapid cooling and solidification, producing a fine-grained durable rock which, although it was first of all at a low level, yet, on account of its resistance to the erosion and weathering of subsequent ages, now remains isolated as the highest point of Britain. This is another instance of the general principle that the Scottish mountains are not true mountains of uplift, but the resistant remains from the erosion of a plateau.

The volcanic outbursts were repeated at intervals over a considerable period of time, so that part of the climbing rock is andesite lava, some very fine-grained and some much coarser, whilst another part is a less resistant agglomerate, a fragmental type of rock which was laid down during the explosive phases. The climbing qualities of the rock are determined alike by their dip (direction and inclination of bedding of the different layers), manner of jointing and surface texture. In all these respects there is great variety on the Ben. The lie of the climbing routes and ledges, as well as their difficulty, bear witness to their geological diversity. The best of the rock, such as the cliffs on the Douglas Boulder, the rocks of the North-East Buttress below the First Platform and on its front facing Observatory Gully, are excellent, although the smoother texture never makes the climbing so easy as on the rough gabbro of the Cuillin in Skye, where one can often glide up surprisingly steep slabs by friction alone. On the other hand, there are parts of the Ben where the rock is unsound and insecure trap, and extreme care is absolutely essential. Those impressive buttresses called the Comb and the Castle are of this type.

For all that the geologists can tell us, it is much better to test the theory by a practical visit to the cliffs themselves, and to treat all rocks with care and respect. The most reliable faces have faults and trap intrusions here and there. These form lines of weakness and of unreliable rock, but they also give rise to easy ledges and chimneys which make several routes possible that would not otherwise have been so. It is well to remember that the processes of erosion and decay are proceeding today as they have done in all past ages, and that their effects are most manifest in such places as chimneys and gullies. Even an unusually heavy shower of rain can loosen stones high up on a cliff, especially if accompanied by a high wind. The pioneer party on the difficult Slav Route was immobilized for about an hour during such a squall at the difficult lower crux of the route. There were several stonefalls, although the month was September and there had been no previous night frost.

Graded Rock Climbs

The older school of British rock-climbers preferred routes along prominent ridges or up gullies. The gullies taught them to climb chimneys as well. A great advantage was that the routes were obvious natural features of a rock face, and consequently very easy to identify. So far as Ben Nevis is concerned, much of the early climbing was done by Easter visitors who were members of the Alpine Club. The gullies, therefore, were primarily of interest as snow and ice climbs and were seldom or never attempted or climbed in summer. This was, perhaps, just as well; for any gully which is snow-filled during a great part of the year is bound to be subject to intense weathering and decay, so that the virgin rock, apart from its covering of scree and rotten debris, is liable to be most unsound.

At least two of the Nevis gullies have proved exceedingly formidable, if not dangerous, as summer climbs. Gardyloo Gully, in its upper section, is one of the more difficult winter routes on the Ben. Dr Graham Macphee, who first climbed it in summer conditions in 1935, describes it as one of the hardest rock climbs on the Ben. It is also dangerous, owing to loose and unsound rock, some of which is very soft. I climbed it with George Dwyer in August 1940, and we were more impressed by the dangers and looseness than by its actual severity, though each condition reacts on the other. Certainly a large party should never climb such a place. This happened in 1944 when a friend of mine, who was not leading, had two stones dropped on him by other members of the party. I heard a similar account of the first summer ascent, the only one before this date, of No. 2 gully which has a very dangerous and severe pitch about half-way up. These considerations dispose of the Nevis gullies as desirable rock climbs for any but cranky experts, except for such easy ones as numbers 3 and 4 (and possibly Tower Gully), which can always be used as quick routes of descent. Of these, No. 4 is an excellent, fast scree run, rather severe on the boots, but useful in bad weather.

The ridges of Ben Nevis, however, are long and sound, and they are wonderfully well graded as regards difficulty. They form the best training ground for rock climbers. The novice is able, not only to learn the rudiments of the craft and the various

BEN NEVIS AND CARN DEARG

GULLIES

o	Zero Gully	2,3,4	Gullies known by their numbers
1	(2 branches at upper End) Observatory Gully top left is Gardy Loo, top right Tower Gully	5	Carn Dearg Gully
		6,7	South and North Castle Gullies

RIDGES AND BUTTRESSES

NEB	North East Buttress	Ga	Garadh na Ciste
OR	Observatory Ridge	ST	South Trident Buttress
OB	Observatory Buttress	GB	Great Buttress of Carn Dearg
T	Tower Ridge	C	Castle
D	Top of Douglas Boulder	CR	Castle Ridge
Co	Comb		

SUMMITS

N	Ben Nevis	CD	Carn Dearg

CORRIES

Between T and CD is Coire na Ciste
The main valley above D is Coire Leis

Slopes of Carn Mor Dearg in foreground fall away gently into the Mhuilinn Glen

types of difficulty, but he can also learn two things of supreme value to the mountaineer who intends, later on, to climb on greater mountains such as the Alps. On easy ridges, like the Castle Ridge and the Tower Ridge, he can learn to take his place, either as leader or follower, in a party which moves safely, and often continuously, whilst using the rope. Later on he can learn to descend such ridges in the same manner. That is how Ben Nevis serves to make climbers into real mountaineers. There is an excellent mixture of easy and difficult; and some degree of route finding is called for, especially during a descent.

The Castle Ridge is the easiest, but one can get into some very awkward places on the descent if one is not careful. The first ascent of the Tower Ridge is best made by approaching the gap between it and the Douglas Boulder from the Observatory Gully side. At a later stage the direct route up the face of Douglas Boulder—a grand climb of 700 feet on very steep and difficult but sound rock—may be made, and then also the Great Tower can be negotiated by one of the western routes. These routes demand some experience, good cragsmanship and dry rocks. At a first ascent the easiest way should be followed on the ridge, avoiding the steepest part of the Little Tower on the left and passing the Great Tower also on the left by the Eastern Traverse. The Tower Gap beyond is fearsome looking, but has good holds.

By this time the rock-climber should have learned to proceed with care and security. Of the other ridges the North-East Buttress is not very difficult if one sticks to the proper route, except for the Mantrap near the top which is a short and polished problem in gymnastics. Here, too, the easy approach to the First Platform from upper Coire Leis is best.

Of all the Nevis ridges the best continuous rock climbing is on the Observatory Ridge. Its lower, slabby nose is a place where one can easily get into difficulty if one misses the central route which is marked by scratches. The upper ridge is delightfully narrow and airy, but not at all difficult. The rock is very sound throughout. The last of the ridge-like routes is the Observatory Buttress, shorter than the former, with a lower stepped portion with very good holds. A fault cleaves the buttress about the middle, and there is just one correct place for crossing it. The upper section is less determinate and is loose in places. A fatality occurred here a few years ago after the two members of the party had unroped. Apparently a block of rock came loose, but the angle of the face is not at all severe, and it is difficult to understand how the accident occurred. I have descended all these ridges, but would recommend careful route finding, especially in the case of Observatory Buttress. The descent of Observatory Ridge is the most interesting, but that too is a matter for experts, both as regards technique and route finding. Whoever leads a party in such an expedition should know the ridge from previously having ascended it, preferably more than once.

Now for the selection of several shorter rock climbs where the technique is more difficult. Nevis has many such, but only a few will be suggested, where the rock is particularly good and sound. Two such places are excellent for practice—the face of

Douglas Boulder and the west face of North-East Buttress below the First Platform. The south-west ridge of Douglas Boulder, bounding the western gully from the Gap on the side of Coire na Ciste, is excellent and moderate. It also gives a quick route of descent for a skilled party. I have descended it alone from the Boulder summit to the scree at the foot of the rocks in eighteen minutes. The Direct route of ascent is graded as very difficult and follows an almost direct line from the lowest point of the rocks to the top, as viewed from a position in the Mhuilinn glen about 100 yards above the C.I.C. Hut. It is delightfully steep, yet the holds are positive and adequate and the belays good.

There are many routes of varying difficulty below the First Platform on the west face of the North-East Buttress. Slingsby's Chimney is loose, especially near the top, and should be avoided. Raeburn's Arête is certainly the best approach to the Platform for experts. The rock is very sound, but there is much slab work, long runs-out of rope and few belays. My first ascent was by this route. I have ascended it several times, once at the beginning of May when many of the ledges still carried snow and some of the slabs had trickles of ice over them. It is a very difficult route for a descent, mainly owing to the featureless nature of the slabs which accentuates the difficulty of finding a route. Between Raeburn's Arête and Slingsby's Chimney are quite a number of recognized routes of varying degrees of difficulty and interest, but all on good rock. From these a choice can be made to suit the capacity of the party, but the routes lie fairly close together, and the directions of the Guide Book should be carefully followed if a certain standard of difficulty is not to be exceeded.

One excellent natural route of a more difficult character is No. 1 Route on Carn Dearg Buttress. It faces the C.I.C. Hut and looks most vertical and severe. But the rock is so sound and rough that steepness and safety go hand in hand for competent climbers. The classification is severe, but I think most climbers would now call it an "amiable" severe. The buttress gets a lot of sunshine and is climbable early in the year; the rock is wonderfully rough. The direct Cambridge start is decidedly severe. Great care is advisable at the penultimate pitch above the big chimney.

Another excellent route is Raeburn's Buttress on Carn Dearg, with an awkward but not difficult approach and a final section which is airy and sensational, demanding considerable care. If one avoids the severe, lower crag, the South Trident Buttress is a delightful route, but the variations on the lower crag are both severe and exposed. I have mentioned the routes in the last two paragraphs as completing the training of the rock climber on Ben Nevis up to the stage when he may be able to tackle the hardest and longest routes, and as showing the immense possibilities of the Ben for turning out a finished rock climber, not only for the best British rock climbs but also for similar work in the Alps. There is also much trap rock on Ben Nevis of varying degrees of soundness, but it is unnecessary to deal with it here.

More difficult Rock Climbs

Detailed accounts of rock climbs have an unfortunate and monotonous habit of similarity, a mustiness of flavour and verbiage which is best confined to the guide books, unless the experience of the reader or some vivid incident can charm the dry bones into life. There are many excellent and very difficult rock climbs on Ben Nevis, and I have for many years been of the opinion that the climbing on that mountain is superior to that which can be enjoyed anywhere else in Scotland, not excluding the Cuillin range in the Isle of Skye. The face climbs are best of all, holding much in reserve for the initiative of future mountaineers. A separate chapter is devoted to some recent discoveries on the greatest of the Nevis cliffs, the tremendous face which sweeps down from the crest of the North-East Buttress to the inner reaches of Observatory Gully, where a small but nearly permanent snow-bed persists throughout most of the summer. All that can be done here is to suggest a few other routes as a representative sample of the more difficult climbing available on the Ben.

In September 1936, Colin Allan, Sandy Wedderburn and I found ourselves at the base of Rubicon Wall, which, at that date, was reckoned to be the hardest rock climb on the Ben. It is a steep wall of rock, flanking the lower half of Observatory Buttress, next to the precipitous, unclimbed gully between the latter and the face of Observatory Ridge, and was first climbed in 1933 by the party of Mr A. T. Hargreaves. We found it somewhat difficult to decide on the exact beginning or line of their route. Starting as close as possible to the gully we soon found ourselves on rather severe slabs. Sandy was in the lead until we overcame these and found a suitable niche, still close to the edge of the gully, in which we sat down to lunch. Colin

then took over the lead, swarming up a flake on the right and
continuing up another 90-foot pitch of steep slabs with small
holds. The steepness and difficulty continued all the way to the
finish of the climb, when we found a small cairn, a few yards
away on our right, which was clearly the end of the 1933 route.
This perfectly sound, exceedingly steep and difficult route can
be highly recommended to a strong party, but there must be
considerable scope for variations on this broad face, as none of
the detailed accounts show good agreement with each other.

Another interesting case of severe routes occurring close
together on a Nevis cliff is the Bottom Tier of South Trident
Buttress. It was first climbed by Dr G. Graham Macphee and
G. C. Williams in June 1934. The next ascent was by W. G.
McClymont and myself in May 1936, and we passed Macphee's
cairn after our difficulties were ended. In September 1938
Wedderburn and I were limited by bad weather to ascending
the Ben by the track, but our day was not wasted. The sun
came out and we descended Observatory Buttress to the Hut,
enjoyed an excellent meal and climbed back over the mountain
by South Trident Buttress, using Macphee's route on the
Bottom Tier. There does not seem to be much to choose
between the two routes, as regards interest or difficulty.

In 1943 the location of most of the doubtful routes on Ben
Nevis was investigated by B. P. Kellett. He had great difficulty
in differentiating the 1934 and 1936 routes on the lower part of
South Trident Buttress, although I had none at all in 1938.
Kellett made the issue still more obscure by claiming a third
new, severe route, distinct from the others. Quite apart from
the perplexities and confusion of routes on the Bottom Tier, the
South Trident Buttress is one of the most interesting and
satisfying climbs on Ben Nevis. The middle tier makes very
good climbing, if taken as directly as possible, and the upper
part, including the Top Tier, formerly known as the Pinnacle
Arête of Carn Dearg, makes a delightful finish.

Most of the more recent, severe climbing on Ben Nevis has
been pioneered by Mr B. P. Kellett, and the original accounts
from his pen and his diaries have appeared in the *Scottish
Mountaineering Club Journals* in the years 1944, 1946 and 1947.
Kellett was an exceptionally able rock climber and his descriptions are meticulously accurate. It is tragic to reflect that he
lost his life in a fatal accident on the Ben in September 1944.
The available evidence tended to show that he was not, on that
occasion, engaged in climbing anything new or especially
difficult.

I had hoped to accompany him on several of his latest routes, particularly his Route 2 on the Great Buttress of Carn Dearg and one of his new discoveries to the left of the Orion climbs, but bad weather and wet rocks made this impossible. It is only fair to say that Kellett's climbing, for sheer daring, was often almost uncanny to watch. He led me up his Routes A and B on the North Buttress of Carn Dearg, and I have no particular wish to visit either place again. It is, of course, hard to disentangle one's impression from subsequent tragic events. His account of the first ascent of Gardyloo Buttress (between Tower and Gardyloo gullies), matter of fact as it appears at a first reading, is enough to bring out a sweat on the brow and the palms of a reader who has seen the place and is aware of the previous unsuccessful attempts on this formidable and sinister cliff. He invited me to join him on a second ascent. It was a high compliment, but the onset of bad weather relieved me from facing a difficult decision!

VII

BEN NEVIS IN WINTER

Introduction

HE WHO HAS climbed Ben Nevis only in summer knows but half the story, for the old Ben puts forth his mightiest challenge when clad in all his winter armour of snow, ice and storm. During one of my early visits to the Alps with Frank Smythe, after a rather tough day when we were only too thankful to reach the hut, having climbed our mountain on a day of storm and bad snow conditions, he said to me, "That shows the difference between the Alps and our British hills. You are glad to get to the top by any way whatever. These mountains really try to do you in." The same thing applies to Ben Nevis in its most wintry garb.

It is no longer a case for relying on the directions from a Guide. Everything is changed. Places which were easy in summer are so smothered in snow, ice and frost crystals that the summer route is no longer recognizable. The Tower Ridge can be an easy way of descent in summer. I have left the summit at midnight in the month of July and chosen the Tower Ridge as an interesting and pleasant way down to the Clark Hut. In winter and spring, especially after an unusually heavy snowfall followed by alternate wind, thaw and frost, the ridge may be quite impossible to ascend, so that parties have to retreat or may be benighted through failure to realize soon enough what they are up against. At other times the weather may change rapidly during an expedition, and what appeared well-considered and practicable at the start may end in a protracted fight to avert accident and disaster.

Climbers who are members of recognized clubs have the advantage of being able to start from the Clark Hut at the very foot of the crags, and thus can make full use of the short winter days. In the pioneering days there was another haven of refuge open to those who succeeded in fighting their way through the difficulties and reaching the summit: warmth, welcome and refreshment were usually available at the old Observatory. Now there is little comfort in the windy, derelict and ruinous remains of the old buildings, although some parties have tunnelled their way inside when entirely submerged in snow, and have lived there in comparative comfort during a New Year's blizzard. For it may prove to be the last, and apparently the easiest problem of getting down from the summit that spells disaster for an exhausted party in bad weather conditions.

On Easter Monday 1925, Smythe and I fought our way to the summit by the track in a blizzard of blinding snow and spindrift. One must experience such a storm before one can hope to realize what it means. My companion considered that one seldom encountered any worse *tourmente* on Mont Blanc. We were comparatively fresh men in the middle of our day. What would such a blizzard have meant to a party which had been fighting their way, without respite, for many hours up ridge or gully? And they would have the additional hazards of gathering darkness and increasing cold. It is no wonder that there have been accidents and fatalities to winter climbers on Ben Nevis, perhaps more especially to those from south of the Border who have had no previous experience of Scottish snow conditions. The really surprising thing is that the tally of winter accidents on the Ben has been so light during the twenty years from 1930. But the warning note should be sounded. The rate of accidents was on the increase before 1939, and the increase is likely to continue with the rise in popularity of winter climbing and improvement of communications.

Easter is the most popular time for English visitors, and much depends on the weather and snow conditions at that period. It must be firmly asserted that a few expeditions on the Alps in summer do not qualify a man for difficult winter conditions on Ben Nevis, and this is all the more true if the Alpine experience is of the guided variety. A great British mountaineer, H. W. Tilman, one of the first party to scale Nanda Devi (25,645 ft), in the Himalaya, had a mishap on Ben Nevis in the spring of 1946, owing to bad weather conditions. Fortunately, there were no serious consequences, but Tilman remarked afterwards in conversation, that a man who could climb safely on Ben Nevis in winter conditions could climb anywhere. So it should not be considered out of the way to suggest that newcomers to Scottish snow might well confine their activities to lesser mountains or easier routes until they gradually acquire some experience of that mysterious entity, the condition of the snow. It is a matter which takes a longer time to learn than rock-craft, mainly because we can never reconstruct the conditions for ourselves, nor can our experience be perfectly translated into words.

My own introduction to snow climbing took place on Ben Nevis, on Easter Sunday 1922. I learned a great deal from an excellent leader, my friend Ernest Roberts, an experienced veteran of the Alpine Club, and for many years the editor of the *Yorkshire Ramblers Club Journal*. Roberts had previous winter experience of Ben Nevis and he understood the vagaries of Scottish snow. As we walked up the track from Achintee a perfectly regular snowline about the 1,500-foot level extended evenly along the hills surrounding Glen Nevis. A little snow fell, but, as we passed the Lochan Meall an t'Suidhe the air cleared and I had my first sight of the splendours of the northeast face of Ben Nevis in winter—great ridges sweeping up in whiteness to a mottled sky and gullies bulging with blue-green ice. It was not the same sort of snow that I had been accustomed to in the plains. It gave a different sort of crunch underfoot. When one looked down the hole made by an ice-axe the colour was a beautiful pale blue. One does not always see this effect, and I was lucky in my introduction to Scottish snow.

We lunched during a snow squall in the hollow of Coire na Ciste. It must have been about the site of the Lochan, but there was nothing visible except a snowy hollow with a small crag, and then steep slopes ahead. Soon we started off up these slopes below No. 2 Gully, for Roberts expected that we should be able to make our way up, although he could not foretell what sort of cornice there might be at the top of the gully. At first the snow was very soft, but it firmed up as the walls of the gully hemmed us in. As the gully narrowed it steepened, the snow becoming much harder. We could no longer kick steps. The axes, hitherto used in the manner of spiked walking sticks, were now to be applied to their main purpose. The surface was tough snow-ice, and Roberts proceeded steadily to cut a zig-zag staircase of steps. As he was not much taller than I the spacing suited me very well. At every turn of the zig-zag was a larger step, where he belayed me carefully over a driven-in ice-axe when I moved up to join him. Likewise, I safeguarded him when he moved in front.

At the steepest part we were assailed by a fierce wind, a sand-blast of icy spindrift, whirling round and coming at us from every quarter at once. Then there was a troublesome section where the snow was deeper and softer. I relied on the experience of the leader who considered that the snow was not badly compacted to the harder layer underneath. In any case, under the prevailing conditions, we could not have cleared the soft stuff and cut into the underlayer, for the steps would have filled up immediately. So we kicked out steps and adopted a style of crawling straight up the slope, helping ourselves with our axes held before us and driven deeply into the snow. In certain kinds of snow I have found this a very safe and useful way of climbing, but it is a good thing to test the cohesion of the soft surface snow to the underlayer. This can always be tried by one member of the party on the rope. With experience one gradually senses the reliability of the snow by the way it compacts or yields when sudden strain is put upon it.

At length we reached the foot of the steep funnel below the cornice at the top of the gully. We were again on hard snow-ice. It was an imposing cornice, overhanging considerably in a wide eave on the left, but not nearly so high and without any overhang at the right-hand corner. Cornices are built outward by drifted snow from the plateau; and the prevailing thaw wind, when the drift snow adheres best, is from the south-west. Roberts made for the easier right-hand corner and was careful to cut good, solid steps. Below the cornice was a hollow lip, and I was left there, securely belayed, while the leader cut the last few holds on the vertical wall and pulled himself up. After securing himself he invited me to follow, and soon we were shaking hands over the success of a very good climb.

The scene was most impressive. For the time it had stopped snowing. Above and behind us were dark, snow-bearing clouds: a dazzling shaft of sunlight streamed up from below through a rift in the lower cloud—the reflection of the sun in the distant waters of Loch Linnhe. Roberts stood there sparkling and ice-bedecked in the sunbeams; exactly like a polar explorer with hair, moustache, eyebrows and woolly helmet all encased in ice. We moved off to the summit of the Ben. The old Observatory was thickly cased in snow with long frost crystals at all the projecting edges. Unlike cornices, these fluted ornaments of fern-like beauty are formed, not of drifted snow but of super-cooled vapour. They build themselves outwards into the wind. They occur on all Scottish hills in winter, but are most beautiful and massive on the higher levels of Ben Nevis. We also admired the huge cornices at the mouths of Gardyloo and Tower Gullies, particularly the latter; and Roberts recalled his last experience on the Ben when his party succeeded, after a hard fight, in storming Gardyloo Gully.

We returned along the plateau and over Carn Dearg. Then we made for the top of the long funnel, occupied in summer by the Red Burn. Down it we enjoyed a magnificent standing glissade, for the condition of the snow was just right. After a short walk to the old Halfway Hut we brewed some tea with a small primus. Duly refreshed, Roberts led me over Meall an t'Suidhe and down by a steep and intricate route to Nevis Bridge and Fort William. Such was my satisfying first experience of Ben Nevis under snow and ice.

Next day we again set out for the Ben, but decided to attempt something nearer to hand. We made for South Castle Gully on Carn Dearg. As the day was calm, crisp and clear, we thought that we might put it to a better use. Traversing out of the gully to the right we had little difficulty in securing a lodgment on the rocks of the Castle. In summer time this may be more difficult, but now very little rock was showing except at the sides of the gully. We gradually worked our way up the centre of the Castle, cutting a line of steps so as to link up the outcrops of bare rock. By this method it is possible to find good foot-holds and stances in the snow pockets amongst the rocks. It saves time and step-cutting. If the snow is in a doubtful state as regards avalanche danger this provides safe stances and additional security. I was already learning to reflect on such things and picking up a good deal of practical technique which proved invaluable to me later on, in the Alps. The immediate object was only to save time and labour, because the snow was icy and the rocks had conveniently bedded ledges.

It was interesting work and we made steady progress, although Roberts well knew that the most serious difficulties lay ahead, where the summit cliffs became much steeper and almost appeared to overhang. We came to a natural halting place which was a sort of narrow cave. The cornices at the edge of the plateau seemed to be little more than 200 feet above us. Roberts asked me to try leading up the next difficulty, but I was soon halted by chimneys of hard, black ice. The rock strata shelved outward and downward and the rocks were filmed with ice. After Roberts had inspected things for himself he thought for a little, shook his head and advised retreat. To attempt to force the issue might, he said, take many hours. So I learned the wisdom, and also the technique, of a timely retreat. Our steps were still good and usable, but we exercised great care on the icy parts. As we walked down the Mhuilinn glen a few hours later the Tower Ridge and North-East Buttress looked magnificent and austere in the evening light.

Next day we had to leave Fort William, but there was time for one more mountain. We left the train at Tyndrum and made our way up the Choninish glen to Ben Lui. I was appointed to lead up the Central Gully in the north-east corrie. The day was again perfect and I enjoyed myself. It was only necessary to cut steps in the narrow, upper section, where we climbed the steepest branch of the gully. Even so, Ben Lui (3,708 ft), was very much easier than anything we had done on Ben Nevis, and the cornice was quite a simple affair. The extra 700 feet of height on Nevis makes all the difference in the world, especially as late in the spring as April, to the hardening of the snow, that peculiar process of transformation into snow-ice which is usually termed "firnification" in the Alps. If the climbing was easier the view from the summit of Lui was unexcelled—embracing Loch Awe, Ben Cruachan, the Glencoe hills, Ben Nevis, Ben Lawers, Schichallion and many other hills.

On Good Friday, 1925, I was with Frank Smythe at Fort William. We opened our campaign with the Castle. The snow was in excellent hard condition. Where Roberts and I had turned back three years previously Smythe and I had some intricate work on iced and snowy rocks with badly sloping holds. Actually, there was little more than fifty feet of difficulty followed by an easy slope to a small cornice at the top, which was easily overcome. So I enjoyed my revenge on the Castle, but, from the summit of Carn Dearg, we were at once faced by the challenge of the Tower Ridge with hardly a spot of black showing above the level of the Douglas Boulder. On that perfect evening it appeared unearthly in its peaceful beauty but also, "as the air, invulnerable".

The Gullies

The Nevis gullies are most useful for learning about the conditions of the snow, the icy channels which are the natural tracks for falling stones and fragments of cornices which have broken away, and the way in which cornices build up, how to climb them or force a way through them. Apart from the two Castle Gullies which I have never climbed and of which the southern is usually considered to be the easier, there are four gullies which are not at all difficult, viz, Nos. 3, 4, 5 and Tower Gully. No. 5 has some short pitches at the narrow section, but these offer little trouble, as a rule. It has a very wide upper funnel, so that an exit can always be made at one point or another. I climbed it with R. M. McIntyre as a farewell climb

on a Monday morning in April 1932. We left the Clark Hut at
five a.m., had some trouble with deep snow and breakable crust
in the middle section, but reached the top of Carn Dearg at
seven a.m. There was a lip below the cornice at the top, fringed
with a beautiful curtain of icicles through which we could see
the morning sun shining brightly on the distant cone of
Schiehallion. It seemed a shame to break the icicles and flog
down the graceful snowy curves of the cornice.

Nos. 3 and 4 gullies are usually easy to descend, No. 4 being
the easiest of all and least likely to give trouble with a cornice.
It is curved at the top, but from below the curve it is generally
safe to glissade all the way to Coire na Ciste. The same cannot
always be said of No. 3, which is perfectly straight. If one
descends No. 3 it is wise to be exceedingly careful until below
the narrow, rocky portal at the foot of the upper funnel. There
is often a considerable cornice at the top, but there are two
upper openings, of which at least one may be practicable for
starting a descent. In icy conditions No. 3 should be treated
with great care, as there may be a polished, hardened avalanche
trough between the portals. On a former occasion I was lucky
to escape with a few bruises and bumps when a standing
glissade got out of control. I retained my axe, but the spike is
not a very powerful brake on a hard surface, whereas any
attempt to use the pick on such a surface would simply jerk the
axe out of one's hand altogether if, as is usually the case, the
slide has developed a certain velocity before the remedy can be
applied. In a hard, icy condition of the snow, which is not so
bad as to necessitate the actual cutting of steps, the safest mode
of descent is to stamp the feet down sideways, edging them into
the surface, remain as upright as possible and secure oneself
continually with the pick of the axe driven in forcibly slightly
above, so that a slide will never start. This warning should
apply to any Nevis gully, even to No. 4, during hard, frosty
conditions, and sometimes to broad, open snow-slopes as well.
One should note that the top of No. 4 gully is at the lowest
point of the rim of the plateau above Coire na Ciste and is next
to the steep rise leading to the summit of Carn Dearg.

The only other Nevis gully which can be recommended for a
practice descent, not without a little difficulty, is the Tower
Gully, on the summit side of Tower Ridge. This gully is easy in
summer, but it carries huge cornices in winter. Everything
depends on the size and continuity of the cornice. If entry can
be effected safely from above the party will probably be able to

descend the rest of it safely. Below the upper part it is necessary
to traverse obliquely downwards to the right, over a steep slope,
in order to get on to the upper snows of Observatory Gully
below the exit of Gardyloo Gully. This may be difficult if the
snow is in bad condition. Observatory Gully is steep, but has
no pitches lower down.

On Easter Monday, 1929, on the occasion of the opening of
the C.I.C. Hut by the Scottish Mountaineering Club, three of
us walked to the summit of the Ben and made our way to the
opening ceremony down Tower Gully. Part of the old cornice
had fallen in, affording us an easy entrance, and Charlie Parry
cut the steps down the gully. There was a fierce, cold wind with
blasts of spindrift. Lower down, where we had to turn to the
right, great care was necessary owing to the masses of new
snow. The mist swayed and eddied around us, but there were
wonderful glimpses of distant mountains and of Loch Laggan,
thirty miles to the east. Once past the dangerous slope we
enjoyed a straight run on splendid snow down the entire length
of Observatory Gully. Owing to the gentle run-out at the
bottom we were able to glissade the whole way, in perfect
control, to the Mhuilinn glen. We arrived at the Hut at four
fifteen p.m., over an hour late, but still in time for the remains
of the feast. But we were not too late for the delightful dinner
that evening in the Palace Hotel, Fort William. Such a dinner,
following a day on the hills by almost everyone concerned, was
permeated by the true mountaineering spirit. Dr Inglis Clark,
mountaineer, explorer and pioneer of Scottish mountain photography, had just come down from the opening ceremony,
despite his age of over seventy years, and he gave us a delightful
and colourful speech in praise of mountaineering and of Ben
Nevis in all its many moods.

The Gardyloo Gully is the most fearsome of the Nevis gullies
when seen from above in winter. Its walls are not far short of
vertical and it is defended by cornices where they are not so.
The name dates back to the old Observatory days, when all
manner of rubbish and discarded material was tipped over the
side into the gully, just as in the narrow streets of old Edinburgh, when open gutters did duty for drains. The tipping of
a bucket of dirty water from an upstairs window was usually
preceded by a shout of "Gardez l'eau" from above. These days
are also in the past as regards Gardyloo Gully, but rusty relics
of old cans, pipes, bedsteads can still be found in the huge
mounds of rocky debris at the foot of Observatory Gully, a

tribute to the action of the geological forces of denudation within our own time.

Gardyloo Gully is narrow and steep, but not over 250 feet in height. Half-way down is a natural rocky arch which is completely buried in snowy winters. When that is so the main difficulty is to climb the wall beneath it. When the archway is clear, there may be a severe ice pitch just above it. I have been three times up Gardyloo in winter, but there was always room to crawl through the archway. My first ascent was on 31 December 1928 with R. R. Elton. We had been ignominiously driven off the Tower Ridge by a gale of wind and ice-crusted rocks. The ice pitch above the Gardyloo archway was a tough proposition. I found myself inside a little chimney curtained by massive icicles, and had to break out of it in order to climb up on the left to an ice slope. Twice I had to retreat, restore the circulation to numbed hands and straighten tense limbs, but ultimately I got through and cut substantial steps in the ice above. The icicles were sufficiently massive to confer some measure of security. When my friend came up, there remained only a short, steep slope to the top, for the cornice had broken away to a short, vertical wall.

That was a day of unequalled visibility to the Cuillin of Skye, Rum, Mull, Jura and all the north-western peaks. We descended by the Arête and traversed the ridge to Carn Mor Dearg, just in time to view a sunset which was one mass of crimson glory in the west. On the following day, clad in shirt-sleeves in warm sunshine, I ate my lunch on the top of Carn Dearg. The day was windless and the north-western hills were perfectly imaged in the calm waters of Loch Eil. On such days Ben Nevis can be truly Alpine and magnificent in its grandeur. Looking at the summit crags from the foot of Observatory Gully, before climbing Gardyloo on the previous day, the racing clouds were flashing with silver and gold in the level sunbeams and bringing to mind Milton's lines on the "crystal battlements" of Heaven. And we were setting out to storm these battlements.

My next ascent was on a gloomy April day in 1932. We vanquished the gully at dusk, and, amid the racing clouds of mist and spindrift, we had an anxious struggle to find and force our way down by the normally easy western slopes. To our shame, be it said, that not a man of the four of us carried a compass. We could proceed only with the utmost care, within sight of, but not too near the edge of the north-eastern precipice,

until we reached the level plateau between Nevis and Carn
Dearg. Then we turned to face the gale, and there was just
sufficient murk of twilight to enable us to distinguish several
of the snow-covered cairns which mark the route of the old
telegraph line to the Observatory. That was the end of doubt
and difficulty, as we raced down the slopes and saw the sombre
gleam of the Lochan Meall an t'Suidhe far below us. We had
emerged through the floor of the cloud. We were descending to
the C.I.C. Hut, but, in the prevailing conditions, our circuitous
route was much safer than attempting to descend by the Carn
Mor Dearg Arête, which may be very difficult to locate and
may even demand continuous step-cutting.

The Great Ridges

The best winter mountaineering in Scotland is on the great
ridges of Ben Nevis. The Castle Ridge is the easiest, as it
terminates nearly 1,000 feet lower than the others. The classic
route is the Tower Ridge which, although fairly easy in summer,
gives a very long and interesting climb under snow and ice. At
mid-winter it is often impossible to climb the steep rocks of the
Douglas Boulder by the direct route on account of ice on the
narrow ledges. In spring the Boulder may be snow-free and
offer a good, difficult introduction for the serious snow and ice
work beyond. The Tower Ridge may be impossible in winter.
In that case one can be certain that no other ridge will go,
except perhaps the Castle Ridge.

My first attempt on Tower Ridge was with Frank Smythe at
Easter 1925, the day after we had climbed the Castle. Several
parties belonging to the Scottish Mountaineering Club were on
the mountain, as it was the occasion of the Easter Meet at Fort
William. Only one party, bivouacking in the now vanished
Half Way Hut on the western slopes, had gone very early to the
Tower Ridge. As we halted, with a number of others, at a huge
boulder above the Allt a'Mhuilinn, called the Luncheon Stone
by the pioneers, we could see Rusk and Rutherfurd high up on
the sunlit ridge. But alas! they were descending, which was a
bad omen for us. We resolved to have a good rock climb to
begin with and tackled the Douglas Boulder. It gave us good
sport and we reached the summit cairn by three p.m In those
days there was no C.I.C. Hut and we had walked from Fort
William.

The day continued fine, so we both voted for giving the ridge
a trial. The gap between Douglas Boulder and ridge is neither

deep nor difficult. We encountered no serious difficulties beyond the gap until we approached the foot of the Little Tower, as the steep rock nose below it carried little snow. The Little Tower was a very different proposition. So smothered was it in snow and ice that we feared it might take hours to overome by direct attack. We were not yet beaten, however. There was a way of descending on the side of Coire na Ciste, not a big descent, whereby we were enabled to reach a steeply sloping band or terrace which trended upwards in the direction of the Great Tower. This is known as the Secondary Tower Ridge, and we hoped that from it we could regain the main ridge just short of the Great Tower. Step cutting was necessary all the way. Smythe feared, with his Alpine experience, that such steeply inclined snow would be sure to peel off in a minor avalanche sooner or later. I assured him that he under-estimated its toughness and dourness (like the Scottish character). We continued and climbed steeply up the band, using side holds on the rocks on our left, where available. The move was successful and we were at the base of the Great Tower by five p.m.

The easiest way of circumventing this all but vertical boss of rock is by the Eastern Traverse, above Observatory Gully. It looked frightful: the idea of traversing a broad band of snow, as steeply inclined as a high angled roof, with a sheer drop over a cliff at the lower edge, gave us pause. Across Coire na Ciste, on the summit of Carn Dearg, a large group of mountaineers were observing our movements with interest. They were going down to Fort William for dinner, and here were we, at least half ignorant of what lay before us, but pretty sure that it was going to take a long time and much hard step cutting before we could even reach the easy summit slopes of the mountain. Could we make it at all before nightfall?

Smythe stepped out on to the steep band of snow. It was gratifyingly hard and firm. The mist closed in about us, hiding all but the frost crystalled cliff of the Tower and the line of footsteps, curving inwards to cross the top of a little gully and then outwards round the next bulge of the buttress. Things were not improving: here and there the snow was very thin and the axe struck bare rock, but there was always a way of some kind that led onward and upward. The snow was tough and sound; I will say that for it. Working hard and steadily, it took us an hour to regain the crest of the ridge beyond the Tower. It was now snowing gently, with nothing visible ahead but an awesome gap in the ridge in front of us, and then the great, white wall of the final rocks. We held anxious converse. The rocks were cased in frost crystals about a foot thick. We knew about the Tower Gap, but we had no idea of the difficulties beyond and we feared that there might be a cornice below the summit plateau.

In all prudence, or perhaps on account of our ignorance, retreat was the only sensible course of action. From the Tower Gap two chimneys descended into the mist in opposite directions. The one on the right I had read about. It was Glover's Chimney, a difficult climb in summer. We knew nothing of the other except that it must lead to Observatory Gully, and we could see nothing. The only sure way of retreat was the way by which we had come. Moving carefully, yet as quickly as possible, we retraced our steps round the Tower. There was no drifting snow and the steps were all good. I shall not detail that descent. The passage of time was only measured by the landmarks of our route. We were soon below the mist. As we got down the last of the rocks by the steep gully from the Douglas Boulder Gap to Coire na Ciste (for we knew too little of the topography of the Ben to select the easier gully leading towards Coire Leis) the setting sun coloured the summit snows of Carn Mor Dearg a deep crimson. Far below us the Great Glen was filled with a lovely violet coloured haze. It was one of those wonderful colour contrasts, soft yet brilliant, which are only seen in our Scottish Highlands in winter or spring, and almost unknown in the drier climate of the Alps.

We got off the rocks by eight p.m. and hurried down the glen in careless contentment. The last wisps of cloud were drifting over the summit of the Ben: the great ridges assumed a pale, spectral hue—intensely cold and aloof. We were profoundly thankful that we had beaten a timely retreat. The last peril of the day was when we were stumping dreamily towards Fort William along the railway track. A belated goods engine crept swiftly and silently up behind us, and we hastily jumped down the embankment. At ten p.m. we met Mr J. A. Parker, President of the S.M.C., in the main street. He was unaffectedly glad to see us, and the word "search party" was not even mentioned!

Needless to say, the challenge of the Tower Ridge, clad in full wintry armour (it had to be so for sporting reasons), was often in my mind. The next trial of strength was at Easter 1929. On the Saturday C. W. Parry and I had ascended Observatory Ridge and descended the North-East Buttress with comparatively little trouble on snow-free rocks in glorious weather. It snowed and blew all that night. We were staying at the C.I.C. Hut, just before the formal opening. Smythe and Roberts were also there, so we set out, all four of us, for the Tower Ridge next day. In doubtful weather we took the easiest approach and gained the ridge beyond the Douglas Boulder Gap. As we got higher a proper blizzard set in. Ledges were all smothered in new snow, which had to be cleared as there was some ice underneath. It became unendurable and we retreated from the rocks of the Little Tower.

In 1932, a winter of ample snowfall, I tried again, in the company of Robert McIntyre, of Perth. We motored to Fort William on a Friday afternoon early in April. We opened the campaign in a rather unorthodox way, going to the local cinema, where we saw a modern American version of something like Shakespeare's *Comedy of Errors*, under the title *Lonely Wives*. We then descended into the basement of the local fish and chip restaurant, commonly known as "Hell's Kitchen". Well nourished, we left the car at Achintee at eleven fifteen p.m. in bright moonlight. As we ascended the track it occurred to us that we might as well test the condition of the snow. We decided to continue to the summit of the Ben. Above the snow-line all feelings of drowsiness left us and we thoroughly enjoyed the latter part of the ascent. Clouds came over the moon and a cold wind moaned across the plateau, which looked completely desolate and arctic in the half-light. We reached the summit at two a.m. and took shelter for a few minutes in the lee of the Observatory. Then we made for the top of No. 3 Gully where there was hardly any cornice, and proceeded to descend. The snow was in good condition and not too hard, so, after cutting a few steps we were able to stamp our way downwards in security towards Coire na Ciste. Conditions were too soft for glissading. The sky cleared again, and we saw the Great Tower, high above us, frost-spangled and gleaming in the moonlight. Surely the conditions were right at last for a successful assault. We were in the Hut by three a.m., trying to coax the warmth back into our feet after much wallowing in soft snow.

We made an early start, climbing the Douglas Boulder quickly by the direct route, there being little snow on the lower rocks. The first steep rocks beyond the Boulder Gap required a little clearing, but the first serious difficulty was again at the Little Tower. We attacked it direct, but all the rocks were heavily plastered and we were soon forced to traverse over steep slabs overlooking the Observatory Gully. The snow was new and dry, of the consistency of flour. It had not been thawed or refrozen and it failed to adhere to the old film of ice on the rocks. Unfortunately, the latter was too thin to be chipped into satisfactory footholds. After about sixty feet of traversing, things improved and I secured a belay of a sort for the axe. I did not like the situation at all and felt obliged to warn Mac that I might not be able to stand the strain of holding him if he had the misfortune to slip. This is always a danger on a long traverse. If a second man comes off on the rope he executes a long pendulum swing before he can be checked. My caution was unnecessary. Mac proceeded with irreproachable precision.

We worked our way back to the crest of the ridge. The rocks were draped with massive icicles which, as we cut them down, bounced on the slabs with a merry, musical tinkle before plunging finally into the gully. It was such a day of gorgeous sunshine that we made light of our difficulties. We were both in splendid form and the Tower Ridge was giving us our money's worth. We, neither of us, wished for an easy passage.

Over an hour and a half was spent on the Little Tower. At length we were proceeding along the graceful, curving eaves of purest snow to the base of the Great Tower. For half an hour we fed and rested in the warm sunshine, gazing contentedly at the Alpine panorama to north and east of us. When we started on the Eastern Traverse the slope was already in shadow, not at all a bad thing for that dangerous-looking, steep band of snow which we must cross. I have known cases where parties have come so far and have been intimidated by that slope, so that they have either retreated or attempted one or other of the much more difficult western routes on the Tower. If one sees the place in summer the ledge-like structure of the lower rock explains why the winter accumulation of snow is generally perfectly stable, despite its steepness. It builds up gradually during the winter so that the successive layers have time to cohere by relegation. Beyond the traverse we gained the Tower crest by iced ledges, and that was the end of all serious difficulty. If only Frank Smythe and I had known what lay beyond the Tower Gap; even with our small pittance of available daylight, we should have been able to complete the ascent in 1925. On this occasion we cleared and crossed the Gap quite easily. Two ugly bulges of vertical snow above it turned out to be firm and good; a beautifully curved ridgeline of snow followed, corniced a little on one side. Then Mac cut a staircase up the final slope and we stepped on to the summit plateau after five and a half hours of actual climbing time.

The Tower Ridge is far from being the most difficult of the great ridges of Ben Nevis, but it is always interesting under snow. It is so delightfully varied, and the ice-boltered rocks at the Great Tower (to copy an expression used by Mr Winthrop Young in his Alpine classic, *On High Hills*) are so exceedingly impressive. The few hundred feet by which Ben Nevis overtops the other Scottish hills in the west makes an enormous difference to the difficulties of the upper parts of the climbs. The rest is due to the storage capacity of the plateau for snow and the strategic position of the Ben on the Atlantic Seaboard. W. T. Kilgour, in his book, *Twenty Years on Ben Nevis*, remarks that there seemed to be only two conditions of atmospheric humidity on the Ben—very dry or saturation. Under the latter and more common condition frost crystals would grow out into the wind at an enormous rate, up to several feet long on all sharp edges of rock, buildings or Observatory apparatus.

There have been several cases of benightment on the Tower Ridge. At Easter, 1937, after a very snowy winter, only one party succeeded in completing the ascent, Mr and Mrs S. H. Cross, of Cumberland. They actually cut steps across the face of the Great Tower, obliquely upwards in a westerly direction. Surely that must have been more difficult than the Eastern Traverse, but it all depends on the previous weather history of the mountain. Their performance was a very fine one. On the same day two friends of my own proceeded too far and too late, with the result that they were compelled to spend a calm, frosty night on the rocks. They were none the worse, for I enjoyed an excellent climb with them two days later up Green Gully by the side of the Comb. There, we only succeeded in fighting our way up to the plateau by seven p.m.

Just before Christmas, 1939, with W. H. Murray and D. Laidlaw, I again climbed the Tower Ridge. After a hard fight we reached the summit in bright moonlight. All around and beneath us was a sea of cloud silvered by moonbeams, from which only the high tops of the Mamores and the Glencoe peaks projected like black islands. Days such as these are indeed rare, but through them one lives to the full. The worries of a modern civilized existence vanish into thin wraiths of unreality and we are back in the dawn of history among the gods, giants and mysterious animism of our remote forefathers, when sagas like Beowulf and the Norse Eddas were composed in a setting of great mountains and savage wildernesses of snow and ice.

On days when the Tower Ridge can be climbed fairly easily

the Observatory Ridge may be quite impossible. This was so in early April 1939 on account of icing on the lower slabs. After many fruitless hours George Dwyer, Dicky Morsley and I abandoned the attempt and completed our day by a rapid ascent of Tower Ridge. At the end of April I was back again at the C.I.C. Hut in a goodly company of climbers. Next day Bill Murray, W. M. Mackenzie and I started for Observatory Ridge. Several ledges required clearing of snow and there was some ice here and there, but I had little difficulty in leading up the lower, slabby nose of the ridge. The others were held in reserve for the snow and ice higher up.

A snow ridge followed, with rocky bosses at intervals. Soon we had to cut carefully up the Observatory Gully side of the ridge and back again to a broad snow stance on the crest, where we halted for lunch. There was now a choice between a difficult route along the crest or another traverse over apparently easier ground on our right into a steep gully. In February, 1938, Murray, Mackenzie and MacAlpine had used the detour, but it had cost them much time and labour. On that occasion the party had encountered masses of dry powder snow which made the going exceedingly difficult, and even dangerous. This must have been the most severe ascent ever made of the Observatory Ridge. It cost the party fourteen hours and they reached the summit of the Ben at eleven-thirty p.m., having been forced to cut steps for several hours by the light of torches on the final slopes of Zero Gully. (Mackenzie gives an account in *S.M.C. Journal* 21: 337ff).

Mackenzie having led before lunch, it was now Murray's turn. We followed him up a wall to the crest of the ridge. In front was an ice-encrusted rocky tower. The snow covering became very thin as we approached its base, and Mackenzie anchored himself. The leader ran out ninety feet of rope, so we had to untie and include an extra sixty feet in our linkage, as we had been tied on a single 120-foot length. First came a delicate traverse to the left, then a direct ascent, partly on rock and partly on notches cut by Murray in the ice, and finally to the lower end of an ice-covered, rocky scoop. This gave the leader much trouble, as it was a nasty place. I fully understood when it came to my turn to follow. This fine lead brought us back into the sunshine. For all that, it was so cold that we continued to wear all our woollies and helmets. Things went much better now. The crest rose in front of us in a beautiful snowy curve, and Zero Gully on our left was no longer at an enormous distance below.

At four p.m. we cut steps across into the bed of Zero Gully. We could see our friends on the Tower Ridge, negotiating the Eastern Traverse. I was now on familiar ground, as Colin Allan and I had climbed the lower half of Slav Route on 4 April 1936, and finished up Zero Gully, being forced to cut steps continuously for three hours and negotiating two ice pitches. I carried a clinometer on that occasion and found that the average inclination of the gully was 56 degrees for a very long way. This is a very steep gradient indeed for Scottish snow and usually indicates a hard surface of snow-ice. On this occasion, however, the snow-ice was in excellent condition. By working without a halt and changing over the lead at intervals, we emerged on the summit at five-thirty p.m. Zero Gully is seldom corniced at the top. Our splendid climb had taken us just six and a half hours, a very different experience from the notable February ascent of the year before. As the strength of the parties involved on the two occasions must have been approximately the same, the difference in time taken can only be ascribed to the very troublesome condition of the snow in the month of February. This dry, powdery snow is common enough in the Alps and must be perpetual on the upper slopes of Himalayan peaks.

Next day Bill Murray and I climbed the North East Buttress. That, too, was an ideal day. We attained the First Platform directly by Raeburn's Arête. In many places great care was required owing to ice on the ledges, but the rock was otherwise dry. Two hours saw us on the Platform. Higher up we encountered a good deal more snow, and it was a little difficult to regain the crest of the ridge from the snowy gully on the left, some way below the Second Platform. We knew the structure of the ridge and the beautifully incut holds available on this wall, when once the snow had been cleared away. To all other climbers who essay the route under snow conditions I should give the advice not to be daunted by the forbidding appearance of this wall. As soon as we regained the crest we had an alternation of snow and rock all the way to the top. The few difficult sections were short. Near the top the rocks were again heavy with frost crystals. Without halts, we gained the summit in two and three-quarter hours from the First Platform. We descended by the Ledge Route from Carn Dearg, normally a quick route of descent when the lower rocks are snow-free. Of course, the North East Buttress would present very formidable problems in winter or early spring after heavy snowfalls. It can always be expected to be much more difficult than Tower Ridge. It is interesting to recall that these two routes were, apart from gullies, the earliest climbing routes on the Ben. The Tower Ridge was first climbed by Norman Collie, G. A. Solly and J. Collier in April 1894 and described by them, in *S.M.C. Journal* 3: 158ff, as "a superb climb of about 2,000 feet of ice, snow and rock". The first ascent of the North East Buttress, by the brothers Hopkinson in September 1892, was obviously not complicated by snow and ice.

In conclusion a word may be said about descending the Ben in winter by the Arête in the direction of Carn Mor Dearg. In severe conditions this may be extremely difficult. Parties have been compelled to cut steps all the way, and it has taken as long as two hours to reach the saddle at the head of Coire Leis. The best descent to the corrie is by a uniform slope of scree some way short of the saddle itself (where there are terraces of crag). Moreover, in mist or twilight, it is not always easy to hit off the correct route to the edge of the Arête. Parties have got into difficulties and accidents have happened when they have gone by mistake to the end of the North East Buttress and attempted to descend its eastern face, which is craggy and may be badly iced.

Many other climbs on Ben Nevis will be done in winter conditions which have hitherto been regarded as purely rock climbs, as there is always progress in mountaineering technique, but sufficient has been written in this chapter to show what a grand field for adventure and unending variety is offered by the truly Alpine, wintry defences of Ben Nevis. They must never be lightly regarded; for a sunny April day with warm, dry rocks can, within a few hours, be transformed into a raging storm of hail, snow and tearing cloud, with a film of ice on the rocks and masses of whirling spindrift. There is yet another danger for the inexperienced. Winter days are short: even April days are followed by long nights. A party may be capable of climbing the lower two-thirds of a route like Tower Ridge, but be utterly outclassed by the icy defences of the last 500 feet. It is then that a weak party may panic and an accident happen to an exhausted member on ground which he could normally descend or climb in comparative safety. It is vital that the decision to retreat should be taken as soon as prudence and commonsense urge its advisability. It takes more than a few, brief visits at Easter time to confer a comprehensive practical experience of snow, ice and weather on a difficult mountain like Ben Nevis.

VIII

THE ORION ROUTES ON BEN NEVIS

ONE HAS A natural tendency to look to Ben Nevis for the longest rock climbs in Britain. The Tower Ridge, including the direct ascent of the Douglas Boulder, must provide about 2,000 feet of vertical ascent, but, in summer conditions, much of it is very easy climbing. There is only one place to search for such a route, if we wish to preserve the height and raise the general angle and the standard of difficulty throughout. As long ago as 1925, when Frank Smythe and I were beaten on the Tower Ridge in difficult conditions of snow and ice, and again in early June 1932, when we had bad weather, we came to the conclusion that this exciting, new rock climb must start from near the foot of a formidable gully which separates the Observatory Ridge from the slabby face of the North-East Buttress. The gully had never been climbed at that date, nor has a complete ascent of it been made up to the present, but, on 5 April 1936, Colin Allan and I climbed it with the exception of the lower part, which was then a mass of prodigious icicles. Continuing the Guide Book nomenclature of the Nevis gullies, without a spark of imagination, we named it Zero Gully, and the name has been, more or less, accepted.

Above the foot of Zero Gully, rather less than half-way up the precipice, there is a large, gently inclined depression in the face of the cliff, which, in spring and early summer, generally retains a small snow-bed when all the other rocks are bare. We focused our attention on this prominent landmark in June 1932 and decided that an ascent to the snow-field, which we called the Basin, was within the bounds of possibility. We could do nothing at that time on account of the weather and the quantity of water which was streaming over the slabs above. If we could reach the Basin we considered that the upper rocks might offer several feasible ways to the crest of the North-East Buttress.

Two years went by without any opportunity of making the attempt. In September 1934 Sandy Wedderburn was entertaining two first-class Yugoslav mountaineers at the C.I.C. Hut. I happened to be there with a guest of my own, and Sandy asked my advice, for he wished to take his guests on a really hard climb, something out of the ordinary. I passed on the new idea, and the result was that excellent discovery, now known as the Slav Route. The start was at the foot of Zero Gully and the lower 300 feet were exceedingly difficult. In the prevailing bad weather, with very wet rocks and a heavy storm whilst they were on the most difficult part, two *pitons* were fixed and used for security. The continuation of the climb, instead of going directly upwards to the Basin, was parallel to Zero Gully and much easier than the lower part. It occupied about the same time that my own party of two, moving fairly continuously, required for climbing the standard route on Observatory Ridge.

The Slav Route, while it did not solve my problem, appeared to decide two questions at least. Wedderburn did not consider that it would be possible to climb straight up to the Basin from Slav Route, and it was clear that good weather and dry rocks would be essential for reaching the Basin from below by any route whatever. My next opportunity was in July 1935 when I was accompanied by Miss Violet Roy of the Grampian Club. She was an excellent rock climber, well balanced and light. We had perfect weather conditions and plenty of time. The structure of the rock determined our general line, for this whole face, as seen from the C.I.C. Hut, is sculptured into huge ribs, running back leftwards from the vertical at an angle of about 20 degrees. One of these ribs passes upwards to the left of the Basin, and we attempted to follow it.

The point of view is very important in estimating the angle of a mountain face. From the foot of Observatory Gully this wall appears to be so nearly vertical that one instinctively regards it as an impossible climb; from the crest of Observatory Ridge, just above the lower nose, it looks quite vertical with some places which appear to overhang the base. From the middle slopes of Carn Mor Dearg, however, the impression is altogether different, and the angle of the face, seen partly in profile, is not nearly so intimidating. It is not exactly inviting, for the eye begins to appreciate the smoothness of the great, steep slabs, and the mind to doubt if they could be climbed, even if set at a moderate angle. The same type of problem faced Edward Whymper during his attempts on the Matterhorn, causing him to persist too long in attacking the Italian ridge above Breuil. Only later was he convinced that the general angle of the Hörnli ridge above Zermatt was little more than 30 degrees, although it had appeared to be impregnable, as seen

The Orion Routes: Ben Nevis (*N.E. Buttress, N.W. face*)

L	Long Climb	SL	Straight Left Route	B	The Basin
E	Easy Traverse	Z	Zero Gully	M	The Mantrap
SR	Slav Route	OR	Observatory Ridge		

The summit of Ben Nevis is above OR. The left skyline is the crest of the North-East Buttress. The figures are standing on a snow-bed which, in most summers, does not entirely melt away. The figures are about 1,600–1,700 feet below the summit of Ben Nevis.

from the Riffel Alp. The result was a successful ascent at the first serious attempt in 1865.

Our problem was a minor replica of his. The most revealing views of the face could only be obtained under two conditions. Either very early or late in the day, in mid-summer, the glancing rays of the sun show up its irregularities. As there is often very little sunshine on the Ben one may also see the rock structure occasionally when mist or cloud is dispersing and re-forming over the crags in isolated blobs and wisps which play hide and seek amongst the ribs, pinnacles and hollows. Such conditions are frequent, both on Ben Nevis and the Cuillin. I have often learned a good deal on such a day, and it has guided my movements on a future climb.

We started slightly lower than for Slav Route and about fifteen or twenty yards to the left. About 150 feet of moderately easy slabs brought us to the first serious difficulty, where our rib swept upwards in a steep, smooth wall. I climbed up to the right of this on slabs with the minimum of holds and succeeded in pulling myself up on to the crest of the rib about fifteen feet higher up. My second did not enjoy this pitch, as she was not yet converted to stocking-sole technique. The easier way, as I have since discovered, is to traverse leftwards round a difficult exposed corner.

The main rib now rose at a uniform angle for a considerable distance without any belays whatever. The rocks were dry and my stockings gave me a measure of confidence. New, soft rubbers would probably have done equally well, but mine were age-hardened and useless on such smooth rock. After running out nearly 100 feet of rope I reached a grassy recess with a huge bollard of rock for a belay. Here we considered our next moves. For the guidance of other climbers I should say that by traversing a good deal farther to the left the ascent to the recess becomes a good deal easier, but no climber worth his salt would take such an unsporting course. In August 1947, when climbing this route with my wife, I was able to maintain a perfectly straight line from the start up to the grass recess, but the lower section was severe and very lacking in positive holds. Pat became a little impatient at the slowness of my movements, but appreciated the reason when she followed in her turn.

Slightly to our right an impressive rib of rock swept upwards at a uniform angle, obviously not far short of vertical. The rock was rough, corrugated and inviting, if only we could make a start on it from the slightly overhanging nose at the base. The alternative would have been to climb a cracked slab straight above us and to attempt to get on to the rib about 100 feet higher, but that would have been less direct and attractive. I went along to prospect and found that the lower front of the rib had just enough small holds and cracks to permit of a lodgment for toes and fingers. It reminded me of the direct route up Eagle's Nest Ridge on Great Gable, but was rather longer and more difficult. The cracks continued and lured me upwards. Airy and exposed to a degree, the slabby rib provided a sufficiency of small but good holds. After running out about ninety feet of rope I came to a perfect stance. Somewhat higher was a belay.

The Great Slab Rib, as we afterwards named the pitch, is clearly visible from the C.I.C. Hut in the corrie, especially when it stands out in the evening sunshine. Seen from a stance of equal height on the Observatory Ridge, it appears to be altogether vertical and impossible. My second came up neatly and easily, but we were both climbing in stockings. I have come up on another occasion in boots, with no sense of security on such small holds, when I was second on the rope.

Above this the climbing became easier, as we trended obliquely upwards to the right towards the Basin. The latter place, where we lunched, is a wonderful eyrie with grand views of the Nevis crags and distant views across the Great Glen to the mountains of the north-west. It was pleasant to eat and rest in the warm sunshine, thinking that the most difficult part was over and that we were sure to be able to find a way to the crest of the North-East Buttress.

We resolved to continue on the line of our rib if that should be possible. It formed the northern rampart of the Basin and proved easy enough until it swept upwards in an overhanging nose, where there did not appear to be any way round on the left. I traversed to the right on very small holds, and then back to the left until I could see an opening directly upwards. This was a difficult piece of climbing, and I took my second much more directly upwards, so as to be able to hold her more securely on the rope. I am afraid that she found this the hardest problem of the day. At one place she came on to the rope altogether, presumably having no holds at all. However, our problem was solved, for the rocks ahead were now splintered into huge blocks, offering free passage to the easier ground above.

It was our last difficulty. As we proceeded, the character of the rock became lichen-coated and weathered like that on the crest of the North-East Buttress which we soon gained. We were very high, above the lower summit cairn on Carn Mor Dearg, but not quite so high as its main top (4,012 ft). In less than half an hour we were on the summit of Ben Nevis, proud of our new discovery and contented after a splendid day's climbing.

That first climb on the north-west face of the North-East Buttress left many unsolved problems, the two most interesting being those of straightening the route up our rib from the northern rampart of the Basin and of finding a direct route from the Basin to the summit of the North-East Buttress. As a result of a good many later expeditions these problems were both solved and several other linking routes were climbed. Rock climbers are, as a rule, neither imaginative nor artistic when it comes to naming new climbs. They have, nowadays, by common consent, agreed to discourage eponymous nomenclature. Since the authors of new routes are no longer allowed to perpetuate their achievements in their own names, many of them have taken a peevish revenge by falling into the alphabetical, numerical or topographical systems which, as that distinguished editor of the *Rucksack Club Journal*, the late J. H. Doughty, once wrote, "are the offspring of the same unhappy union—a marriage of impoverished imagination with the scientific spirit". Is it possible to avoid the dilemma when there are a whole group of unnamed new routes, linked together like a network? I do not know, but I made the attempt by foisting a little astronomy on to the tolerance of the climbing community, and lumping all the routes together as the Orion climbs, from a certain resemblance between the principal lines and junctions of the network and the arrangement of the stars in that oldest of our constellations.

The direct continuation of the rib was climbed by George Dwyer and myself in August 1940. It involved some delicate progress along a tenuous groove, just below the crest on the north side, and culminated in a short, severe pitch on minute holds, by which we climbed up into a smooth scoop which gave direct access to the upper rocks. The solution of the other problem, which was required in order to complete the upper half of the most interesting and direct route from the foot of Zero Gully to the top of the Ben, was effected by John Wilson and myself in June 1940. We thought that we were justified in calling it the Long Climb, and its description is the natural sequel to that of the earlier route to the Basin, in 1935.

John Wilson and I enjoyed perfect weather and we carried a surveying aneroid for the purpose of determining the altitudes at various points. We reached the Basin in about two and a half hours from the foot of Zero Gully, climbing mostly in rubbers but occasionally in stocking-soles. Having eaten our lunch in the Basin we considered the upper face of the mountain. Again there was a natural line for our guidance, the objective being a prominent tower-like projection to the left of the apparent summit of the North-East Buttress. An easy, rocky buttress would lead us to a long, steep, slabby rib which we might use as a sort of staircase for overcoming a vertical step in the cliff, after which things might be expected to be somewhat easier. This plan was good enough for us to be going on with, at any rate.

All went easily to the base of the steep rib, but this did not prove to be a staircase. It was overhung on the right by a vertical wall and had a similarly steep edge on the left. Directly above the rib was another short, steep wall which promised a few niches for holds. The slab rib was about ninety feet high. Climbing was easy at first until I gained the upper edge of the rib, but this soon swept upwards in a vertical line. Vainly, I felt about with outstretched fingers for any positive hold that might help me to pull up beyond the short, vertical section. There seemed to be nothing there but a smooth, unbroken surface. I was compelled to work my way horizontally to the left on very small ledges, leaning outward over vacancy until I was able to swarm up into a smooth hollow in the rock. Soon I regained the crest of the rib and found a secure belay.

The next problem was to climb the wall above the rib. This proved to be a very difficult piece of balance climbing on smooth inclined ledges, with the meagre assistance of palm friction on similar ledges higher up. There were no positive, in-cut holds at all. No doubt, the friction of stocking-soles and of the palms of the hands was more than adequate to counteract a slight leaning outward from the wall, but one never felt altogether sure about it when moving a foot, particularly when stepping up. Progress was by zig-zags, but we got up eventually. On a subsequent ascent I discovered that a direct upward route, though it looked more difficult, was really better, as the holds were more satisfying, despite the steeper angle.

We were now on much easier ground, and our next objective was a still larger and more conspicuous slab, far above us on the left. From a grassy ledge, upon which reposed a mammoth boulder, we edged our way upwards with alternate traverses and ascents. There was only one exposed move, across the top of an open, vertical corner. We were unable to climb the upper slab, but found a feasible way up its right-hand side, leading finally to a niche near the top. Here there was another severe move for the leader, a short, horizontal traverse with no handholds at all. But it led to a perfect stance and belay. Our aneroid showed that this upper slab was about 200 feet high. Both of these great slabs on this upper route can be readily distinguished from the C.I.C. Hut on a sunny summer evening, and also, of course, from the crest of the Observatory Ridge.

We were now approaching the tower-like projection or bulge near the top of the North-East Buttress, and had soon climbed to a position directly beneath it. The final steep pitch was a difficult, vertical wall, where some projecting nodules of quartz, strongly reminiscent of the Cobbler climbs, helped us considerably. Then the climbing degenerated into moderate scrambling, and we cast off the rope at five-thirty p.m. at a height of 720 feet above the Basin. In a few minutes we gained the crest of the North-East Buttress, well above the Mantrap, and raced to the top of the Ben. It was five minutes to six.

We had completed the longest face climb on the Ben, a climb of 1,480 feet to the cairn on the top of North-East Buttress, of which only 400 feet, partly at the top and partly at the bottom, had been easy scrambling, and practically all the rest had been continuously difficult, with several pitches of undoubted severity. The actual climbing time was six and a quarter hours, under favourable conditions, for a party of two. For a glorious hour we relaxed on the summit, fanned by a gentle breeze from the Atlantic, and then began to descend by the Observatory Ridge, so that John might take a few photographs of our route. The whole face was illuminated by the glancing rays of the evening sun. At eight-forty p.m. we recovered our boots from where we had left them at the foot of Zero Gully, and strolled down to the Hut for a leisurely supper.

Towards midnight we came outside again before turning in. The great face, on which we had striven for so many hours, stood high above us, dark grey in its impassive aloofness and mystery. We felt at one with Shelley as he contemplated Mont Blanc from the Vale of Chamonix:

> Power dwells apart in its tranquillity,
> Remote, serene and inaccessible:
> And *this*, the naked countenance of earth,
> On which I gaze, even these primæval mountains

Teach the adverting mind . . .
. . . The secret Strength of things
Which governs thought, and to the infinite dome
Of heaven is as a law, inhabits thee!

In August 1947 I was able to arrange for a photographic
party on the Observatory Ridge while my wife and I repeated
the Long Climb. The start was the same as before, but we were
able to work out a new, very difficult and entirely direct ascent
to the foot of the Great Slab Rib below the Basin. It was a
windless day with dry rocks, but a fluctuating bank of mist
made photography difficult at the critical positions and times.
Despite these handicaps, J. Earl MacEwen secured an excellent
photograph of us on the upper part of the Slab Rib, using a
Contax camera with a long focus lens. The mist prevented any
successful photography above the Basin, and we should have
preferred the rib photograph to have shown Pat on the more
difficult, lower section of the rib.

On the first rib above the Basin I led the pitch, using the
same traverse to the left as on the first occasion, but Pat, who is
an excellent and fearless climber, came straight up the edge
without traversing at all. She suggested that I could easily have
done so myself, if I had only been confident enough to place
reliance on a certain minute fingerhold. In 1944 the climb was
led by B. P. Kellett, who was a better climber than myself, with
Miss N. Ridyard as a second. She was the first to climb this
edge directly, secured by the leader who, although, like myself,
he had been up the climb before, did not care to do it directly
without a rope. It is not a particularly dangerous place; there is
one very delicate movement and no more.

Our 1947 climb finished in dense mist, rather higher on the
North-East Buttress than the 1940 finish, and with more
difficulty at the end. We never saw the upper slab, though we
must have passed very close to it on our left.

IX

GLOVER'S CHIMNEY ON BEN NEVIS

THE SUNDAY AFTER Easter 1947 was not a promising day for climbing. Four of us—John Wilson, the skier; Bill Thomson, the photographer; my wife Pat and I were slowly plodding up the Coire na Ciste below the north-east face of Ben Nevis. We had breakfasted well in the C.I.C. Hut, and it was only half-past ten by double summer time. The summit crest of the Ben was swathed in cloud, swirling along in front of a fierce west wind. We had thought of attempting the Observatory Ridge, but the prospect of meeting that wind high up on the narrow ridge, just where we might expect progress to be very slow owing to iced and snow-covered rocks, made us think again and seek a more sheltered, if not an easier route, on the upper cliffs of Coire na Ciste. On our right was a gentle, snowy depression covering the frozen lochan, just as it was twenty-five years before when I did my first winter climb up No. 2 Gully of Ben Nevis under the tutelage of my friend, Ernest Roberts. Then we had lunched in a hollow above its surface. The gully made a grand climb, and I was now hoping for just such another good day's sport. On my last climbing visit to the Ben, in August 1944, the weather had been so hot that we had completed our day with the refreshing shock of a dive into the clear waters of Lochan Coire na Ciste. Quite a short swim in the icy waters was sufficient, for they lie at a height of 3,000 feet above sea level and are never warm, even in the hottest summer.

Above us were snow slopes leading up to the beetling crags of the Comb, with its overhanging nose of black cliff. To the left of the Comb the slope steepened to the narrow, twisting rift of No. 2 Gully. John was ahead, attentively studying the icy face on our left, which rose up sheer for 1,000 feet, to the crest of the Tower Ridge. He was looking at the Tower Gap, from which a vertical groove, snow- and ice-filled, fell away straight down towards us. This was the difficult Tower Gap West Chimney, far better known as Glover's Chimney, and named after Colonel George Glover who led the first ascent on 27 June 1902. Even in summer conditions, with dry rocks, the climb is by no means easy. There are awkward rocks at the bottom, and the final chimney is both steep and narrow.

Glover's Chimney was connected with one of the most exciting adventures in the early annals of the Scottish Mountaineering Club. On 28 December 1907, Messrs T. E. Goodeve, Charles Inglis Clark and J. H. A. M'Intyre, were climbing the Tower Ridge under snow conditions. When they got to the base of the Great Tower, they did not care to face the difficulties of the usual winter route round the south-eastern side of the cliff. So they worked their way across some ledges on the Coire na Ciste side, being gradually forced downwards into the upper part of Glover's Chimney, although they do not appear to have been aware of the difficulty of their position. The original account has it that, "Stretching far below, there seemed to be a splendid snow gully to descend, which we could follow with our eyes about halfway down to Coire na Ciste."

It was already approaching nightfall. They hopefully and carefully descended the steep gully until, at length, the leader could descend no farther. The icy rocks bent over in a convex curve, becoming sheer, vertical cliff. They now realized their position and danger. It was a starry night of keen frost. There was nothing for it but to retrace their steps, climb up the gully and attempt another way of escape to the summit plateau. So long as they could keep moving they would keep warm. They had neither lantern nor torch, but found that the stars gave sufficient light on the snow. At the place where they had entered the gully they turned off to the right and discovered that the system of ledges continued gently upwards in that direction. After incredible difficulties and much step-cutting they succeeded in extricating themselves shortly after midnight. But their troubles were by no means over. The summit plateau of Ben Nevis is a confusing place in the dark. They descended southwards instead of westwards, landing in a steep and difficult gully where M'Intyre slipped and Goodeve sustained several cuts and bruises. However, they continued the descent and reached easy ground above Glen Nevis by daylight.

Throughout the night a number of parties of the Club were searching the likeliest places on the Ben for the missing men. The first party to find any traces included Dr W. Inglis Clark, the father of one of them, and a well-known pioneer of Scottish mountaineering. About four a.m. one of their lanterns showed up a line of fresh footprints in the snow of the summit plateau. Closer examination proved that three men had made the tracks, and a further search traced the footprints back to a cornice of snow at the edge of the cliff. When a lantern was lowered over the side it did not seem possible that anyone could have climbed up that ice-encrusted cliff. But the missing men were safe. They were out on the Ben for a stretch of thirty hours, and the cross route from the foot of the Great Tower to the plateau is still known as Goodeve's Route.

I had never climbed Glover's Chimney in its entirety under icy conditions. The first complete winter ascent was made by Dr Graham Macphee's party on 17 March 1935. They took eight hours to climb the gully from bottom to top, and experienced great difficulties. At Easter, 1938, I led a party up the lower severe section, but it was late in the afternoon. We had no time to finish, so we beat a prudent retreat. Next day the climb was completed by another party using our ice steps for the lower section. It cost them many hours, for they experienced severe difficulty in the upper chimney. In fact, the leader, as the hour was very late, was glad to accept a steadying rope from a member of another party who were crossing the Tower Gap, on the normal route up the Tower Ridge. He was a good climber, and, in my opinion, would have succeeded without any assistance, for he was already within ten feet of the Gap. I don't think that John was acquainted with all this history. I kept the knowledge to myself, in the full expectation of a very good day's sport.

Underneath the foot of the Chimney is an easy snow slope, leading downwards to the top of a cliff which sticks far out into the corrie like a black island in the snow. The early explorers, men acquainted with the Alps, called this the Garadh na Ciste, from its resemblance to similar isolated rocky islands on Alpine glaciers, which are locally known as *Jardins* (both words meaning garden). On the Alpine *Jardins* there are beautiful flowers in summer, but I have never yet found much sign of plant life on the Garadh na Ciste. We gradually kicked our way up the steep snow slope until we reached the base of the rocks. A gentle snowy curve descended to the summit rocks of the Garadh. John had already started to cut a ladder of steps in the green bulge of ice. Bill was entrenched in a shallow fissure between rocks and snow slope, and was securing John with the rope, the end of which was passed over an ice-axe driven deeply into the snow. It was necessary for safety that John should have enough rope to get past the icy part, so that he could drive his axe well down into hard snow, as a safe belay for securing Bill when it came to his turn to move. We decided that Pat and I should follow quite independently on our own rope.

John was in good form and did his work well. Our position was not too pleasant, as the chips of ice loosened by John from above, as well as a hail of smaller particles, kept showering down upon us. Such is always the lot of the followers during an ice climb. We accepted it stoically, but when I looked up and saw a fair-sized stone coming spinning and rebounding down the gully, far above John's head, I was not so happy about our chances. I looked carefully at the ice and found a trickle of water underneath. The west wind was having some effect. Even at this height there was a slight thaw. If it became pronounced, and if the wind rose to gale force, we should find ourselves in no enviable situation, progressing slowly for hours up that difficult gully and exposed to whatever missiles might be liberated above by wind and thaw. Gullies can be death-traps under such conditions. I had never believed that the danger could be really formidable on Ben Nevis. John was so engrossed with his labour that he had not noticed the falling stone which did not come near him. He was still on the ice-covered rocks, well to the right of the true gully. I watched anxiously for a long time. Not another stone fell. In fact, we found everything securely frozen as we got higher.

After a long wait, Bill followed on, joining his leader. When it came to my turn, I knew that John was well up to the day's work. Both he and Bill were taller than either Pat or myself, so the steps were rather wide apart for us. An extra intermediate step, here and there, was required for our greater security and comfort. We used 100 feet of line. After two stretches of this we ascended an icy groove between two large, rocky masses. Then an awkward and icy stretch to the left took us into the long, middle section of the gully. There, Pat took over the lead. The bed of the gully was firm, hard snow, over which we made good progress. There were two short, icy bits, but nothing to cause much trouble. The gully cut deeper into the surrounding cliffs, which were all draped heavily with snow and ice. We were completely sheltered from the wind, but became gradually enveloped in thin mist or cloud, into which our forerunners had vanished. At length an opening appeared in the cliff on our left, and another, just opposite on the right. This was the historic Goodeve Ledge Route of 1907, which cuts right across Glover's Chimney from the base of the Great Tower. A good name would be the Goodeve cross-roads. The others were just ahead of us now, still on good, hard snow, but just underneath the upper Chimney which rose like a narrow, vertical shaft to a small, white nick on the skyline.

We called a halt for lunch, as we were still in shelter and required some sustenance, so as to enable us to face the formidable task ahead. If I had doubts about the outcome I kept them to myself. I had been up the Chimney before, but never in such icy conditions. Everyone was very cheerful, and there was the usual lighthearted banter. It was about half-past one when the advance guard prepared to start, this time with Bill in the lead. I rather suspected that the Chimney would take a long time. We were standing on a very steep slope, and the upper part appeared to lie back at a deceptively easy angle. It was, in reality, badly foreshortened, an illusion of perspective that concealed the truth that it was not far short of vertical.

At first there was a vertical step of about eight feet in height. After much hacking at the ice with the pick of his axe Bill got up, but there was little enough to hold on to. In summer one would have jammed and wriggled upwards by friction against the narrow, enclosing walls. These were now heavily coated with dense, polished ice. Some distance higher there was some snow-ice in the bed of the Chimney. The ice-axe could secure a grip on that. John was brought up to the same position, just behind the leader. I asked if the axe was firm. Bill was not entirely reassuring, but John could at least gain some additional security by wedging tactics.

Something like fifteen feet remained to be climbed. The walls were closer together, but still heavily coated with ice. There was no snow-ice now. The back of the Chimney was a flat slab of rock set at an angle of about seventy degrees, coated with about an inch of solid ice. I learned that there was a crack at the lower left-hand corner of the slab, but it did not extend very far. For what seemed like an age of waiting we watched Bill chipping away at the ice on the slab, using the pick in order to fashion a double staircase of thin, icy notches to serve as handholds, and later as footholds. With incredible slowness his head approached the level of the white notch. We paid no attention to the hail of ice chips that continued to fall upon us, although my face received quite an array of small cuts here and there. At last the pick gripped the icy notch of the skyline. Then Bill's shoulders rose to the same level, and with a final heave he was sitting astride of the crest. Victory was assured us, but it had been a hard fight and a magnificent lead.

Then John crawled upwards, reached the gap and disappeared. He was going on to lead the last section of the Tower Ridge. It was now my turn for going into action on the first vertical step. Again, I knew what it meant to follow a leader who was taller than myself. I used the axe to clear away an additional hold on the rock walls in two places. There was little comfort to be had from any of these slippery push-holds. After the long wait below I was feeling rather chilled, especially my hands which were protected by thin leather gloves, already saturated with water. The vertical step was a severe proposition, but at last I reached the snow-ice below the slab. Well secured, I took in the rope from below and held Pat while she climbed up beside me, very rapidly, too. I suppose that the gentle tension of the rope was some slight encouragement.

The last man does not get the best out of a ladder of ice steps. They get worn and rounded. I was very careful about the next six or seven feet. I could only get my knee on to a little rocky ledge on the left, and using one's knees is always bad for the balance of the body. Besides, my gloved hands could find little purchase on Bill's ice notches. I was able to fashion a new one of the correct size in the rocky crack on my left, but I was still about six inches too short for that first step. Pat wedged herself in and offered me her left knee as a stand. I accepted the offer unashamed, to my great benefit. The step was much easier, and I was soon perched on the ice notches, each of which I enlarged and sharpened as I ascended. When I reached the gap I was more than ever impressed with the excellence of Bill's lead. Again Pat came up cheerfully and rapidly, with the rope no more than safely taut. Astride of the gap, I could have held the heaviest of men on the rope if he had come unstuck in that Chimney.

There was now only the final part of the Tower Ridge to be climbed. The steps led round the corner on the left, and then steeply back to the crest of the ridge. The snow was of doubtful consistency on the steep part, but the axe could be driven in deeply. The crest of the ridge was easy until it abutted against the last icy wall. There Pat took over the lead and proceeded round a corner and up a steep, narrow groove of snow-ice to the edge of the plateau, where we all met and shared our satisfaction in the successful issue to a hard climb. We took off the ropes and coiled them up. There was a strong west wind on the summit, with drifting cloud and hardly any view.

John and Bill had gone on ahead. When we reached the old

Observatory we found no sign of them, but on the leeward side of the snow-covered ruins was a boisterous party of four girls and a man enjoying the Nevis weather. Two wore slacks, but the other two girls only ankle-socks and skirts, while the man wore shorts. They were grouped for a photograph. In answer to our inquiries after our friends came a broad Yorkshire response: "Ay, they're in there", with a wave of the hand pointing to a small aperture in the ice-encrusted walls of the Observatory. Soon a pair of purple legs issued backwards from the opening, and a fifth girl came out, full of admiration at the interior of the cave. They were knowledgeable people, as well as tough, for the young man, after surveying us briefly, asked if we had come up by the Tower Ridge, and then informed the others that we were the *real* mountaineers. I don't know so much about that, for neither Pat nor I would have cared to climb the Ben in their rig-out.

When they had all gone we crept into the cave, which, from being a cheerless, broken-down relic of one of the rooms of the old Observatory, had been transformed into a fairy grotto of crystal walls and stalactites of ice. There sat John and Bill, eating sandwiches, and looking like two trolls of the Jotunheim or, if you like, "two abominable snow men" of the Himalaya. When we were all refreshed we emerged and plunged downhill towards Achintee over some of the most execrable, breakable snow-crust that I have ever encountered. Now the crust held our weight, but with the next step it cracked and submerged us to the knees. The easiest way was a curious dancing or tripping kind of progress. When we came to the steeper slopes down the corrie of the Red Burn it was just possible to glissade down the soft snow on our seats, which, of course, became thoroughly soaked. But we had our day and enjoyed it all.

X

SKYE AND THE CUILLIN

Introduction and Geology

THE TRAVELLER WHO catches his first glimpse of the northen
end of the Cuillin range from Sligachan sees a fantastic skyline
of jagged, black pinnacles and cliffs, all the more impressive by
contrast with the bare, rounded hills and rolling moorland
which are the only visible part of the interior of the island, as
seen from the road between Kyle, Broadford and Loch Ainort.
Often he sees nothing but a mass of dark, drifting cloud,
followed by an intriguing vision of the sharp pyramid of Sgurr
nan Gillean, seen for an instant and again swallowed up in inky
blackness. No wonder that Sheriff Nicolson, most famous of the
early pioneers of climbing in the Cuillin and himself a native of
Skye, exclaimed that Sgurr nan Gillean ought by right to have
been at least 10,000 feet high from its appearance! If one has
already seen the skyline of the Cuillin from the sands of Morar
or from a mainland peak, as far away as Ben Nevis or even
beyond Glencoe, it is difficult to understand how such mountains can remain so well concealed from the usual route of
approach. They are, of course, a small range, as regards area,
tucked away into a southern pocket of this big, sprawling island,
between the sea inlets of Loch Slapin and Loch Brittle, and
much more conspicuous from the south and south-east than
from the north. Small as they are, they have drawn to themselves many artists and lovers of mountains and amongst them
not a few distinguished names.

Dr Samuel Johnson, on his journey to the Western Isles in
1773, was not impressed, unless by the bareness and primitive
desolation of the island. Sir Walter Scott was conducted to
Loch Coruisk in 1814 and was overcome by the rugged grandeur of the place. He put his impressions on record and
persuaded many others to go and see for themselves.

The first well-known mountaineer to visit the Cuillin was
Principal J. D. Forbes. As Professor of Natural Philosophy at
Edinburgh, and later Principal of St Andrews, he was a famous
Alpine explorer and investigator of the flow of glaciers. At his

first visit in 1836 he climbed Sgurr nan Gillean by what is now known as the Tourist Route, but which most modern tourists, and some climbers as well, have found sufficiently difficult. After several years of travel and Alpine exploration he returned to Skye in 1845, explored the Cuillin thoroughly and made a map of the range. Sheriff Alexander Nicolson did much more than Forbes, returning again and again, continuing his exploration and pouring forth his love and enthusiasm for the Cuillin both in verse and prose. He climbed Sgurr Alasdair in 1873, the highest point of the island, which was later named after him. From a bivouac by Loch Coruisk he climbed Sgurr Dubh, experiencing no small difficulties, especially during the rough descent through Coir'an Lochain in growing darkness. Nicolson absorbed the very spirit of these mountains when he wrote, "There is an ever changing life in the play of the clouds that float serenely through the blue sky or hurry frantically across the riven peaks, or descend softly like darkness into the bosom of the hills."

Perhaps the best known of the long line of explorers of the Cuillin was Professor J. Norman Collie, a distinguished chemist, but equally notable as a mountaineer in the Alps, the Rockies and the Himalaya. Collie came to Sligachan to fish, but the fine weather drove him to climb the mountains. In later life, when he had given up climbing, but still returned again and again to Skye, he used to say that at one time he "had got into a bad habit of climbing mountains and only in his old age had he become sane again"! We may well rejoice over the long years of Collie's insanity, for he made many great expeditions on the Cuillin, including the Bhasteir Tooth, the Thearlaich Dubh Gap, the first ascents of the great southern face of Sgurr a Ghreadaidh, the north-west ridge of Alasdair and the Cioch pinnacle. Many of these were made along with John Mackenzie of Sconser, a Highlander of the old school and almost the only Scottish professional mountain guide. Collie and Mackenzie grew old together and passed away within a year or two of each other during the recent war, for Collie returned to Sligachan in 1939 to live his last years within sight of his beloved hills.

For many summers Collie lived at Glen Brittle Lodge with his friend Colin Phillip, the artist. He himself was no mean performer in water-colours, and this explains the intensity of charm and the truth in his description of his favourite mountains.

"The individuality of the Cuillin is not seen in their summits, which are often almost ugly, but in the colour of the rocks, the atmospheric effects, the relative largeness and harmony of the details compared with the actual size of the mountains, and most of all the mountain mystery that wraps them round." Collie had climbed on the Alps, the Rockies and the Himalaya, and he knew what he was talking about, so that he could sense "the secret beauty born of the mists, the rain and the sunshine, in a quiet and untroubled land". Whoever has climbed on the Cuillin and got to know and love them should not fail to read the entire article in the *S.M.C. Journal*(4: 259ff).

Many other distinguished mountaineers have climbed on the Cuillin, including Charles Pilkington who first ascended the so-called Inaccessible Pinnacle of Sgurr Dearg in 1880 and W. W. Naismith, the founder of the Scottish Mountaineering Club. It was A. P. Abraham, of Keswick, who first popularized the Cuillin for climbers with the publication of his *Rock Climbing in Skye*. The first *S.M.C. Guide to the Isle of Skye* appeared a little earlier, in the year 1907. Subsequent years, with the exception of the war years when Skye was a restricted area, have seen an ever increasing flow of climbers to the Cuillin, both from England and Scotland.

It is worth asking why there is such superlatively excellent climbing on the Cuillin, for nowhere else in Britain is the rock so perfectly rough and sound. From one point of view a rock-climbing novitiate spent in Skye is a doubtful advantage. One is led to expect too much from other mountains. One gets into bad habits, relying on the perfect soundness of small holds for pulling up with the arms, without testing all holds with care, preserving one's balance at all times, developing habits of neat and accurate foot-work and not relying on the friction of abnormally rough rock on rubbers and trouser knees. One should not expect to be able to climb easily and safely on such steep rock faces on other hills or mountains—certainly not in the Alps.

A few remarks on the geology of the Cuillin may not be out of place. Except for a few rocks near the coast, the great mass of Skye rock is igneous in origin and belongs to the Tertiary epoch, very recent when compared with the main rock masses of the Scottish Highlands. In early Tertiary times vast floods of lava poured out of fissures and covered over two-thirds of the island. Similar rocks are still to be seen among the hills of the northern part of Skye, where the rock pinnacles of the Quiraing are worth visiting, but not for climbing purposes.

In later Tertiary periods there were great intrusions of coarsely crystalline gabbro, which cooled under the pressure due to the great weight of overlying basalt (lava). There was also an intrusion of granite, partly cutting into the gabbro, chiefly on the eastern side. Since these remote times there has been an enormous amount of erosion. The earlier sheets of basaltic lava have been removed, and the tough, resistant gabbro now stands up as the peaks and ridges of the Cuillin. Here and there it is interrupted by more recent and minor intrusions of smooth, brittle basalt.

It is the hardness and the roughness of the coarsely crystalline gabbro that makes this rock unique in its excellence for the purpose of the mountaineer. Apart from the Cuillin it occurs only in lesser masses in the mountains of Rum and at one point of Ardnamurchan, but the grand climbing available on the peaks of the Lofoten Islands off the Norwegian coast is also dependent on gabbro rock. The granite of the Red Hills near Sligachan is in striking contrast to the Black Cuillin, for it has weathered into long talus slopes of red scree which clothe the hillsides and protect the rounded hills from further erosion. The actual shape of the Cuillin peaks is frequently determined by the subsequent intrusions of basalt or trap rock, which cause planes of weakness, not entirely without their uses for the climber, as they may offer easy lines of attack and passes across the mountain chain. The highest summit, Sgurr Alasdair, is made of trap and also the Inaccessible Pinnacle of Sgurr Dearg, so that the above principles should not be taken as an infallible guide to the texture and resistance of the rocks.

Even after the main contours of the Cuillin were developed there have been noteworthy changes owing to the erosive action of rain, streams, frost and ice. Most spectacular are the huge boiler-plate slabs with glacial markings in the Coir' a' Ghrunnda and Coire Lagan and at Coruisk, which is a typical rock lake produced by glacial erosion. The gabbro of the Cuillin retains the impress of the last ice age better than the other Scottish mountains, owing to its hardness, but the ice ages affected most of Britain.

Easy Climbing—the Holiday Spirit

My first experience of the Cuillin was very fortunate, so it may serve as an introduction for others. I attended a Meet of the S.M.C. at Sligachan in June 1923. We arrived on a stormy evening and heard reports of heavy snow on peaks and ridges, only the Tourist Route being possible on Sgurr nan Gillean. There was a grand, climbing atmosphere about Sligachan. The Inn was a real home for mountaineers. Next morning we sallied forth along the track to the Bealach a' Mhaim, not expecting much of the weather, but determined to get to the top of Bruach na Frithe (3,143 ft), the easiest peak of the range. The mist began to lift as we walked up the grassy Fionn Choire. What a magnificent view from the summit for my first experience of the Cuillin! Large, wool-pack, cumulus clouds were lifting off the western tops. There were the black, jagged peaks and ridges, unique and distinguished in form, and far beyond them lay the azure western sea. As the authors of the Skye Guide remark, "Fine weather in Skye is worth waiting for." It is an island of beautiful surprises.

Off we went, six of us, down the western ridge over Sgurr na Bhairnich and An Caisteal with that entrancing view still before us, until we became engrossed in the difficulties of the narrow ridge over the three tops of Bidein Druim nan Ramh (The Peak of the Ridge of Oars). Not that this ridge is normally difficult for a competent party, but now the ledges were smothered in snow and it took us a long time to traverse the peaks. By this time the view had again changed, and we looked straight south over Loch Coruisk to the sea loch of Scavaig. It was hard to say which was the more entrancing shade of blue, for the depth and purity of these Skye colours must be seen in order to be believed. It was late afternoon when we halted on the Bealach na Glaic Moire (2,510 ft), the easy pass across the ridge connecting the Coruisk valley with Coire Tairneilear (The Thunderer), to the north. Then the mist enfolded us again as we picked our way carefully down the latter corrie, keeping close under the rocks of Sgurr an Fheadain, so as to avoid difficulties. One can never reckon on finding a Cuillin pass that is altogether easy to descend in mist. There is often only one easy way down, which ought to be properly memorized beforehand. We were hours late for dinner, but Mrs Campbell, of Sligachan, was used to the ways of climbers.

On the first day we had expert guidance from the veterans of the Club, but, on the Monday, four of us, relatively inexperienced, were turned loose on Sgurr nan Gillean to fend for ourselves. A long walk over the moors, keeping to the left of the spectacular, deep gorge at the foot of Coire a' Bhasteir, led us to the base of our climb; I had selected the Pinnacle Ridge for the day's work. After lunch we found things quite easy until we reached the top of the Third Pinnacle. Now there was to be some real rock climbing, starting off with an awesome descent. Two of the party disliked the prospect, descended to the southeast, by-passed the difficulties and finally rejoined us at the last gap between the Fourth Pinnacle and the final slope of Sgurr nan Gillean.

The warm sun was fast clearing the snow off the ridge, with the result that we had little difficulty with the descent, for the holds are ample. Its bark is far worse than its bite, a common experience with the excellent rock of the Cuillin. In dry, summer conditions one can traverse round Knight's Peak (the Fourth Pinnacle) without ascending it, but there was too much snow on the ledges of the north face. So we climbed it and had to spend a good deal of time over the following descent, the snow being now in a slithery condition. It also meant that our reunited party of four was slow on the long final ascent to the top of Sgurr nan Gillean (3,167 ft).

The mists were eddying around the summit, but the repeated clearances displayed a succession of Brocken Spectres, as the sun and wind were just in the right positions. So far as I know, Sgurr nan Gillean is one of the best situated peaks for this phenomenon, as the west wind throws out a screen of cloud perfectly illuminated by the afternoon sun. In the evening our President referred to these appearances as being most gratifying to one's personal vanity, for if two of us stood fairly close together, each saw a huge composite shadow of both projected on the background of luminous cloud, but only his own head was surrounded by a brightly coloured halo. Each could thus rest assured of his own peculiar odour of sanctity, and that the other man, of a certainty, must be filled with enmity and lying when he claimed the pre-eminence for himself. I have seen these spectres on many other Scottish hills and on Alpine peaks, but I still think that those on Sgurr nan Gillean were the finest. The last of the clouds went racing over the Red Hills to the east of us, climbing up like an unending procession of woolly sheep over Glamaig and pouring down the other side in the direction of Marsco. To the west the sea shimmered in the sun, and the Long Island, as they often call the Outer Hebrides, was a clear, pale blue from Barra Head in the south to the Butt of Lewis in the north. How fascinating were the pale brown moorlands, the hills of Trotternish and the long arms of the sea lochs of Skye in all directions!

Two of our party descended by the south ridge, or Tourist

Route. Ronald Burn, who had accompanied me over the Pinnacles, was not an expert on rocks, but his ambition, later fulfilled, was to climb all the Munros and Tops. At the other end of the arc of the Cuillin horseshoe was the Inaccessible Pinnacle of Sgurr Dearg. That had to be included, and Burn was gaining his qualification. So he readily agreed to proceed by the narrow, western ridge, from which we descended by the easy Nicolson Chimney. It was not entirely a scree gully, however, as Burn had expected; so he incautiously wagered me a bottle of beer that we had not descended the authentic Nicolson Chimney. After this had been paid I was, of course, in honour bound to take him up the Inaccessible.

Next day Ronald Burn succeeded in adding Am Basteir and the Bhasteir Tooth to his collection of Munros and Tops. We were led by W. N. Ling, who used to partner Harold Raeburn in the earlier, difficult, guideless ascents in the Alps, and who also achieved with him two notable pioneering campaigns in the Caucasus prior to the 1914–18 war. There were also present Henry Alexander, author of the Cairngorms Guide and later Lord Provost of Aberdeen, and Sheriff G. D. Valentine of Skye, whose knowledge of the Cuillin and its wild life, and especially of the golden eagle and its haunts, was unrivalled. It was a most enjoyable day. We went up the west side of the Bhasteir Gorge, paying a visit to the Caves, and traversed Am Basteir from the col between it and Sgurr nan Gillean, continuing by a short, difficult descent to the Tooth and then into Lota Corrie by the original route, returning over the Bealach nan Lice and the Fionn Choire. I should say that all three days' climbing, covering the Pinnacle route to Sgurr nan Gillean and continuing by the west ridge, Am Basteir, the Tooth, Sgurr a Fionn Choire, Bruach na Frithe and the Bidein peaks to the Bealach na Glaic Moire is eminently suitable, in good weather conditions, for novices who have had previous experience of rock climbing and the use of the rope. Most of the rock is of moderate standard, and no part is very difficult. It is more direct to descend the western face of the Tooth by Naismith's route, but this is precipitous and more difficult. Certainly the holds are sound and adequate, but they are easier to find by doing the route upwards to begin with.

We younger men, E. C. Thomson, C. Phillip, Burn and I, walked over to Glen Brittle next day and ascended Sgurr Dearg, after which I got them all up the Inaccessible Pinnacle by the short and difficult side. There is an excellent block for a belay on the small summit, the whole ascent being possible on an 80-foot length of rope. By common conspiracy we persuaded Burn that he must stand upright on the small block on the summit, or he could not be credited with having climbed this important peak. The top of the Pinnacle is at least twenty feet higher than the summit cairn of Sgurr Dearg on the adjacent mountain top, so it is the Pinnacle and not the other which is the true summit of the mountain. Burn took no chances and fairly climbed the two tops.

On the descent to Coire Lagan we were in dense mist, which thinned out as we got down to the upper corrie above the lochan. It is well here to keep close under the ridge for a little way in order to secure an unbroken scree slope to the corrie floor. As the mist lifted the westering sun shone along that wonderful cliff of Sron na Ciche, casting a huge shadow of the Cioch Pinnacle on the great slab. This must have been how Norman Collie first discovered the existence of the Cioch and wondered "what Titan cast that shadow". He answered the question himself when he made the first ascent in the year 1906. Coire Lagan filled us with admiration and delight. Facing us across the lochan were the huge buttresses of Sgurr Alasdair and Sgumain. Beyond the barrier of whale-backed slabs at the outlet of the loch was the Sron na Ciche, its sheer skyline dipping into the Atlantic.

Such a paradise for rock climbing, warm sunny days with picnic meals and a swim in the green waters of the lochan, it would be impossible to match anywhere else in Britain. It is the epitome of that irresistible attraction which has brought the same people back to Skye, year after year, and has inspired their dreams when they were far away. Many have paid their tribute in verse or in prose to that compelling charm; sometimes those who had not been known to break into verse upon any other occasion. There is, for instance, a simple directness and sincerity in the following lines by I. M. E. Bell which must appeal to all who have felt the magnetism of the Cuilinn:

Oh, the spirit of the Cuillin, her tryst with you she keeps
In the heart of Corrie Lagan, where the jade-green lochan sleeps,
And you lose all sense of weariness as in its depths you lie,
For there's magic in the lochans on the misty Isle of Skye.

There are days when the Black Cuillin are afloat in silver mist
And a fairy wand has turned them into isles of amethyst;

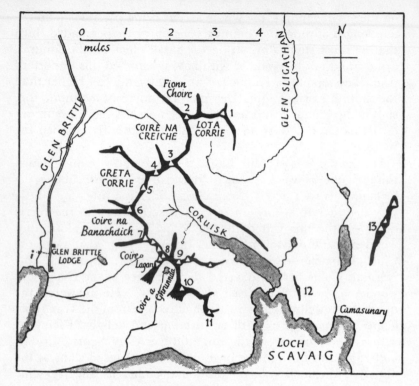

THE CUILLIN

PEAKS

		height in feet
1	Sgurr nan Gillean (peak of the young men)	3,167
2	Bruach na Frithe (brae of the forest)	3,143
3	Bidein Druim nan Ramh (peak of ridge of oars)	2,850
4	Sgurr a' Mhadaidh (foxes' peak)	3,010
5	Sgurr a' Ghreadaidh (peak of clear waters)	3,190
6	Sgurr na Banachdich (smallpox peak)	3,167
7	Sgurr Dearg (red peak). Inaccessible Pinnacle is close at hand	3,226
8	Sgurr Alasdair	3,251

8 3 peaks in line downwards are, in order, Thearlaich, Alasdair and Sgumain, the first named after Charles Pilkington, the highest after Sheriff Nicolson. Next to 8 going towards 7 is Sgurr Mhic-Coinnich, named after John McKenzie, the Skye guide.

9	(From this) Sgurr Dubh na Da Bheinn, the ridge of the Dubhs branches to the right (black peaks)	3,069
10	Sgurr nan Eag (notched peak)	3,037
11	Gars-bheinn (echoing mountain)	2,934
12	Sgurr na Stri	1,623
13	Blaven (hill of bloom) with Clach Glas to north	3,042

You can perch on top of Dearg and watch the clouds roll by
As they fill each lonely corrie on the misty Isle of Skye.

We stayed with Mary Campbell at Glen Brittle. Ravenous as
we were with our day's exertions, we enjoyed an ample and
excellent dinner. Then, as we were settling down to fill our
pipes, the door opened again and Mary entered with a second
meal of two boiled eggs per man, scones and tea. These were
the days when it was good to be young and carefree. We could
not offend our good hostess, so we set to again and did our best.
Towards midnight Philip and I strolled out on to the beach.
The moon was up: a line of silver spangled and shimmered
across Loch Brittle, with the faint outline of Canna beyond and
one light winking across at intervals—as full of mystery and
charm as any fairyland. The Alps and the Caucasus have shown
me grander scenes by far on a bigger canvas, but Glen Brittle
has never lost that more intimate appeal, a grandeur and peace
of its own, perfect in its blending of mountain, moor, sea and
sky.

Our last day was a simple ridge walk back to Sligachan by
way of the tops. We were not a fast party and it was a hot day,
perfectly suited to lingering on the tops. We traversed Sgurr
Banachdich, Sgurr Ghreadaidh and the first top of Sgurr a'
Mhadaidh, descending into Coire Tairneilear from the Thuilm
ridge. We reached Sligachan at eleven-thirty p.m. and they
gave us a full dinner! Most of us, too, had an early breakfast in
order to catch the seven-thirty a.m. boat from Broadford.

Harder and Longer Ventures
In July 1924 I was again in Skye, this time with Frank Smythe,
whom I had met in 1921 at Wasdale, when he had given me
my first taste of difficult rock climbing. After a day spent on the
round of Sgurr nan Gillean, Am Basteir and the Tooth we
moved to Mary Campbell's cottage at Glen Brittle. G. Barlow
and E. W. Steeple, joint editors of the first edition of the S.M.C.
Guide to the Island of Skye, were also staying there. We did not
climb with them, but they were grand people to come back to
in the evenings—those long summer evenings when we never
troubled to descend from the ridges until after sunset, and when
after-dinner talks went on until after midnight. Those evenings
with gorgeous sunset colours and the long views across the
Atlantic to the pale blue hills of Harris and South Uist were
part of a life at the opposite pole from the industrialism,

ambitions and alleged progress of a modern age. Which of them was the real world? We could not be sure, but we were content to live life to the full. It is, perhaps, this atmosphere of careless contentment, so typical of summer days in Skye, that explains why fewer new climbing routes have been made in the Cuillin than in any other principal climbing area of Britain during the thirties and forties of this century.

For the first few days we could not forget the rain which hardly ceased to shroud the hills. Barlow's theory was that fine weather might be expected when the barometer was at its lowest. He and Steeple went out every day, but not to climb. They prowled about in lower Coire Lagan, playing an entertaining game. They looked for surveyors' bench marks. Each scored a point when he found one. It was surprising how long the game lasted, but at length the bench marks failed them. Then they proposed to place competing rain gauges in the corrie. We approved of this idea, on the principle that rain, like other unpleasant things, must be guided by the law of perversity. So far we had done only minor climbs, but now, as if by magic, the weather improved. We at once planned to traverse all the main ridge of the Cuillin in one expedition. This great expedition, the longest of all British rock climbs, although of only moderate, average difficulty, was first carried out by A. C. McLaren and L. G. Shadbolt in the year 1911. Starting from Glen Brittle they traversed the thirty-odd peaks and tops from Gars-bheinn in the south to Sgurr nan Gillean at the northern end of a seven and a half miles' long horseshoe of mountain ridge and descended to Sligachan in about seventeen hours. T. Howard Somervell, the Mount Everest climber, had done it in two hours less in 1920. Smythe and I were no record makers: we just wanted to do the main ridge. Barlow and Steeple chaffed us on our lack of originality, suggesting that we should rather cross all the passes, swim in all the lochans and avoid all the peaks, to which Smythe replied that we would stick to the ridge, but might, for a wager, carry with us a complete edition of the *Encyclopaedia Britannica*!

I shall not describe our successful traverse of the Main Ridge in detail; I actually did it again eleven years later. Mary Campbell awakened us with tea and eggs at one-thirty a.m. on a dismal morning of drizzling rain, with mist within 200 feet of sea level. We ate the breakfast and went to sleep again. At a quarter to five Smythe roused me to a brighter prospect and we started within half an hour. At eight o'clock, on the summit of

Gars-bheinn, sea and sky were a deep, pure blue. A yacht lay
at anchor on Loch Scavaig. We imagined that we could have
thrown a stone down her hatchways. Scavaig was a marvellous
tracery of interlacing wavelets, sparkling in the morning sun.
Eigg, Rum, Canna and the Outer Hebrides were all clear.

We used the rope on four occasions: for the descent of the
short side of the Thearlaich-Dubh gap, for the ascent of King's
Chimney on Sgurr Mhic Coinnich, for the descent by the short
side of the Inaccessible and for the Naismith route up the
Tooth. It was a grand day of sunshine and north-westerly wind.
We carried no water with us, but used a rubber tube so that we
could suck up small quantities from rock pools. Later, we had
to descend for water at the Glaic Moire Bealach, and again
before tackling the Bhasteir Tooth. Smythe did not descend on
the latter occasion and was quite parched on Sgurr nan Gillean,
as a result. He used rubbers throughout the expedition and
they were worn out at the finish. We reached Sgurr nan Gillean
at seven p.m., but took a long time for the leisurely descent to
Sligachan where they gave us a grand dinner, after Smythe had
borrowed a pair of trousers for use whilst his own were being
mended. It was a great ambition fulfilled, which we did not
neglect to celebrate before retiring somewhat unsteadily to bed
up a narrow and steep staircase at the back of the hotel, the
most difficult pitch of the day!

We had already made a new variation route on the west ridge
of the Cioch. On our return to Glen Brittle we again set out for
the Cioch and Smythe led it by the direct route from below.
This is one of the best-known standard four (or severe) routes.
After lunch it was my turn to tackle the Crack of Doom, an
intriguing, narrow rift, first climbed by Pye and Shadbolt in
1918. They rated it as pretty severe but short. Every inch of
height in that almost holdless crack was gained by strenuous
contortion and wedging, with a hard pull over a chockstone to
finish. We ended the climb by the direct route, made some time
before by A. S. Pigott and John Wilding.

After the Cioch Direct and the Crack of Doom we had only
one full day left for climbing. That same evening, just before
sunset, we were looking at the skyline of Coire Lagan from Glen
Brittle Post Office. On the face of Sgurr Sgumain we caught
sight of a long, intriguing, vertical crack with a shorter parallel
crack at a lower level on the left. We knew of no routes on that
face. But for the long, revealing shadows of approaching sunset
we should not have spotted the cracks. The eye of faith grasped

the possibility of a new route. Next morning was fine and we put the matter to the proof. It led to the most thrilling day's climb of the holiday and a genuine, new, natural route, with a character all its own.

We did not rush things on such a fine day, but bathed in the cool, green waters of Lochan Coire Lagan and lunched at leisure on the hot slabs. The approach was by the easy traverse from the Lochan towards the Sgumain Stone Shoot, a route that should be known to all Skye mountaineers. Soon we were at the lowest rocks of the climb, but the sky was now becoming overcast with threatening clouds. Leading by turns, we started up the steep rocks which soon approached the vertical on both sides, a narrow chimney offering the only line of advance. This was the immediate objective, approached by steep slabs and a mantelshelf problem.

At this point the Trap Dyke, which is the main feature, or as one might say in musical language, the recurring theme of the whole climb, first appears high up on the left, cutting through the gabbro wall like an overhanging piece of ornamental masonry. We were now hemmed in on both sides by unclimbable walls, but a steepening groove continued straight ahead to a thin, vertical chimney. This proved to be the crux of the climb, and it almost defeated us at our first attempt. It was the knowledge that it was the only way which caused us to persevere and find the key to the problem, in the form of a hold for the right hand in the hidden narrows of the cleft. It was then possible to raise the left foot high up on to a hold on the opposite wall. As in many similar pitches one must never get too far inside the cleft. The rest of the chimney was strenuous but feasible.

We were now fairly launched upon our venture, devoutly hoping that the rest of the route would "go". Neither of us wished to contemplate a return down that chimney. We left a small cairn to mark the route. The next pitch went up a crack behind a huge flake of rock, rather like a miniature Kern Knotts Crack. It lent variety to the route and led us out on to an open, slabby face. A few moves upward and to the left brought us into the line of our Trap Dyke, and a most interesting place it was, too. I have never seen such a perfectly preserved specimen of its kind, and a veritable staircase for tired mountaineers—or so we thought at the time. The Dyke was built of horizontally jointed, columnar basalt. For a height of nearly seventy feet it led straight up like a ladder at an angle between sixty and seventy degrees, entirely unsupported on the left side, with a gabbro wall on the right which offered occasional handholds, as every good hand-rail should, except that this one was fitted to the wrong side!

There were still pitches to be climbed, as our staircase had to accommodate itself to the contours of the edifice, which was built of gabbro with alternate terraces and intervening walls. After crossing the first terrace we had to ascend an exceedingly strenuous, ten-foot, vertical corner. Later on came another pitch where the stairway had become wildly contorted, loose and overhanging. The solution was by a steep, difficult climb up the gabbro wall on the left, but the gabbro slabs, though very steep, were also extremely rough and firm. So it went on, until the angle eased off and we gained the crest of the West ridge of Sgumain, a narrow but easy ridge of shattered pinnacles which abutted against the foot of a vertical cliff, some 200 feet high. We did not see it all clearly, as there was now a blustering wind which was swirling the mist across the ridges. The hour was advancing, but we were sure that we could not be far beneath the summit of the mountain and we wished to finish our climb by as direct a route as we had pursued from the start.

After fifty feet of scrambling we were up against the sheer wall. Above us was a terrifying chimney, so much undercut that there seemed to be no way of even reaching its base. Again the gabbro was rough and excellent. Climbing straight over steep slabs to the left, there were just enough holds for pulling up into the niche below the chimney, and there was even a spike for a belay. I cannot say how I managed to lead the chimney itself. I remember pulling up with all my weight on a spike of gabbro which projected somewhat *downwards* towards me. This sounds ridiculous, of course, and was only possible by reason of the rough, sharp crystals which projected everywhere from the surface of the rock. Another spike protruded against my body, and I had to swing round past it to the right in order to raise myself sufficiently to secure a foothold on the right wall of the chimney. The next move had to follow at once, but when once the left foot was planted on the other side, I could rest for a moment.

The remainder was orthodox but very strenuous. Above the chimney and out to the left was a huge bollard for a belay. More welcome still was a small cairn of stones. It was as comforting as the patch of moss which Mungo Park found in the West African desert. Someone had been here before, and that was enough to put new heart into us. Still another chimney remained to be surmounted, strenuous and undercut at the bottom, but safe in spite of its steepness and narrowness. Then we turned round into a square, open corner, climbed an easy wall of trap and came out on the ridge, quite close to the summit of Sgumain. In blustering wind and rain we raced down the easy side of the mountain, stumbling over the unstable blocks of the Sgumain stone shoot and trudging across the sodden moor to Mary Campbell's cottage and a good supper.

Between the years 1935 and 1948 I was unable to visit Skye. The outline of the Cuillin reasserted its spell at once as we crossed over the moors from Carbost to Glen Brittle in the last light of a glorious evening in May 1948. We were hospitably entertained By Mrs MacRae at Glen Brittle, and the atmosphere was the same as when I made my early visits. When we started climbing next day on the Window Tower and the South Crack of the Inaccessible it seemed incredible that I had managed to forget the Cuillin for so many years. So I made up my mind to revisit the West Trap Route on Sgurr Sgumain. I was with my wife and my old friend Colin Allan. We had some difficulty in getting properly started on the climb, the initial part proving wet and strange. The crucial chimney was as impressive as before, and it was time to return to Glen Brittle for dinner when we reached the base of the North-West Tower below the final section. However, we returned to the attack next day after doing a new variation on the White Slab Route in Coir' a' Ghrunnda. Certainly I managed to lead the chimney, but, at the end of the day, my wife was so impressed that she forbade me ever to do so again! I had conveniently forgotten the existence of the upper chimney, and that had been the last straw, a sort of insult added to injury after a hard day's climbing. This final tower was first climbed in 1920 by E. W. Steeple and G. Barlow. They do not waste more than a sentence or two on the description, saying that "The climb is somewhat severe, on very rough but clean-cut rock with few holds." We all agreed that it was somewhat severe.

The best of the difficult rock climbing in Skye is certainly on the Sron na Ciche. On the whole, the guide book is fairly lucid, but routes are apt to become difficult to disentangle from each other on the Western Buttress. Colin Allan and I set out to find a route which had been only once climbed before. We had a most enjoyable day and some very good climbing, with one steep groove which nearly defeated us altogether. From the top

Carn Dearg of Ben Nevis
Climbing the South Castle Gully

Summit Cornice, Braeriach

Winter

The Tower Gap, Ben Nevis

Summer

The Cioch, Sron na Ciche, Skye

Black Spout Pinnacle, Lochnagar

Resting mountaineers, Sgoran Dubh
Left to right: C. M. Allan, the author, D. Myles

The Buttresses of Coire Mhic Fhearchair, Beinn Eighe

The Chasm, Buachaille Etive Mor
Below converging walls

Glover's Chimney, Ben Nevis
Skyline of Tower Ridge

The Long Climb, Ben Nevis
Mrs Bell and the author on the great slab

of the Sron we ran down to upper Coir' a' Ghrunnda and enjoyed a perfect swim, diving from a huge boulder into more than eight feet of clear, cold water. The loch lies at a level of 2,300 feet. When we returned to Glen Brittle and puzzled over the diagram of Sron na Ciche we decided that we had been on three different routes linked up and completed by one new section which contained *our* very difficult groove. We could not be certain of finding it again.

On another day we visited lower Coir' a' Ghrunnda and climbed the White Slab route direct, a most enjoyable climb, but not so difficult as the guide book led us to expect. We then crossed over the Sron and descended the Sgumain stone shoot, proceeding over the Girdle Traverse of Sron na Ciche. This is altogether delightful in its variety of situations. Only on the Western Buttress is it not so well defined. We used the opportunity to make a loop on the climb by ascending the Crack of Doom and returning to the Girdle by the Kelly route on the Cioch upper buttress. I found the Crack much easier than when I first did it eleven years before, most likely because I kept farther out, used my eyes better, finding one or two press-holds for the hands which I had failed to notice on the former occasion, a tribute to the gain in balance and experience during the intervening years. I think Colin expended more effort than I did, trusting to the strength of his more powerful arms. All these climbs are well worth a visit, especially the Mallory Slab and Groove route on the Sron. Coir' a' Ghrunnda is exceedingly impressive with its huge boiler plates of glaciated slabs.

Whoever has been on the Cuillin Main Ridge will wish to explore the crags and corries on the Coruisk side, and also the outlying group of Blaven and Clach Glas. I have enjoyed grand days in both places. Colin Allan and I started our 1934 holiday in a rather unorthodox way after motoring up from the south. It almost seemed as if we were wasting a fine summer evening in the Inn at Broadford, but we tore ourselves away in time and set up camp by the shore of Loch Slapin. Then the third member of the party, Dr Myles of Forfar, turned up. After supper we went for a stroll in ordinary walking shoes, up the hillside to the west. Myles turned back to camp, and we went on with the intention of climbing the nearest hill, just for the view! We had consulted no map, although we had a rough, general idea of the layout of the Blaven range. Our first peak had a sharp, serrated ridge-line with a delightful view to the east. The greater ridges beyond looked intriguing and impressive against the colours of sunset.

The night was ours to use as we pleased. Our energy and faculties were enlivened by the cool evening breeze and the after-effects of a good supper. We decided to try an overnight traverse of Blaven and Clach Glas. After descending to the next col we were in doubt about a sharp-ridged peak on our right. We had never been here before and it might be Clach Glas. We made sure by climbing it and returning the same way. It was not Clach Glas after all. Proceeding along the other, or southward ridge, we began to run into difficulties near the top. It was never really dark on that glorious June night. At true midnight the northern horizon was a flaming band of orange and the Outer Hebrides were clear and black beyond the western ocean. In between were the dim, black, serrated ridges of the Cuillin.

There was hardly a breath of wind. The slabs of Clach Glas slowed us up, but were not really difficult. There was just enough difficulty to keep us from becoming drowsy. It was good, interesting climbing on perfect rock all the way to Blaven, the higher top of which we reached at half-past two. A contented somnolence half overcame us during the descent by a sheltered gorge and easy slopes of moorland, with the early morning songs of the birds and the growing light to remind us that a new day of our holiday had started and that we had made a good beginning. Without disturbing our friend we crept into our sleeping sacks at four a.m., sleeping on the dry turf without troubling about a tent. After a swim in the sea-water of Loch Slapin before breakfast we felt as fresh as ever. Myles wanted to climb Blaven that day, and only with our protests that it was Sunday, and therefore a day of rest, did he begin to suspect how we had passed the midnight hours. The map showed us that the bag for the night included Sgurr nan Each, Garbhbheinn, Clach Glas and Blaven.

In June 1935 we had another unorthodox day. We were camping at Glen Brittle and rising rather late in the mornings. On this morning we heard that a motor boat was going round to Loch Scavaig at ten a.m. With a great rush we caught the boat and proceeded to eat our breakfast as we slipped down Loch Brittle and round the Rhu. Again it was one of those perfect summer days of blue sky and hot sun. When we landed at Scavaig we crossed over the little peninsula to a secluded bay under the cliffs of Sgurr na Stri. This is the most delightful swimming pool that I know. Great, black slabs of gabbro bend over and drop straight into deep, clear, pale green water with a sandy bottom. At one place there are caves. The year before, with Dr Myles, we had spent a Sunday on Sgurr na Stri, a delightful little hill, only 1,623 feet high, with perfect rock for a first day's climbing practice both on the Scavaig and the Camasunary sides, and the finest view possible of the main chain of the Cuillin from the summit. That day had included a perfect swim in the little bay of Scavaig, and we had marked it for a return visit.

The effects of luxury bathing early in the day are demoralizing, however. We ate our lunch by the shore of Loch Coruisk and both went to sleep for the rest of the afternoon. At 5 o'clock we roused ourselves and set out for our intended rock climb on the steepest buttress of Sgurr Coir' an Lochan. There we ran into serious difficulties and were obliged to retreat from an impossible, steep groove which proved to be a *cul de sac*. Only by roping down twice did we reach *terra firma*. Clouds were pouring over the main ridge and darkness was not far away. Before everything became blotted out we laid down our course for the Bealach Coire Lagan, but we were soon swallowed up in drifting mist. At length we had a fresher breeze in our faces and a great blur of darkness on our left. We were on the main ridge, but it was too broad to be the pass at which we were aiming. We immediately began to descend on the other side, hoping for the best. There were steep rocks on our left which forced us more and more to the right, down a slabby face. After much difficulty we came out below the mist into a bare, rough corrie without any lochan. It was the Coire na Banachdich, and we had forgotten the guide-book injunction to keep well under the cliffs of Sgurr Dearg. As the book remarks, the Glen Brittle side of the pass is unsuitable for tourists. We got to our tent by midnight.

My most enjoyable day's climbing from Coruisk was in September 1933 with Sandy Harrison. We climbed slowly up the Banachdich corrie through a curtain of mist which began to disperse as we halted for lunch on the northern summit. Coruisk was still a seething cauldron of cloud. At intervals the stately ridge of Sgurr a' Ghreadaidh would emerge from the vaporous stew, and we could even catch a glimpse of the Bideins and of Sgurr nan Gillean. We had a long day ahead of us, so we quickly ran down to the Banachdich-Thormaid Saddle and then, ever downwards, by an easy scree gully to within 1,000 feet of the floor of Coruisk. It was a warm afternoon when we sought the start of our climb up the south face of Ghreadaidh near a little rowan tree. It was reputed to be the longest climb in the Cuillin, with a past history of at least one party which had been benighted before completing it.

Every Skye enthusiast should pay at least one visit to the upper glen of Coruisk. The southern peaks of the Cuillin are much more impressive than when seen from Glen Brittle. They seem to tower above one with their huge impending cliffs and long lines of savage boulders and scree. The impression was deepened for us by the fleeting battalions of cloud and streamers of sunshine which poured through the jagged rents. The notched skyline of the ridge seemed stupendous in its remoteness and height. As Norman Collie wrote, "Fortunately the Cuillin are never inferior mountains. . . . It is the atmosphere that adds both dignity and charm to these Scottish hills, making them appear far bigger than they would be in the clearer air of the larger mountain ranges, and giving them the softened colour and perspective so necessary to emphasize the real beauty of true mountains."

We started our climb, soon running up against a steep nose of slabby rock. After a short traverse to the right the way upwards became clear enough, by an 80-foot chimney of trap rock which required very careful handling. The continuation was up long grooves, by which we attained the crest of the buttress. It is needless to attempt to describe the long, middle part of the route in detail, as we experienced little difficulty on the long backbone of the buttress until we reached the little saddle underneath the final, steep nose below the northern summit of Ghreadaidh. We had to be wary of loose rock on the left face of this 150-foot nose. The final ascent was on a steep ridge of excellent rock. The Long Climb had taken us little over two hours.

The climbing, on the average, is only moderately difficult, but the scenery of the Coruisk face makes it a grand route. Any difficulties are in route finding rather than in detailed technique. It makes a first-class mountain traverse, with a choice of routes for descent on the Glen Brittle side. Our return was by An Dorus and the Ghreadaidh corrie, with a delightful bathe in a pool below the great gorge in the lower corrie. For climbers visiting Glen Brittle, who are fond of river pools for swimming, this one below Greta Gorge is almost perfection, besides being accessible in less than ten minute from the main road. Just as

good are the Fairy Pools in Coire na Creiche, not so very far
upstream from the bridge on the main road to Glen Brittle.

This rambling chapter on the Cuillin seems at times to stray
a good deal from the serious business of rock climbing. All this
must be attributed to the charm and carefree atmosphere which
seem to have much the same effect on all holiday makers who
come under the spell of Skye. One infallible cure is the traverse
of the Main Ridge. In 1935 Allan and I hoped to include Blaven
and Clach Glas, as well as the outliers Sgurr Dubh Mor and
Sgumain, in the expedition. This was my second traverse of the
Ridge, but the additional items were cut out by a sudden
change of weather, scudding rain and a sou'wester bursting
upon us as we were traversing the Bidein peaks. We continued
to Sgurr nan Gillean and then returned to our base at Glen
Brittle. As we passed the Lodge gates Mr MacRae asked us
where we had been. When we told him he shook his head and
asked us why on earth we had done it.

We did not camp that night. Mary Campbell gave us a
glorious supper of ham and eggs, and we slept in comfort. I
awoke about six a.m., very thirsty. Outside it rained, but there
is a convenient little burn at which I filled a jug. Colin still
slept when I came back with the water. Without opening his
eyes he held out a hand and raised himself a little on the pillow.
I held the water to his lips and he drank nearly a pint before
relapsing into sleep. Our next awakening was six hours later,
when, despite the continued rain, we betook ourselves to Loch
Brittle for a swim before breakfast. I hope to traverse the Ridge
again, for the third time, whenever I get the opportunity.

The first complete traverse of the Ridge with the addition of
Blaven was effected on 12 June 1939, by Ian G. Charleson and
W. E. Forde, starting from a camp below Gars-bheinn and
finishing at a camp in Harta Corrie. In September of the same
year W. H. Murray and R. G. Donaldson repeated the expedition from Glen Brittle, again using a destination camp, already
prepared in Glen Sligachan. Since then Mr S. Thompson has
done the whole expedition alone, starting from and returning to
Glen Brittle in a little over twenty hours, in August 1944. The
most troublesome part was the return to Glen Brittle at nightfall
from the head of Loch Scavaig round the base of the hills.*

So far, nothing has been said of the charm of the Cuillin

---

* Accounts of these expeditions are to be found in B. H. Humble's *The
Cuillin of Skye*.

when coated with spring snow. The weather may be capricious in March or April, but the reward of a fine day of spring sunshine on these glorious, sparkling ridges, set high above azure seas, must be superlative. I draw on the experiences of my friend John Wilson who has visited the Cuillin several times in the month of March. He finds three types of weather: (1) like poor summer conditions with cold, wet rocks and occasional ice, but with snow confined to the higher ridges, (2) mixed weather with a north-west wind and snow below 2,500 feet, when one battles along the ridges against blinding snow scurries (a section of ridge, easy in summer, may become an inferno of driving snow and ice-plastered rocks under these conditions), and (3) a north-east wind may be followed by several perfect, sunny days of pure delight. Even in perfect conditions the Banachdich section of the ridge demanded a long afternoon of effort, with much step-cutting and places where roping-down tactics were necessary to ensure any progress at all. He concluded his account with a climb on Bidein Druim nan Ramh: "Coruisk lay at our feet. All about us the peaks of the Cuillin danced to the blue of the vault above. Heaven and the world were ours."

XI

THE CAIRNGORMS

THE CAIRNGORM MOUNTAINS are the nearest thing we have in Britain to an isolated, self-contained range of an almost continental type, as regards climate, flora and fauna. They are far enough from the western sea to ensure a tolerably dry climate, and the mean height is sufficient to guarantee a hard winter with plenty of snow remaining on the heights until well into the spring, thus rendering possible very good skiing on large areas of their higher slopes. There is an air of remoteness and vastness about them which inspires both respect and exhilaration, despite the fact that the contours of their summits are somewhat rounded and unimpressive in form.

There are many satisfying, distant prospects of the Cairngorms. The view from Craigellachie behind Aviemore is, perhaps, the most accessible, but if a hill road be taken northwards from the main road, just north of Loch Alvie, proceeding up the hill far enough to see things in their proper proportions, there is no finer view in Britain of a great mountain range. In the foreground are the woods around Loch Alvie, then the forest of Rothiemurchus stretching south-west beyond Loch an Eilein and eastward to Loch Morlich. Beyond are the massive outlines of the Cairngorm giants, blue in the distance and not too easily distinguished, the one from the other, until we get to know them well by walking and climbing amongst them. Cairngorm is on the left, Ben MacDhui merging with Braeriach, with its many western corries, in the centre, and, across the gap of Glen Einich, Sgoran Dubh on the right leading the eye across Glen Feshie to the lower hills beyond.

It is an impressive façade which, however, leaves us still puzzled without explaining the real charm of this range of hills. In his *Scenery of Scotland* Sir Archibald Geikie chooses this view to drive home his main conclusion about all the Scottish mountains, that they are remnants of a dissected plateau, worn down by ages of combined erosion by the action of sun, wind, rain, frost and ice. Only the resistant portions are left today and they, too, have been sculptured into rounded forms. But these forms are by no means ugly or ungainly when we get to know them. Professor Norman Collie once wrote of them as follows: "To many people the Cairngorm Range is composed of shapeless, flat-topped mountains, devoid of character. They do not rise like the Matterhorn in savage grandeur, yet the sculptured sides of Braeriach, seen from Sgoran Dubh Mhor, are in reality far richer in beautiful, intricate mountain sculpture than the whole face of the Matterhorn as seen from the Riffel Alp."

This is praise with a vengeance, but Collie was a painter as well as a mountaineer and scientist of distinction, and his people came from Deeside. He had no doubt that the ancient mountains of Scotland showed a wonderful strength and repose in their outlines, "so that the bigger mountains seem to rise without effort from the moors and smaller hills that surround them". The Cairngorms, like all lands of far distances, should be seen in fine weather with enough blue sky and cloud to bring out the aerial perspective and the play of shadows on their vast masses of rolling upland. It is then that one realizes what Fiona Macleod, writing of the mountain charm in the month of June, called the "blueness of blueness" of distant hills. Hence the origin of the name Cairngorm (the blue mountain), although the local name, from the colour of the granite cliffs, is Monadh Ruadh (the red mountains).

The appearance of these mountains is very similar to lower hills to the south of Deeside. There, too, we have difficulty in recognizing the giants of the picture, obscured as they are by the lesser, rounded foothills. Surely the key to the charm of this belt of country is rather in the valleys than on the summits, for there are many beautiful and impressive glens; clear, rushing rivers and wild, secluded lochs, not only in the lower valleys but high up in the bare corries beneath the summit plateaux. Nowhere in Britain is there a more attractive country for high-level walking, for long days on the heights, going from one peak to another, and for that most genuine and delightful form of travel which starts from one valley, crosses a pass or a mountain top and descends by a different glen to some other place amid contrasted scenery in a different valley.

Difficult climbing has not been much developed in the Cairngorms. Great distances must be covered from the available places of habitation in order to reach the most interesting corries where rock climbing is possible. Good roads do not penetrate far into these mountain sanctuaries, although there is an abundance of good paths and rights of way. The same obstacles prevent a good deal of first-class winter climbing. Weather changes can be rapid on the mountains, especially in winter, so that the utmost precautions should be taken on an expedition to the high Cairngorms in mid-winter. There have been many tragedies and near-tragedies, nearly all caused by the lack of reasonable care and forethought as regards clothing, equipment, food and general fitness.

In my earliest climbing days the Cairngorms exercised a great fascination over me. My first venture was a cycle trip from my home in Fifeshire, with the object of catching a glimpse of the big peaks with the interesting names. Going north in the evening I spent an hour or two at the summit of the Cairnwell Pass on the way to Braemar and breakfasted by the Linn of Dee. The southern aspect of the Devil's Point and the higher hills behind made a deep impression and gave birth to a resolve to explore them fully. Then I carried on westwards across the watershed and down Glen Tilt to Blair Atholl. A year later I climbed Ben MacDhui from Derry Lodge by Loch Etchachan and enjoyed a grand view of the corries of Braeriach and Cairn Toul. Two years later came the opportunity to explore the former after a night spent at Alltdruie Bothy (now wholly in ruins), situated in a beautiful meadow surrounded by forest, dominated to the south by Carn Elrick and the Lurcher's Crag, the majestic northern outposts of the Larig Ghru Pass.

In mixed weather, with much wind and cloud, Mr R. P. Dansey and I crossed the Larig and climbed over slopes of huge granite boulders into the Garbh Choire Dhaidh where the infant Dee plunges over the edge of the plateau of Braeriach in a 600-foot cataract. About half a mile back from the edge are the Wells of Dee, the true source of the river, which we visited after climbing up fairly easy slopes beside the waterfall. The summit plateau of Braeriach is the greatest British mountain area around and over the 4,000-foot level. It is a thinly eroded expanse of red granite, consisting mostly of sand with a scanty covering of mosses and other lowly plants. The Wells are close under the 4,000-foot level, little mossy hollows in the plateau with several small streams flowing out of the ground and soon uniting together to form a vigorous young river of clear, cold water.

There is a strange charm about this vast, arid expanse, so close to the sky and the clouds, with far prospects on every side of the massive, everlasting hills. This roof of Scotland is not altogether desolate. It is the haunt of the snow bunting, the dotterel and the ptarmigan, which can often be surprised with a brood of yellow-brown chicks in early July. Overhead one may occasionally see the golden eagle sailing swiftly over the plateau with hardly a perceptible flicker of his wings, but seemingly intent to remark any small creature which may be moving amongst the stones, when he will swoop down suddenly upon the prey, even from a height of over 1,000 feet. Once, close to the summit of Carn a' Claise, on emerging from behind a huge boulder on the ridge, I surprised an eagle perched on the summit cairn. Photography was not possible. The bird stared at me for only a second or two before vanishing at a great speed.

The other great, high plateau of the Cairngorms lies between Ben MacDhui and Cairngorm. This we visited on our next expedition, ascending easily from the Larig track over the Lurcher's Crag to Ben MacDhui and taking a somewhat lower route on our way to Cairngorm, so as to enjoy the view from above of Loch Avon (2,377 ft), one of the wildest scenes right in the heart of this mountain land. Cairngorm is the northern outpost of the range, with a long, easy ridge running down northwards to beautiful Loch Morlich, by which route it can be very easily ascended. All these mountains can be readily climbed from Speyside by a strong walking party, properly clad and shod for the hills.

The best route for Braeriach is either from the summit of the Larig Ghru track or from Glen Einich at the point near the site of the lower bothy (now destroyed), just beyond where the road crosses the main stream, by following the line of the Beanaidh Beag and striking up into Coire Ruadh for the summit. It is even better to make for Coire an Lochain which encloses the highest British loch at a level of 3,250 feet, a wild rocky hollow overhung by great crags, which are still more impressive in spring when huge ice-floes cover the loch, and the gullies and ledges are all snow-covered.

For Cairn Toul it is best to proceed to the end of the Glen Einich road, just short of the Loch, where the Upper Bothy once stood before it was burnt down during the recent war. A good path strikes up to the left by Coire Dhondail. This takes one steeply up to the stony plateau between Braeriach and Cairn Toul, so steeply that the backward views across Loch Einich to Sgoran Dubh are exceedingly impressive, as the Einich wall of that mountain has five great rocky buttresses which give very good climbing.

For those who wish to enjoy some rock scrambling of an easy nature, the Fiacaill Ridge between Coire an Lochain and Coire an t-Sneachda, the two main, northern corries of Cairngorm, offers an interesting route to the summit of Cairn Lochan (3,983 ft) and thence to Cairngorm. It is one of the few, narrow rock ridges in this group of mountains.

Long Hill-walking Expeditions

The Cairngorm mountains are ideal for very long expeditions, either passes between Deeside and Speyside or traverses of several peaks in one day. The hardest and longest of these is the traverse of the six highest Cairngorms, which was first effected in a single day by Messrs H. J. Butchart, L. J. Davidson, H. G. Drummond, H. Kellas and I. M. McLaren, all of Aberdeen, starting from Loch Builg at midnight on 21 June 1909. They crossed over Ben Avon, Beinn a' Bhuird, Cairn Gorm, Ben MacDhui, Cairn Toul and Braeriach to the lower bothy of Glen Einich, a distance of twenty-eight miles, involving 9,000 feet of climbing in nineteen hours. A similar traverse taking Cairn Toul last (after Braeriach) and finishing at Corrour Bothy in Glen Dee was effected in fourteen and three-quarter hours by R. P. Yunnie and a party of three in July 1932. No one appears to have started and returned to the same base, which would make the expedition a good deal longer.

The making of records is against the whole spirit and tradition of mountaineering, but a long hill traverse such as this is the nearest thing we have in Britain to mountaineering or exploration on the greater mountain ranges of the world. It is in the course of such an expedition that one really gets to know the contours of the landscape and the changing aspects of the hills from different points of view. As the day advances we acquire an additional source of information, not always accurate but strangely insistent, in our sense of muscular effort. Towards the end of a long, hard day we become acutely sensitive to any slight increase of gradient or roughness on our route. This sense is ever with us in a minor degree, but enables the trained mountaineer to progress always with a minimum of effort and a fuller appreciation of the ground than an unskilled person. I have always wished to effect the traverse of all six Cairngorms, but the opportunity has, thus far, eluded me, so that I have had to be content with two partial successes.

On 8 June 1946, John Wilson and I camped in our car on the

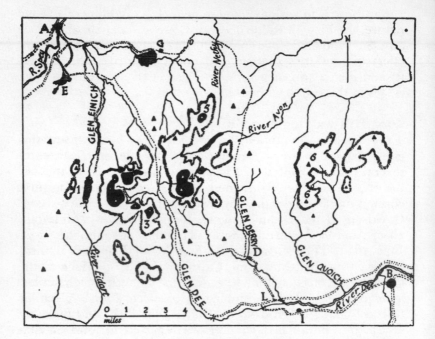

THE CAIRNGORMS

MOUNTAINS

		height in feet	
1	Sgoran Dubh Mor (two tops)	North top	3,635
		South top	3,658
2	Braeriach (several tops)		4,248
3	Cairn Toul		4,241
4	Ben Macdhui		4,296
5	Cairn Gorm		4,084
6	Beinn a' Bhuird (two tops)	North top	3,924
		South top	3,860
7	Ben Avon		3,843

A	Aviemore	G	Glenmore Lodge, on Loch Morlich
B	Braemar	I	Inverey Village
D	Derry Lodge	L	Linn of Dee
E	Loch an Eilein		

PASSES

From A southward to Glen Dee or Glen Derry is the Larig Ghru. From River Nethy southward to D is the Larig an Laoigh.

Derry Lodge road above Deeside. We had no definite plans and
it was a rainy evening, but John hankered after an attempt on
the big six Cairngorms, with a return to our base, an almost
impossible programme as we had to motor south on the
following evening. The project was made still more unreason-
able by the fact that I had only a pair of rubber-soled walking
shoes available. The weather cleared about three a.m. and we
started an hour later on a dank, cold, misty morning. We struck
eastward through the hills by a long, straight, V-shaped cleft
leading from Glen Derry to Glen Quoich, a curious place which
I learned was part of a great fault crossing Scotland by Loch
Lubnaig, Loch Tay and Glen Tilt. Deer looked down from the
edges of the defile, birds sang cheerfully and the clouds parted
in front of us, revealing the smooth, elephantine bulk of the
southern shoulder of Beinn a' Bhuird.

As we swung to the left, contouring over the moor before
descending to the upper part of Glen Quoich, the huge mountain continued to dominate the scene, overlooking a mysterious
sanctuary of old Scots pine trees, still partly concealed by
isolated masses and streamers of morning mist. We missed the
old bothy which is marked on the map but has now disappeared. What a grand place for a bivouac and a camp fire,
redolent of peacefulness, freedom, great spaces and the kindlier
aspects of wild nature! Both John and I agreed that it was a
valley to live in. The gently rounded contours of the mountains
were more akin to the atmosphere of these wooded valleys than
any of the more naked and abrupt hills of the west. Deer were
numerous above the woodland, and we watched a small herd,
the movements of which were impeded by a hind which was
encouraging a young fawn.

It was very cold on the plateau when we reached the south
top of Beinn a' Bhuird at seven a.m., but the distant view was
exceedingly clear, with all the beauty of shimmering cloudlets
above the south-eastern valleys. On the way to the northern or
main summit, two miles to the north of us, across a stony,
undulating table-land, we admired the huge cliffs of the eastern
corries, especially those above the Dubh Lochan, which
gleamed like a mirror in the morning sun. Great snow wreaths
encircled the rim of the plateau, and we promised ourselves a
return visit in order to explore the buttresses of rock and the
steep gullies.

By now our ambitions were trimmed to a measure of equality
and reasonableness. We decided to leave Ben Avon alone and

to be content with Ben MacDhui. A strong, fresh, south-east wind kept us on the move. We did not mean to miss any intervening peaks, of which the first was Beinn a' Chaoruinn, three and a half miles away, with an intervening drop to 2,650 feet from our stance at 3,924 feet. That stretch was rough going though fairly easy, but the succeeding descent carried us into the deep V-shaped valley traversed by the Larig an Laoigh track from Glen Derry to Nethy Bridge. We crossed the track at an altitude of about 2,300 feet, followed by the steepest climb of the day to the summit of Beinn Mheadhoin (3,883 ft), which we accomplished within the hour. The last of our scanty store of provisions was consumed at the outlet of Loch Etchachan (3,058 ft). There was now a regular path to the top of Ben MacDhui (4,296 ft) which we attained at two-fifteen p.m. This is the highest of the Cairngorm mountains and, until the year 1810, was believed to be the highest Scottish mountain, although the issue was not decided in favour of Ben Nevis until the Ordnance Survey of 1847.

We met several parties on the summit and John Wilson considered that he had never before enjoyed a finer view as regards distant visibility. To the south were the Lomond Hills of Fife and the Ochils, to the west Ben Vorlich, Lawers, Ben More and Schiehallion, then Ben Alder, Creag Meaghaidh and Ben Nevis, which was partly in cloud. The Five Sisters of Kintail and the mass of Mam Sodhail were clear to the north-west, and Morven in Caithness to the north. The Garbh Choire of Braeriach carried a lot of snow. Our return route was over Cairngorm of Derry and the long ridge to Derry Lodge in its surroundings of scattered pine forest. We regained our car at five-thirty p.m., after twenty-three miles of walking and 7,000 feet of ascent, a satisfying day, filled with variety and enjoyment.

Our other attempt on the "big six" was no more likely to succeed, but there was no harm in trying. Such a programme can always be shortened if necessary, as soon as the inexorable realities of space and time begin to overpower the ill-considered ambitions of map-reading mountaineers. With us was Ian Charleson, who had not climbed for several months. We were staying at the hospitable cottage of Mrs Lorimer, beautifully situated amidst the pines on the shore of Loch an Eilein, and the date was early October 1947. The only thing in our favour was a third quarter moon, so we decided to start at three-thirty a.m.

It would weary the reader to go over the expedition in detail. There was plenty of time and much thoughtless hilarity at the breakfast table, but we were only ten minutes behind schedule on starting out. The first seven miles took us to the foot of Coire Dhondail at the head of Glen Einich, so that the actual climbing did not begin until about six a.m., and the moon had remained persistently obscured all the way. The Dhondail track is really excellent, a graded progress to a height of about 3,300 feet. The clouds were ominous, with a fierce, cold, west wind, but the cloud level kept above us as we rose. Losing a little time by getting too far up on Braeriach, we reached Cairn Toul at eight-thirty a.m., an exceedingly chilly spot for our second breakfast. We visited the Wells of Dee on the way to Braeriach and enjoyed our most comfortable siesta of the day by the Pools of Dee at the top of the Larig Ghru Pass. By now it was obvious that the Eastern Cairngorms were out of the programme. In June things might have been different.

Rain and flying scud met us on the last lap before reaching Ben MacDhui at one-thirty p.m. We had been warned, but the clerk of the weather was evidently satisfied with our submission, for he allowed us to finish the day peacefully by including Cairngorm, where we assembled at four p.m. Ian and I returned over Cairn Lochan, descending by the Fiacaill Ridge. He had gone very well indeed, although he needed a little coaxing to get him across the slopes of the Lurcher's Crag and on to the Larig track before dark. When we neared the Cairngorm Club Bridge over the Allt na Beinne, Ian appeared to savour the prospects of a good supper and fairly took the bit between his teeth, striding along the forest path at a pace which stretched me to the utmost. We had done the "big four" if not the "six" and we all enjoyed ourselves to the full. When I measured it out on the map I found that our day of sixteen hours had included 7,700 feet of ascent and thirty-one and a half miles, most of it fairly rough going. I hope there is still time for the longer expedition!

In mid-June 1938 I spent a long day, entirely by myself, on Braeriach and Cairn Toul, approaching from White Bridge in Deeside. It is on such occasions that the spirit of the mountains enters into one's very being, unhindered by even such distraction as the presence of a like-minded companion. There was no cause for haste and I spent some time in the Corrour Bothy, that famous haunt of mountain men and hikers, below the crags of the Devil's Point. The visitors' book of the Dundee University

College Rucksack Club made good reading. One band of New Year enthusiasts had made themselves very comfortable, although the frost was keen. The entry in the book said, "Tonight we have a fire, a magnificent fire. In its fiercest moments it has driven us into the back of the bothy. Shirts have been abandoned. The 'old dogs' are suffering from burnt knees." These were the stalwarts of the Ptarmigan and Creag Dhu Clubs of the Glasgow area.

I made my way onward and upward into the Coire Bhrochain of Braeriach. After a shower of hail the Black and Braeriach Pinnacles were clearly defined against a background of swirling mist. I progressed easily up the lower slabs of the former, and then up a narrow crack about forty feet long, where the holds were just sufficient and which kept a yard or two to the right of the true nose. The latter was too steep to climb with its roof-tile structure of smooth slabs. Easier rocks continued to the teeth on the Pinnacle crest. It is a good climb and not too difficult. This is also true of a flank attack on Braeriach Pinnacle which I climbed next, but not of the sharp, vertical edge at the end of its ridge. The highest summit of Braeriach is immediately above.

In bad weather, scudding cloud and repeated showers of sleet, I made my way round the rim of the plateau over Sgor an Lochan Uaine to Cairn Toul. Then the sun came through and showed up a brilliant Brocken Spectre as I rested by the cairn. Every step down the rocky ridge was sheer delight in that lovely evening, with all the distant hills intensely clear in their rain-washed colouring of blue and purple. I got back to the car after nearly twelve hours' absence.

I had still to make a promised call at Thistle Cottage, Inverey, the home of Maggie Gruer* and the best-known hostelry in the Cairngorms. Bill Mackenzie and I had stayed there the previous night and our hostess had given us a ham and egg breakfast at six a.m. Bill had been ticked off for attempting to sign the visitor's book in pencil, as the ink was solid in the bottle provided. This evening I had little time to spare, but the kettle was on the fire and a welcome brew of tea appeared in a few minutes. I took out a lump of gingerbread

---

* Maggie Gruer was the friend of generations of walkers and climbers in the Cairngorms. She welcomed them at all hours of the day and night, and somehow there was always room for everyone. She died at her home in March 1939 at the age of seventy-seven.

from my sack and my hostess gracefully accepted a slice, at the same time going to a cupboard and placing before me a plate of butter, which I spread on my own slice. I noticed that she herself took jam. In fact, she told me that she preferred jam, at the same time fixing me with a humorous twinkle in her eye. Then I took a bite and understood. It wasn't yesterday's butter! But I stared her out, even taking another slice and some more butter. Meanwhile, she chatted away about the great figures of the past who had come to Deeside, from Queen Victoria and Mr Gladstone to the latest mountaineers from Aberdeen. She was surely entitled to her little joke at my expense.

XII

CAIRNGORM GRANITE

FOR ALL-ROUND MOUNTAINEERS the Cairngorms, along with which, for the purpose of this chapter, is included the mountain mass of Lochnagar to the south of Deeside, offer great attractions, both in summer and winter. Good rock climbing is available, but one must be prepared to walk a long way in order to find it, or else pitch a tent or bivouac in some remote corrie. Lochnagar belongs to the same granite formation as the Cairngorms, the rock structure and scenery being very similar. The southern boundary of the granite lies beyond Creag an Dubh Loch and Broad Cairn, above the uppermost recesses of Glen Clova, near Bachnagairn. Lochnagar and Creag an Dubh Loch provide, in fact, the best rock climbing of the whole district, and the 700-foot crags of the north-eastern corrie of Lochnagar are outstanding in every way, both for summer and winter climbing. The other most attractive and accessible area is the long face of Sgoran Dubh above Glen Einich, with its five great buttresses of rock and numerous gullies.

Granite climbing is by no means easy, for the crags, at a first attempt, may appear to offer very little between easy scrambling and vertical walls of imitation masonry. There is much loose rock in many places, and the rounded edges offer few belays. None the less, the climbing can be both difficult and safe for those who have mastered the technique and faced the limitations of the material. Vegetation is often found on ledges and in chimneys and cracks, but this is avoidable and not at all troublesome. Difficult climbs should not be attempted in wet weather, as the granite is often coated with a thin green or greenish-black patina of lichen which becomes very slippery when wet. A similar caution should be extended to the use of any vegetable holds in wet conditions. Plants cannot root themselves deeply on granite. Only a few notes can be given on the location and character of several typical climbs, for the Cairngorms will always be a paradise for the hill walker rather than a popular area for rock climbing.

Sgoran Dubh

The Glen Einich road is closed to motors, but a bicycle can be very serviceable. From Aviemore to Loch Einich is about ten miles, but the nearest of the five buttresses (No. 1) is not quite so far. In May 1932 we held a week-end Meet of the Perth Section of the J.M.C.S. and thoroughly enjoyed our six-mile walk beyond the locked gate up Glen Einich. Near the upper limit of the forest there is a sharp bend to the right which discloses the snowy dome of Sgoran Dubh, flanked by its buttresses of rock, one of the noblest vistas in the Scottish Highlands. We camped on piles of dry heather in the stable of the Upper Bothy, short of Loch Einich. Both bothies have now disappeared, casualties of the recent war when this region was used as a training ground for mountain warfare troops. After our evening meal we visited the loch with its beautiful beach of granite sand. The moon was glancing down over the shoulder of Braeriach and there was a strong ripple on the waters. To the right was the black, serrated outline of the Pinnacle Buttress and, beyond the southern end of the loch, the faint, whitish streak of the waterfall descending from Loch nan Cnapan—as wild a scene as Loch Coruisk in the heart of the Cuillin hills of Skye.

Next morning, after an ample and leisurely breakfast, Colin Allan, Dr Myles and I crossed the stream at its outlet from the loch and toiled upwards to the foot of the rocks. It is quite easy to recognize the five buttresses, but by no means so simple to identify the known climbing routes. Between Nos. 2 and 3 buttresses is a prominent, deep gully which drains an upper corrie. Centrally placed in this corrie is a conspicuous mass of rock which, as seen from the direction of the Upper Bothy, is shaped rather like a diamond. Our objective for the day was to climb the Diamond Buttress situated in the Fan Corrie, for rock climbers are optimists and have no scruples about naming a climb whilst it is still no more than a hopeful figment of the imagination. Of course, we considered that we might have some success with the lower rocks as well before starting on the real business of the day. It would be time enough after that to traverse into the Fan Corrie, rather than to reach it by an easier but less interesting route.

I shall not recount our troubles on the lower rocks. We failed to find any of the established routes, although we did come upon a cairn which seemed to indicate the upper end of one of them. We encountered many difficulties on the slabs and ribs of that complicated buttress and were repeatedly compelled to execute difficult, horizontal traverses (several of them even in a downward direction) when we were utterly defeated by the smoothness and steepness of the face above us. It was very good sport and we thoroughly enjoyed our lunch above the lower rocks. We began to understand why most of the early routes on Sgoran Dubh, generally climbed at Easter-time when the days are not long, did, in fact, avoid the greater difficulties which would appeal to the modern rock climber.

As we crossed over easy rocks into the Fan Corrie our buttress rose before us, looking more attractive than ever. It began with an *arête*, pleasingly interesting but fairly easy. We moved continuously, all together, to the foot of the steep face beyond. Then we roped up and put Colin on the lead. The wall rose with exceeding steepness for close on 100 feet, but the leader progressed steadily on small but sufficient holds to a secure stance with a belay at forty feet. Then came a 15-foot chimney. The climbing was difficult and interesting, and the whole of this face was airy and impressive. Above the steep part was an easy, upper ridge with one or two small gaps, leading to a short snow slope and an easy cornice of snow below the rim of the plateau. Less than 200 feet of walking took us to the cairn of Sgoran Dubh Mor (3,635 ft).

Allan left us soon afterwards, but Myles and I continued over Sgor Gaoith (3,658 ft) and descended to Loch Einich by the fifth or Pinnacle Buttress. The Pinnacle, which is conspicuous from the Glen Einich road, is easily climbed from its upper neck, but is even easier to avoid altogether. On another occasion I climbed it directly from below, which involves a very difficult, short pitch. The slabs below the Pinnacle are very awkward to descend, the best plan being to keep well to the south. For those who want a long, interesting climb of moderate difficulty the Pinnacle Buttress can be cordially recommended. It is best to choose a route on the lower slabs a little to the left of the Pinnacle and to cross the neck behind it before resuming the ascent.

As I have already stated, the Sgoran Dubh routes are, in general, not easy to identify, as there are so many ribs and ridges which look so much alike when seen from the Einich road.

There is, however, one such continuous rib, some little distance to the right of the gully between Nos. 2 and 3 Buttresses, which can be cordially recommended as giving a

500-foot climb, perfectly continuous, on sound rock of no more than difficult standard. The foot of the rib can be identified from the road near the site of the upper bothy, as it lies above a long, thin, sandy groove running down to the moor. The rib ends below and not far to the right of a little grassy saddle overlooking Fan Corrie. When my sister and I climbed it in September 1941 we crossed this saddle and finished our day by a lateral route which joined the original route on Diamond Buttress below its upper ridge.

The only other route on Sgoran Dubh which I propose to describe here is quite easy to identify on No. 1 Buttress, and is typical of Cairngorm granite at its best and soundest. No. 1 Buttress is split by a long, deep gully, overhung by impossible-looking cliffs on the left, and by the clean-cut edge of Roberts Ridge on the right. The nomenclature of the cliffs of Sgoran Dubh would have been simpler if the two halves of No. 1 Buttress had been numbered separately, thus corresponding to Nos. 2 and 3 Buttresses which are also separated by a narrow gully.

Ernest Roberts, Denis Howe and I made the first ascent of this fine route on 24 April, 1938, a day of perfect weather and dry rocks. We named the climb in honour of our friend's sixty-fourth birthday. He had retired from his profession within the previous year, but not from mountaineering. On this climb he thoroughly enjoyed himself. The route, 450 feet in height, keeps as close as is practicable to the edge overlooking the gully and finishes in a short, steep ridge. We took two and a half hours to complete the climb.

The first objective is a small rowan tree growing out of the base of a chimney, about fifty feet up. The tree is not only useful as a belay, but assists the leader in reaching the niche behind it. The chimney is rather difficult and the rocks above it are somewhat exposed, without very satisfying holds. One must beware of anything loose on such a steep face. The route goes somewhat leftwards, with one very bad step to the right on to a slab with a belay. We are now above the steep, lower wall. The intermediate section, set at a more moderate angle, offers many good stances and leads directly to the upper wall, which is almost severe in standard at isolated places. It seems possible to avoid this by keeping more to the left. The main pitch exceeds sixty feet in height and involves the ascent of a long fissure, not deep but not far short of vertical, with a very awkward part below the middle but a sufficiency of good holds near the top. It is perfectly sound rock, with no vegetation.

There now remains a short, steep wall leading to the slabby roof of the end block of the ridge, but there is a surprise at the end, for the block is almost completely isolated from the main mass of the mountain. There is a vertical drop of about eight feet to a sharp, rock edge, leading over to steep and easy rocks which run up to the summit plateau. It is not a pleasant descent for the last man, for the knife-edge has a long, steep drop on both sides. The view through the notch, past the savage crags of the next buttress to Loch Einich, with the massive, rounded outline of the flank of Braeriach beyond, is one of the most impressive in the Cairngorm region. Our party went to the top of the mountain and returned along the ridge to its northern end which overlooks Loch an Eilein and the woodlands of Rothiemurchus, as fine a panorama of a very different type.

Other Climbs in the Cairngorms

I have already mentioned the climbing in Coire Bhrochain of Braeriach. A good deal of exploration can still be done in this remote, savage corrie, as well as on the crags in the innermost recesses of the Garbh Choire. There is also an interesting ridge leading to the summit of Sgor an Lochan Uaine. On the northern ramparts of Cairngorm there is more accessible and splendid winter climbing below Cairn Lochan in the corries which flank the Fiacaill ridge (which is very easy), the rock climbing being mostly found above the huge slabs of Coire an Lochain. Visitors to the Shelter Stone at the head of Loch Avon will find opportunities on Shelter Stone Crag and also above Loch Etchachan, where the routes are, however, very short.

The Garbh Choire lying at the northern base of Beinn a' Bhuird is full of possibilities, the Mitre Ridge being the finest and best known of these. It was first climbed by two parties, by separate routes in the lower section, in July 1933. The more direct route, by Messrs E. A. M. Wedderburn, P. D. Baird and E. J. A. Leslie, was particularly difficult on the lower slabs. I myself climbed it by the shorter, side route in May 1935 and was greatly impressed by the narrow, steep ridge on the upper part, where a delicate traverse and a thin crack on the precipitous western wall had to be negotiated in order to circumvent a tower. There are also fine crags above the Dubh Lochan on the eastern side of the South Top of Beinn a' Bhuird, in a corrie where I enjoyed a grand snow climb in early May 1948.

Lochnagar

Lochnagar and its subordinate peaks are ideal country for hill walking, as well as for rock or snow ascents. The best way to get an idea of the country is to traverse the mountain, either way, between Glen Muick and Glen Callater. A good path ascends the north side from Allt na Giubhsaich (on the opposite side of Glen Muick from Spittal, which is the end of the driving road, about nine miles from Ballater in Deeside), mounting by an easy gradient to the summit. Those making for the rock climbs above the Lochan, at 2,575 feet above sea level, should leave the track at the commencement of the Ladder or zig-zags beneath the Cuidhe Crom summit, and cross the neck between that peak and the Meikle Pap to the right of it. There is a wide summit plateau, the highest point (3,786 ft) being beyond the main mass of the crags. The southern descent to Loch Callater is also by a good track, about six miles long, over wild moorland. At one point there is a glimpse down a valley to the east to the Dubh Loch, which is dominated on the south by the equally impressive line of 700-foot crags of Creag an Dubh Loch. The Dubh Loch is also accessible by path from the head of Loch Muick. Loch Callater is connected by a rather inferior road to the main Cairnwell road, about two miles south of Braemar. The Glen Muick approach is much better, both for camping and climbing. The Lochnagar corries and gullies carry a great deal of snow in winter, but the gullies are not good for climbing in summer.

Most of the rock climbing is either fairly easy or very difficult. Considerable experience is necessary for the latter, and it is not a very good place for the training of novices, owing to the general lack of good belays and prevalence of rounded holds. The Eagle Ridge of Lochnagar, to which is devoted a separate chapter, is a good example of the very best climbing on granite, or on any other kind of rock for that matter. It is almost unique in Britain as a long, severe climb on a steep, narrow ridge. In the limited space available in this chapter it is only possible to direct the rock climber to a few other selected routes of varying grades of difficulty.

The gullies are not to be recommended, as they are loose and the rock is usually unsound. The most formidable is the Douglas Gully of Lochnagar. A strong party may be able to climb fairly easily to within 150 feet of the top, and yet be defeated by a short wall of smooth, loose, slabby rock. In August 1946 a climber had to remain there, unable to move up or down, for

The Cliffs of Lochnagar

1 Eagle Ridge
2 Parallel Buttress
3 Tough-Brown Ridge
4 Raeburn's Gully

5 Black Spout Pinnacle
6 Black Spout
7 Black Spout Buttress,
  (West Buttress on right)

eight hours before being rescued. Mr C. Ludwig made the first ascent alone in September 1933, but he maintained that the top section was unjustifiable. The Black Spout is perfectly easy, but may offer difficulties in winter owing to a cornice at the top. Raeburn's Gully makes a good winter climb. There does not seem to be much sense in attempting Douglas Gully as a rock climb, when it is flanked on either side by such excellent face and ridge routes as Eagle Ridge and Shadow Buttress B. The latter is rather typical of many Lochnagar buttresses, having an exceedingly steep and difficult lower wall followed by an easy upper section.

It will be better to mention one or two buttress or face routes of moderate difficulty, so that a visitor may get an idea of the topography of the mountain and the feel of the rock underfoot. The classical route of this type is the Tough-Brown Ridge, first climbed by Messrs Tough and Brown in August 1896. The route demonstrates the difficulties of climbing on Lochnagar granite; for the lower part of the ridge (which would be much more accurately described as a buttress) was not climbed by the pioneers. They started up the rocks near the base of Eagle Ridge (which is a true ridge but was first named Eagle Buttress), traversed to the right along a gently sloping shelf beneath Parallel Gullies and Parallel Buttress, and gained the crest of their buttress by a very steep climb. The upper continuation was perfectly easy. In June 1939 W. H. Murray and I descended from this buttress into Raeburn's Gully by a steep, but not specially difficult route, but the direct route up the lower wall of the buttress was climbed only in July 1941 by Miss N. Forsyth and myself. It proved to be one of the hardest climbs I have ever done. Parallel Buttress, first climbed in 1939 by W. H. Murray and myself, showed different features, having a short severe section near the top. For those who hanker after the impossible there is always the challenge of the terrifying wall of Black Spout Pinnacle, above the foot of the Black Spout, (climbed in August 1949 by W. D. Brooker and D. A. Sutherland).

I fear that I have been diverted from moderate routes for moderate climbers. Shadow Buttress A or Black Spout Buttress are excellent climbs of this standard. There is some very good and variegated climbing on the West Buttress. The routes are often linked by ledge traverses and are difficult to describe, so that hard and easy ways are often close together. On the west side of Lochnagar the Stuic Buttress above the green loch is worth visiting.

Creag an Dubh Loch is much less explored than Lochnagar. The granite appears to be more closely jointed, tending towards a roof-tile, slabby formation with correspondingly increased difficulty. The Labyrinth, a long, fascinating climb of about 700 feet, goes up a curious, inner amphitheatre of the mountain on very sound rock, and finishes close to the summit. Miss Forsyth and I found it exceedingly difficult at our first ascent in 1941 (*S.M.C. Journal* 23: 32ff), and it was pleasant and interesting to have our opinion confirmed a year later by Mr S. Thompson, a very good climber, who had not read the account of our ascent. His route was almost the same as ours.

A Winter Climb on Lochnagar

Raeburn's Gully was first climbed in November 1898, when there was very little snow and the main difficulty was a great,

vertical wall of rock across the gully at about middle height.
Harold Raeburn's party used combined tactics, the leader being
obliged to hook his ice-axe by the pick over the edge of a
jammed block above him in order to overcome the pitch. There
were lesser difficulties, and a through route between large
boulders above this point, but there was, of course, no cornice
of snow at the top.

A mixed party of four of us set out from Allt na Giubhsaich
for Lochnagar on 23 April 1939 with Raeburn's Gully as our
objective. There had been a fresh snowfall during the night and
it was a morning of dull skies and hard frost. A cold wind
helped us to maintain a good pace to the saddle between the
Cuidhe Crom and the Meikle Pap. Then the sun came out and
revealed the great horseshoe of crags, all plastered with snow
and ice, with gleaming white streaks where the sun shone
through the upper notches of the gullies on to the buttress.
After a laborious traverse round the steep slopes below the
rocks we gained the snowfield at the foot of our gully. We could
only hope than an accumulation of old, consolidated snow had
built up against Raeburn's rock wall, so as to allow us to cut
steps most of the way to the top of the pitch, but we could not
see so far from below on account of the narrow, curving line
and the lofty rock walls of the lower gully.

The snow was in good condition, as the coating of new
powder was comparatively thin. We made good progress by
kicking steps until the gully narrowed and steepened, after
which every step had to be slashed out with the axe. In the
centre was a snow-filled trough or runnel, clearly a channel for
occasional snow slides or minor avalanches. As it was almost
certain to be lined with ice we kept well above it, on the right.
The gully now curved to our left and revealed, high above us, a
wall of ice extending right across, with a cave underneath it at
the right-hand corner. This was obviously the crucial problem
for the day, and its aspect was rather discouraging. However,
we persevered and soon climbed into the cave, which proved a
commodious shelter and a safe anchorage for the rest of the
party while the unfortunate leader was attempting to climb the
ice wall.

Some refreshment was obviously desirable before tackling the
pitch, so we ate in comfort and listened to a series of humorous
tales from Dr Myles. Long after I had left the comforts of the
cave, and was uneasily perched on the face of the icy cliff, I
could still hear the ladies laughing at some droll occurrence

among the farm "touns" of Angus, racily put across by a native of the same county. I could only hope that they were paying some attention to my rope as well, as I had little other sense of security.

I traversed along underneath the wall, armed with an ice-axe and a small pick. The latter is an exceedingly useful tool when one must cut both hand and footholds at close quarters on a wall of ice. It was a slater's hammer with a short shaft, the hammer having been burned off short in an oxy-acetylene flame. My friend Dick Morsley presented it to me after our first ascent of Green Gully on Ben Nevis. At the far side of the gully were one or two rock holds which helped me to make a start on the ice. I doubt if the ice wall exceeds fifteen feet in vertical height, but such ascents are better counted in inches when one considers their duration and severity, accentuated as they are by the cramped and tiring posture of the climber.

At one point I was able to insert a forearm through a hole into a cavity behind some massive icicles, but all the other holds had to be cut, and made both capacious and insloping, as it was no place for risking a fall. With a horizontal run-out of rope from the cave I should have fallen a long way before the rope tightened. At length I was able to reach over the top and feel for holds over a sloping granite slab, but it, too, was coated with a thin veneer of ice. This was the crucial movement, as the pick of my axe had but a slender grip above the slab and the short axe was badly placed. The frost rendered the holds perfectly secure, in spite of the fact that I was climbing a wall composed of a whole row of icicles cemented together. Somehow I managed to swarm over the slab and obtain a satisfactory anchorage in the snow-ice above it.

Having cut two huge steps and buried my axe to the hilt in the hard snow I summoned the next member of the party. Everyone came up safely, but the pitch had taken us an hour and a half to overcome. The next stretch was much better: steep, hard snow covering a chaos of huge boulders. There was no sign of any tunnel. Where the rocks were extra large they protruded from the snow and we pulled ourselves over the ledges, avoiding the ice in the crevices between the blocks. Then the gradient steepened again and the gully floor became one uniform slope of snow-ice. It meant hard and continuous step cutting for the leader and took a long time, but the upper end of the gully was now in sight and there were no intervening obstacles. Here and there a covering of powder snow had to be swept aside before cutting the steps, but conditions were surprisingly good on the whole.

A lad appeared on the cornice at the head of the gully, watching our labours with interest. He told me that he had come up the Black Spout by himself, finding it fairly easy. Then he disappeared again. The cornice was not particularly large. For most of the way round the top of the funnel it was overhanging, but, at the left corner, it was just vertical and not at all high. Our labours continued, only two persons moving at a time, the first and third or the second and fourth. We could not afford to take risks. Soon we came to a small, rocky neck, about fifty feet below the cornice, and our last good anchorage. The encouraging lad had re-appeared after being "awa for a danner round the taps". He came to see the finish.

I cut steps to the left corner of the cornice, swarmed up on to a long hummock of icy stuff and crawled along it beneath the overhanging eave of snow. Very gently, for the snow was powdery, soft and dry, I wriggled upwards through the gap and over the wall to freedom and the mountain top. We were all on the plateau at six-twenty p.m. after a grand climb of six hours' duration. The weather had been perfect with little wind and continuing frost. Towards the south-east the horizon was bluish-black with promise of further snowfall.

NOTE. A considerable rock-fall in Raeburn's Gully occurred previous to the summer of 1946, sweeping away the great pitch altogether. One or two pitches of a minor character have been created lower down.

XIII

THE EAGLE RIDGE OF LOCHNAGAR

ALTHOUGH IT IS still possible to make new and difficult routes on Scottish crags they are generally somewhat artificial and seldom follow a conspicuous natural line or architectural feature. A climbing friend once commented on the year's discoveries, saying that it appeared to him to be much more meritorious to discover and climb a natural route of moderate difficulty than a severe, gymnastic problem of an artificial nature. He was right, of course, but could not suggest where such an ideal discovery might be made. Surely not in the overworked regions of Glencoe, Ben Nevis or the Cuillin Hills of Skye.

Perhaps something might be hoped for on Aberdeenshire granite which has a bad reputation amongst rock-climbers for cliffs that look attractive and imposing at the first view, but, on closer inspection, offer nothing whatever between impossibly vertical faces without any holds at all and easy ways interspersed with heather, grass and loose blocks, offering little of interest to the serious climber. Without any definite plan of campaign, but in the hope that something good had been overlooked by former visitors, three of us went to Deeside in early June 1936 with designs on the cliffs of Lochnagar.

Along with my old friend, Dr Myles of Forfar, was Mr W. G. McClymont, an enthusiastic mountaineer from New Zealand. After hearing his tales of pioneering in the New Zealand Alps we had to do our best to put up a good show with the mountains of the old country. The weather played up to perfection as we camped in a pleasant pine wood close to the road in Glen Muick. On a lovely, sunny morning we breakfasted in a copious, leisurely manner until we were approached by two gamekeepers with a polite but urgent request to pack our tent and remove all evidence of our sojourn as soon as possible. We realized the fairness of the request, and hoped that the estate Factor would not come upon us and get the keepers into trouble.

In any case, Lochnagar is a good two and a half hours distant from Allt na Giubhsaich, and the earlier we moved off the more time would be left for the rock climbing. There was a delightful, fresh breeze as we moved up the well-worn track towards the mountain. We were not the only ones on the hill on such a glorious morning, but we soon left the route below the Ladder and crossed the Saddle between the Cuidhe Crom and the Meikle Pap, entering the great corrie beneath the horseshoe of granite crags.

This is one of the finest mountain sanctuaries in Scotland. Beneath the great arc of cliff lie slopes of huge boulders, scree and heather ending at the shores of a dark lochan, 2,575 feet above sea level. Small wonder that the youthful mind of the poet Byron, who spent long periods of vacation in the district, was deeply impressed by "the crags that are wild and majestic, the steep, frowning glories of dark Lochnagar".

A great buttress of rock with grand, sweeping lines caught the rays of the sun. It rose just beyond the steep rift known as the Douglas Gully. We did not carry the new edition of the *S.M.C. Guide Book*, but I felt pretty certain that such a magnificent buttress could not have been climbed without the Scottish climbing fraternity (including myself) hearing something about it. There was no need to look anywhere else. We decided to attempt it, although the time was a little past one o'clock. A few yards above the lowest rocks I led off from a patch of snow in the gully, soon landing on steep slabs with very little in the way of holds. That was all to the good, for the climbing became interesting at once. We climbed a steep, little chimney, then a steep crack and the going became easier to the crest of the buttress, about ninety feet up.

Traversing above Douglas Gully was impossible, and the edge of the buttress rose above us in an almost vertical, smooth wall. The remedy was to climb a little gully on the other side, and another chimney. The wall above us on the left was now steep and holdless, but the route continued across the western face of the buttress. Of course we wanted to climb back to the crest, and I ultimately succeeded in doing so by another succession of chimneys, reaching the crest at a narrow notch with a precipitous view into the recesses of the Douglas Gully. Twenty feet higher the crest of the ridge became steep, exposed and holdless. We had to consider our chances, and especially the time factor. There was definitely no possibility of avoiding the vertical section by a traverse above the Douglas Gully. Prospects of continuing our upward traverse on the western face were much better, and included a rib by which we might

hope to climb to the top of the buttress. Not a very enterprising
or direct attack, it may be said, but we felt that we had no time
to be fastidious. There were even protests from the rear of the
party against any more holdless walls and smooth chimneys. It
was useless for me to assure Myles that he was really a much
better climber than he thought he was. We wanted to climb the
buttress by any possible route and we could not tell when we
might still be forced to retreat.

The upward traverse worked well enough. Far ahead was a
corner above some exceedingly steep rocks which seemed to
hang over a deep gully on our right (now called Parallel Gully
A). As there were no more possible openings on the slabby cliff
to our left we were inevitably confronted by these rocks. If we
could not climb them the buttress must be abandoned. With
the closing of any avenues for indecision the morale of the party
improved wonderfully and, within the next 200 feet or so, we
enjoyed the best climbing of the day.

An awkward corner led to a secure stance beside a huge
pyramidal block of granite which was delicately poised and
could just be rocked very slightly. It proved to be the key to a
very difficult situation, and I used it safely as a take-off for
swarming up to a scoop and a difficult crack somewhat higher
on the face. Another difficult crack led to a secure stance and a
perfect belay for the rope. This time there was no protest from
the rear, and my friend came up as if he were really enjoying
himself. The ensuing rocks were very steep, but provided with
small and satisfying holds. The last steep crack resolved all our
doubts, the end being both speedy and dramatic. We stood
together on the broad summit of the buttress at five forty-five
p.m. A later inspection of the Guide Book proved it to be an
entirely new route.

Of course the Eagle Ridge could not be left without some
attempt being made to improve the route, straighten it out and
climb it, as nearly as possible, on the crest of the ridge. We had
climbed it by a sort of flank attack on the side of the buttress.
Although we had enjoyed an excellent, difficult climb, we had
not savoured its true character.

In the autumn of 1940 I was surprised and delighted to
receive a letter, to the effect that Messrs W. S. Scroggie and
J. G. Ferguson, of Dundee, had enjoyed a hard tussle with it in
rather poor weather conditions in August of that year. Their
climb was exceedingly meritorious under the prevailing conditions of rain and wet rocks, and they had made the route a good

deal straighter. The new section was reported to be severe in standard, as rock climbers rate their difficulties. There were few belays, but the rock was sound. They had secured their advance by the use of four *pitons*, and they had climbed in stocking soles. As I expected, they had climbed back to the crest very soon after crossing it on the line of our route. There they had met severe difficulties which had ultimately forced them to abandon the crest, traversing again along the west face over steep rock and grass. They regained the crest by climbing a crack, and then mounted easy slabs to the summit.

It appeared, therefore, that the route up the Eagle Ridge was not yet entirely direct. But I respected the Ridge, and also the achievement of the men of the Corrie Club of Dundee, so I had little hope of doing better. Opportunities were few during the war, but on 24 July 1941, I had an excellent partner in Miss Nancy Forsyth. We had done one or two other climbs on Lochnagar, and weather conditions were perfect.

The first part of the climb—slabs, chimney, crest and subsequent chimney—was exactly as before. The smooth, steep wall on our left, decorated with a few hair-like cracks, had not been climbed by the Corrie Club men. It looks impossible. We soon found a *piton* lying loose on a ledge, doubtless dislodged by frost and sun from the cliff above. This we collected for a later emergency. Then we ascended steep, discontinuous ribs on our left. The climb to the crest was difficult, but not more than that. We soon reached the little cairn which had been left by the former party at the point where they reached the crest.

The Eagle Ridge now began to display its mettlesome quality. Almost at once the crest rose up before us in a steepening, narrow wall, easy at first, with big flakes of rock offering grand holds on their cross-cut edges. Then came a sudden steepening to the vertical where it was necessary to pull up over a sort of mantelshelf into a steep, smooth, holdless groove. Here we found another *piton*, securely fixed in a crack of the rock. I was unable to move it. In the prevailing conditions, with dry rocks, I was able to climb the pitch without touching the *piton*. The former party, of course, had vile conditions of rain and wet rocks, and the *piton* was well placed for securing the leader's rope over the next forty feet of severe climbing.

I soon realized this when I was compelled to traverse a yard or two to the right on very small holds. A return traverse, even more delicate, was made to the left at a higher level, with a final, severe pull up to a large, enclosed niche which provided perfect anchorage for man and rope. This severe section required fifty to sixty feet of rope. My second enjoyed it thoroughly.

Now the ridge thinned down to what is generally known amongst climbers as a knife-edge. There were occasional cracks and roughnesses on the flanks, making progress airy but not very difficult. The crest then rose in another smooth wall, leaving us with a ledge for a passage along its right base. This could not go on indefinitely; the gangway ended at a corner in front of a smooth, vertical wall.

Further progress was only feasible by a steep, difficult crack which split the wall on our left. It did not look at all hopeful, but I climbed the crack and surveyed our diminishing prospects from the sharp crest of the ridge. On my left was a sheer drop, slightly undercut, into the depths of Douglas Gully. The knife-edge crest on which I was sitting astride was neatly fitted to the middle of a triangle of blank, vertical cliff in front.

Here, if anywhere, our predecessors would undoubtedly have made use of another *piton*, but, although there was a suitable crack for the insertion of such an implement, there was no sign of its having been used. They must, therefore, have already traversed along the right face before they reached this point.

We were at the crux of the climb, but the wall in front was only about ten feet high. The rock was smooth, for the most part. Beside the crack where a *piton* could be used, but more to the left, was a small excrescence which might, perhaps, hold a boot nail. At the top of the wall, and somewhat to the left, was a sloping scoop with a raised edge on its left side. If that edge would provide a sharp, in-cut handhold it could be used for pulling up. There appeared to be a slight overhang about the wall, so that one secure foothold at the correct height on the left, as well as a steadying hold on the right, was absolutely essential before making the crucial pull. There would be only one critical movement; once the body was in the scoop the angle eased off, and I felt confident that safety lay within reach.

British rock climbing, as practised by its best exponents, has rightly set its face against the use of artificial safeguards, steeple-jacking methods and the use of ironmongery on the crags. So far we had used none. The Eagle promised to become one of the finest of all British ridges as a difficult rock climb, yet this difficulty was inescapably a part of the route. It was on the right of way. Almost before I knew what I was doing I had removed my boots and lowered them to my partner in a rucksack. Balance would be a critical consideration. I found a handy lump of granite, stood up against the wall and hammered in our one *piton*. Slipping a snap link into the ring and my rope through the link I felt a good deal safer. If the top handhold proved unsound I should have a clean drop on the side of Douglas Gully, but the rope, held by my second through the snap link, would soon check my fall.

My right foot had a good hold, but not a high one. The hold for the left foot sloped badly. By raising my right hand to a higher crack on the face it was possible to get my left foot up to a small toe-crack. Here the balance was extremely delicate, as I reached up with the left hand and grabbed the edge of the coping above the scoop. It was a perfect hold. My right foot used the *piton* as a steady while I heaved myself up, pulling now with both hands side by side on the coping and hunching up my knees on to the scoop. There is no pausing in such a situation, for the scoop had only press and friction holds. Persistent effort, friction and wriggling put me within reach of another perfect handhold and I was safe. About fifteen feet farther along, the narrow crest gave me a good stance and a belay for the rope.

Then I hauled up the rucksacks and boots on the rope, which ran directly down the scoop and so afforded a complete safeguard for my partner. Nancy came up perfectly, as I expected she would, but she did more than that. She knocked the *piton* loose with another lump of granite and took it out before climbing straight up on the thinnest of holds. All I did was to maintain a taut rope to steady her balance. It was a wonderful performance. Thanks to Nancy we had not defaced a perfect climb by leaving any signs of mechanization upon it.

Her performance made me wonder if I could lead up the crux without an artificial aid, with the knowledge that the upper handhold was reliable. In April 1948 I was again at Glen Muick and took my wife up Eagle Ridge. The climb impressed me as much as on the former occasion. Again I inserted a *piton*, but I used the correct holds at once, never touching the *piton* at all, the rope being slack all the time. When it came to my wife's turn to join me she reported two things. The *piton* was rather loose in the crack, and the end block of the coping, the crucial handhold, seemed to move very, very slightly as she pulled up on it. One cannot be too careful about pulling holds, especially on granite.

The difficulties continued, one after another. The next vertical step meant a move to the right and a stiff pull up another mantelshelf. Then came a minor replica of the crux, where I again took off boots. A coping slab protruded above the wall, and I managed to pull up, using the far edge of an inclined slab beyond. This led back to the crest and a succession of smooth slabs shelving steeply downwards to the Douglas Gully. Stocking soles are a great comfort on such places. I rested for a few minutes from the strain of the contorted posture needed for crawling up these slabs. When Nancy joined me we both commented on the grand, downward view along the narrow, serpentine ribbon of the ridge and the precipitous drop over the abyss of the Douglas Gully. We were near the end now. Steep but easy slabs landed us on the broad top of the ridge, level with the summit plateau of Lochnagar.

We had enjoyed three and a half hours of the very best of rock climbing, without any halt, for about 700 feet of ascent. We felt a luxurious and contented fatigue settle down upon us. The strain of the climbing, unheeded at the time, had left its mark. We had not come upon any further traces of the passage of the Dundee men, so we could not tell where they had left or regained the crest of the ridge, but we felt certain that everything above and including the crucial pitch was virgin ground.

My enthusiasm for the Eagle Ridge of Lochnagar has the same character of complete satisfaction as the experience of a great work of art. I remember a professor of mathematics who became almost lyrical over the beauty of some new, convergent, infinite series, by means of which he had solved an intractable problem. I think he was right in applying the concept of beauty to his solution. The achievement of a direct ascent of the Eagle Ridge, which indeed I shared with all who had climbed on it, was not the main factor in this enthusiasm. The ridge itself, unique amongst long, precipitous mountain ridges in Britain, was the object. The Eagle Ridge is very steep and narrow, with a symmetrical curving crest. There is a joyful variety about its climbing problems, a magnificent exposure and a persistent suspense about the outcome which is maintained almost to the very last moves. The surrounding rock scenery is grand on all sides and the distant prospect wide and satisfying. If the general character of the rock had not been sound and reliable the climb would not have been justifiable.

Of course this climb would have one drawback in the opinion of the friend whose views I quoted in the first paragraph. Although a natural route up the mountain, the standard of difficulty was more than moderate!

XIV

ARRAN GRANITE

THE GRANITE PEAKS of the Isle of Arran, rather like those of the Cairngorms and Lochnagar, have acquired a bad name with some rock climbing purists, on account of unsound rock, lack of belays and vegetatious ledges. At the same time, mountaineers love the Arran hills for the excellence of the ridge walking, the attractive character of the summit views and the scenery of the glens.

Arran climbing started with Lugless Willie Lithgow who climbed Goatfell (Goatfield Hill) in 1628. He dilates on the marvellous view of Northern Ireland, the Isle of Man and the hills of Cumberland, "Three Kingdoms at one sight". Other pioneers speak of the delightful contrasts of such views from Arran peaks, embracing rocky hills, green Glen Rosa, the yellow sands of Brodick Bay, the sunlit slopes of Corriegills and the surrounding seas.

Serious rock climbing started about 1891 when W. W. Naismith and Gilbert Thomson, founders of the Scottish Mountaineering Club, began their explorations on the north-east face of Cir Mhor (the great comb), the central hub of the Arran peaks, and one of the most stately of Scottish mountains, though but 2,618 feet in altitude. By 1894 many climbers were engaged on the Arran cliffs, and in 1895 the best of the classic climbs, the BC Rib of Cir Mhor, was climbed by Bell, Boyd, Green and Napier. They went up by a series of steep slabs and narrow ledges, but good belays were lacking for the rope. The best known climb of those days was the Oppenheimer Chimney of Beinn Nuis, led in 1901 by E. A. Baker. The party was all-English, consisting of Baker, Puttrell and Oppenheimer, and was almost defeated at one point. It does not seem to be clear whether the climb was ever repeated. The rock of Beinn Nuis is rather unstable and treacherous and it may well be the case that a rock-fall has, since then, altered the configuration of the place. Harry MacRobert was the leading spirit in the exploration of the southern gullies of the A'Chir Ridge between 1908 and 1911.

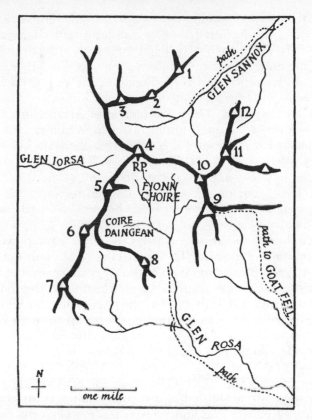

ARRAN RIDGES

PEAKS

		height in feet
1	Suidhe Fhearghas	2,081
2	Ceum na Caillich (Witch's Step)	2,300
3	Caisteal Abhail (Castles)	2,817
4	Cir Mhor (Great Comb)	2,618
5	A'Chir	2,335
6	Beinn Tarsuinn	2,706
7	Beinn Nuis	2,597
8	Beinn a' Chliabhain	2,217
9	Goatfell (Hill of the Wind)	2,866
10	North Goatfell	
11	Mullach Buidhe	2,688
12	Cioch na h' Oighe (Maiden's Breast)	2,168
RP	Rosa Pinnacle	

For a long time nothing new was reported from Arran and, meanwhile, the favoured type of climbing had changed from gullies to faces. In 1939 A. S. Pigott and B. K. Barber made the first route on the east wall of Rosa Pinnacle, Cir Mhor, and in 1940 J. F. Hamilton and G. S. Roger, of the younger school of Glasgow mountaineers, climbed its South Ridge, the finest face of rock on the island. The main revival of Arran climbing was due, however, to a small group of naval engineers who were stationed at Largs for several years during the war. The leaders and recorders were G. H. Townend and G. C. Curtis. They made many new and excellent discoveries and established Arran, once and for all, as a grand centre for climbing on sound, rough rock with routes of all degrees of length, interest and difficulty.

Arran has a remarkable variety of rock formations, both sedimentary and igneous. The great Highland Fault cuts right across it from Blackwaterfoot on the west coast, by the line of the String road to the east coast near Corrie. To the south are the lesser, rounded hills of the Old Red Sandstone. To the north is a great nucleus of granite, thrust up through beds of shale and sandstone, tilted at an angle, with the slate next the granite. Here and there are basalt dykes in the granite, forming chimneys at A'Chir and elsewhere. Sir Archibald Geikie points out that the two sets of joint planes in the granite are inclined at an angle in a somewhat irregular manner, so that the processes of weathering and erosion have broken up the rock into characteristic, rounded blocks, like huge piles of masonry with edges which are both rounded and etched. The structure varies a good deal, for the south faces of Cir Mhor and A'Chir are wonderfully sound and rough, with good belays (especially on Rosa Pinnacle) and very little vegetation. Beinn Nuis and Cioch na h'Oighe are not at all sound. There is a close resemblance to the cliffs of Lochnagar and the Cairngorms and also, curiously enough, to the ancient Torridon sandstone ridges of Ross and Sutherland.

Even for beginners there are many interesting expeditions, but Arran granite is not the best place for novices in rock climbing. Goatfell (2,866 ft), the highest peak, is an easy excursion from Brodick or Corrie, and can be combined with a ridge walk over North Goatfell to Mullach Buidhe and Cioh na h'Oighe (2,168 ft), the rocky peak overlooking lower Glen Sannox. As the latter has precipitous cliffs the walk had better be done in the reverse direction. Both Glen Sannox and Glen

Rosa are beautiful valleys surrounded by mountains and traversed by clear, rushing streams. They meet beneath the Saddle (1,413 ft), connecting Cir Mhor with North Goatfell, and both can be traversed in a grand walk between Brodick and Sannox. The main ridge of the Arran granite peaks bounds these glens on the side opposite from Goatfell, and the keen hill walker will wish to traverse it from end to end. It demands great care in mist, but all technical difficulties of a rock climbing nature are easily avoidable. This horse-shoe of mountains is a far shorter and easier proposition than the Cuillin Ridge of Skye, but it does make a good, hard day on the hills with any amount of variety and a succession of glorious views of mountain, glen and sea.

In May 1945, George Collie, Charlie Gorrie and I left Sannox shortly after ten a.m. An easy heathery climb, followed by an upper grassy shoulder, took us to the first summit, Suidhe Fhearghas (the seat from which King Fergus the First surveyed his domains). Easy going continued to the top of Ceum na Caillich (the witch's step), from which there is a steep and moderately difficult descent to the next gap. An easier way is possible, lower down on the northern slopes, but no real climber should have much difficulty, and, presumably, the Caillich got over the place easily enough. A long, rocky ridge from Glen Sannox to the summit is now named Broomstick Ridge. A long ascent from the gap took us to the top of Caisteal Abhail (2,817 ft), where we halted for lunch amongst the weird granite tors on the wide, flat summit. We were enveloped in dense mist, which deprived us of one of the finest views of the island, towards the grand, steep, northern face of Cir Mhor with its fluted cliffs.

We took a compass bearing before leaving, for The Castles, as the mountain is usually named, can be a very confusing place in mist, a meeting place of four ridges, with steep cliffs falling away to upper Glen Sannox. Running down an easy scree slope, we were soon out of the mist and enjoyed bright sunshine for the rest of the day. Cir Mhor (2,618 ft) was the next halting place at two forty-five p.m. The way was now easy to a saddle before the rise to A'Chir. Here again, a traverse round the base of the cliffs on the western side, above Glen Iorsa, would avoid all difficulties, but we were determined to have some rock climbing in our day's expedition.

We thoroughly enjoyed ourselves on the A'Chir Ridge. The rock and the holds are good. The ridge is not at all difficult—

least of all the apparently sensational bridging of the A'Chir Gap. The ridge is very narrow in places and the changing views, both near and far, are entirely delightful. There is one interesting traverse on the Rosa side before reaching the summit, but the rock holds are very good all the way. The actual summit block presents a little gymnastic problem for those who are purists in such matters. The hour and a half we spent on this ridge seemed to us far too short. Rather a dull, sweaty ascent followed to the top of Beinn Tarsuinn (2,706 ft), and in little over half an hour we were on Beinn Nuis (2,597 ft), our last summit for the day, at six p.m. We refreshed ourselves for the final three-mile walk to Brodick by a delightful swim in a long, deep pool of the Rosa burn, at the turn of the glen.

Next day George Collie and I returned to the base of the southern cliffs of Cir Mhor with more serious intentions. Hamish Hamilton had assured me that the South Ridge of Rosa Pinnacle was one of the few top-rank discoveries of the century in Scottish rock climbing—an incredibly steep climb of nearly 800 feet on grand, sound rock, narrowing at places to a veritable knife-edge! We had a perfect, sunny day with a gentle breeze, ideal conditions for a difficult climb. After lunch on the warm heather slopes beneath the crags we left our sacks and started off in rubbers for the climb, aiming at the foot of a prominent S–shaped crack, which is the main feature of the lower tier of cliff.

It is a formidable crack, soon approaching the vertical. The cross section is awkward, a central rib flanked by two narrower cracks. The positive holds were soon left behind, but the rough walls gave plenty of friction grip. Near the top I found a spike on which I was glad to belay the rope as I rested for a while, for the final upward move on to a slab on the right was very awkward and exposed. Immediately above the slab was a great triangular flake of massive proportions with a comfortable niche behind it, a perfectly secure stance for bringing up George.

We were now about the centre of the steep, lower cliff, in a comfortable and agreeable situation, with a splendid view over the nearer hills across the Firth of Clyde, but with no answer whatever to the urgent question: where next? I failed to get very far to the left. To the right was a delicate corner with a flat triangular slab beyond. Just above George was a steep slab, split by a crack and ending under a slightly overhanging wall, about eight to ten feet high. The crack narrowed and split the wall, forking like a letter Y below the top. It was not a very

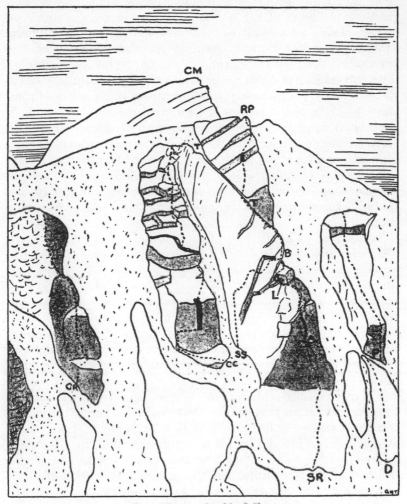

Rosa Pinnacle Cir Mhor

This diagram has been borrowed from the Scottish Mountaineering Club Journal (1945), Vol. 23, p. 242. Some of the lettering, therefore, is not relevant to descriptions in this chapter. The full key is, however, included, and interested readers may refer to the original source for routes not described here.

CM	Cir Mhor Summit	L	Lay-back Crack (not on route described)
RP	Rosa Pinnacle Summit		
SR	Start of South Ridge	B	Three Tier chimney
A	Severe Crack	TT	Easy Terrace
		SS	Sou'wester slabs

Not described: CR, Cubic Route; CC, Caliban's Creep; P, Prospero; D, Prospero's Prelude. Cubic and Caliban are just difficult, D is easy, but P is severe.

high wall, but the crack was too narrow for anything but sideways wedging of the toes and there was no guarantee of positive holds above the Y. Neither Collie nor I knew where Hamish Hamilton's route went, so we chose to explore the traverse on the right rather than to risk falling off the overhang. The traverse turned out to be fairly simple, leading to steep flakes of rock which brought us out above the Y crack. From the easy slabs above George safeguarded me on the rope as I descended to explore the holds above the lower crack. They were clean-cut and perfect. Later in the week we met Curtis, who told us that Hamilton had led the Y crack directly, a very fine piece of climbing which was justifiable because Hamish had been up the other way on a former occasion and had, no doubt, assured himself of the good holds above that very severe crack.

We were now at the foot of the middle tier of cliff on Rosa Pinnacle. Townend had told us something of a good lay-back crack by which it could be ascended from the left. We found another overhanging crack straight above us, but could not identify the Townend pitch. So the middle tier was again solved by a traverse to the right and a very steep climb up the east wall, where the holds were extremely sketchy in places. The final tier of cliff to the crest of the Lower Pinnacle was delightful climbing by the Three Tier Chimney and a blunt knife-edge below the top.

There remained the conical wall of the Upper Pinnacle, approached by an easy ledge. Steep slabs led up to the right, but I was unable to force my way to the crest in that direction. A short traverse to the left admitted us to a slab, up which we climbed to the edge of the vertical eastern wall. The climb finished along a beautiful knife-edge on the upper crest. The Upper Pinnacle occupied us for fifty minutes out of a total climbing time of three hours and forty minutes. Hamilton was right, and the South Ridge of Rosa Pinnacle will take its place among the classics of British rock climbing.

Those who do not feel equal to trying conclusions with the S Crack may still taste the delights of an ascent of Rosa Pinnacle. At the end of our holiday week George had taken to photography and Charlie, who had a game leg as a result of his war experiences in North Africa, wanted to climb Rosa Pinnacle, but could not rely on his injured limb for anything too strenuous. Townend and Curtis, those indefatigable explorers, had designed the Sou'wester Slabs Route to meet such a case.

It starts from the scree higher up and farther to the left than the direct route and attacks the buttress on the flank. Curtis and two of his friends were also with us as a separate photographic party. The climb is nowhere above "very difficult" in standard, the rock is perfect and the situations are delightful. We rejoined the direct route at the foot of Three Tier Chimney on the upper band of cliffs of the lower Pinnacle. I lost the way on the Upper Pinnacle and involved Charlie in a short, severe pitch after all, but he pulled up all right, and we finished by a huge, upper slab, exactly at the top of Rosa Pinnacle.

There are many other excellent rock climbs in Arran. I cannot speak of the north-east face of Cir Mhor, but believe that the BC Rib is excellent. George and I enjoyed a grand climb of over 500 feet on the face of A'Chir above Coire Daingean, near its head. Townend had recommended Pagoda Ridge to us and we found it excellent. It runs up between Nos. 4 and 5 gullies, and looks almost impossible, as seen from near the top of Beinn a' Chliabhain. George and I found that it had a sort of roof tile slab structure, with any amount of incident and difficulty on steep, sound rock, taking us at least two and a half hours to climb. On another day we had good sport on long ribs of steep slab leading up from Glen Rosa to Goatfell. These climbs are all much better suited to rubbers than to nailed boots.

If Arran granite, like Skye gabbro, encourages the care-free holiday spirit in the rock climber, it may be as well to sound a note of warning. Charlie and I went off one morning to seek out one of two new routes by Townend and Curtis on Cioch na h'Oighe. Their names were Midnight Ridge and Twilight Slabs, presumably because both had been first climbed very late on a Saturday night, so as to lose nothing out of a short week-end. We could not identify either climb, but negotiated a severe and nearly vertical pitch of almost ninety feet on a loose rock wall above a little rowan tree. It was the worst, hardest and least secure piece of rock climbing during the entire holiday. Townend told us that the face of Beinn Nuis was of a similar character but worse.

On that day we travelled from Brodick to Sannox on a bus. Charlie carried the rope and excited the interest of another passenger who *knew* something about mountaineering. The conversation proceeded roughly as follows:

Mr X: "You will be all right since you have boots and a rope. It won't matter at all if it rains."

Charlie mentioned that we also carried rubbers, but this evoked a peculiar and dubious look from the stranger.

Mr X: "The rock is very rotten all over Arran."

Charlie: "I am not sure about that, but isn't it as good as on the Cuillin in Skye?"

Mr X: "Oh yes, for Skye rock is very rotten, too. Have you been on Rosa Pinnacle of Cir Mhor?"

Charlie: "No."

Mr X: "That is the very worst rock in Arran."

Charlie: "Where can one find the best rock?"

Mr X: "It is best on Beinn Nuis."

We had seen Beinn Nuis. We haven't climbed on it. We do not intend to!

XV

THE NORTH WEST

THIS CHAPTER DEALS with the rugged, shapely mountains of north-west Scotland, beyond the line of the Dingwall–Skye railway. They are, for the most part, sharply distinguished from the main mass of the Scottish Highlands, and they also differ from such local regions of volcanic and eruptive action as the Cuillin of Skye, the granites of Galloway, Arran and the Cairngorms or the good climbing porphyrites of Glencoe and Ben Nevis. They are well worth a visit from all three points of view—scenic, climbing and geological.

They presented very difficult problems to the earlier geologists, and out of these arose more than one famous controversy. Hugh Miller, author of *The Old Red Sandstone* and other geological publications, who was a native of Cromarty, once thought that the striking scenery of Wester Ross and Sutherland was founded on a western extension of the Old Red Sandstone which plays such a large part on the east coast of Scotland from the Shetlands to the Borders. But the great mural precipices of Suilven and Liathach, most characteristic of this interesting region, proved to be a much older rock and much more resistant to denudation. In Sutherland it stands up in great, isolated peaks, mountains that so impressed Dr John Maculloch between the years 1811 and 1821 that he wrote of ". . . mountains which seem as if they had tumbled from the clouds, having nothing to do with the country or each other, in shape, material, position or character".

Whoever obtains his first glimpse of Suilven, either from the sea to the west of Lochinver or from the moors between Oykell Bridge and Alltnagealgach, must agree, if the appreciation of mountain form is engrained in his nature and enthusiasms. The same can be said of the first sight of Liathach across Glen Torridon, of the view of the great corries of Ben Bhan of Applecross from the road between Lochs Carron and Kishorn or of the Teallachs from the gorge above Dundonnell. In the latter examples the mountains group themselves into larger ranges rather than isolated peaks, but the tremendous frontage of wall-like precipices of horizontally terraced, dark red or purplish rock is the same in all cases.

My own introduction to the Torridon Red region was fortunate and made a great impression upon me. The Easter Meet of the Scottish Mountaineering Club in 1923 was arranged for Kinlochewe and Loch Maree, with the option of a start at Dundonnell and a cross-country journey to Loch Maree. Ernest Roberts was with me, but no one else went to Dundonnell. There was a breath of spring in the air as we reached Little Loch Broom, and plenty of snow on the higher tops as we started out for An Teallach on the following day.

Whilst Roberts was in the post-office my ice-axe caught the attention of a passing tramp. Hearing that the axe was used for cutting steps on the ice of the mountains he looked puzzled for a moment, but brightened up eventually and said, "I see, you are fishmongers. You cut out big lumps of ice, carry them in your sack and sell them to the fish shops in the city." We pushed on, but when I looked round I could see him still staring after us rather quizzically, as if not quite satisfied.

A good track through the woods led us up the hillside, with the spiky tops of An Teallach to the west. The range opens out towards the north-east, enclosing two magnificent corries, the northerly one below the highest summit, Bidein a' Ghlas Thuill (3,483 ft) and the other, more impressive corrie ringed about with crags enclosing the waters of Toll an Lochain. This was our objective as we made our way up successive, slabby terraces of rock to the lip of the corrie. We lunched by the shore of the lochan in warm sunshine. In its still waters were reflected the snow-terraced cliffs of Corrag Bhuidhe of An Teallach, one of the most fascinating visions of mountain architecture in all Scotland. The sandstone is of a dark purple hue and horizontal in its bedding. Many of the sheets of rock overlap the lower ones. A thousand feet of cliff were clearly delineated by the snow-covered ledges. It was a mountain face to be admired rather than climbed. Several of the terraces may be accessible to the mountaineer, but they often contract to the thinnest of ledges, hardly a break in that vertical sweep of precipice. Torridon sandstone has few positive holds; they are mostly rounded and there are few, if any, belays. No climbing route goes directly up Corrag Bhuidhe from the lochan.

Reluctantly, we turned our attention to a steep, snow-filled gully on the right. Here we made rapid progress to a fork where the left branch soared up to the skyline in a series of impossible-looking pitches. After some interesting climbing up the right fork we reached the summit ridge and attained the little rocky nose called Lord Berkeley's Seat. Pleasant and interesting scrambling followed over Corrag Bhuidhe (the yellow finger, 3,425 ft), across a little saddle, and finally, on to Sail Liath (the grey heel, 3,100 ft), the last top of the range. We had no time to include the highest top, which was far behind us. The ridge took a good deal of time, as the sandstone had weathered, in many places, into huge piles of biscuit-shaped slabs—unstable heaps where an incautious step might easily unbalance the whole edifice and bring it down about our ears.

The view from the summit was one of delightful contrasts— westward over a loch-studded moorland to Gruinard Bay and the islands, north-west to the intriguing, isolated peaks of Coigach and Assynt which I hoped to explore in the near future, and southward across a tortuous maze of mountain country where lay our next day's journey. One prominent feature concerned us most, the rocky cone of Beinn Dearg Mhor above the flat valley of Strath na Sheallag. At its base lay the cottage of Larachantivore where we hoped to pass the night. A rapid glissade down a snow slope helped us over the first stage. After a longish walk we reached the flats, crossed the stream and were groping our way at dusk across the half-mile of boggy ground towards the cottage.

We had a big programme for the next day, but we laid a good foundation with a breakfast of porridge, eggs, scones and butter. Before eight a.m. we started for Beinn Dearg Mhor, aiming for the crags on the side of the big, northern Coire nan Clach. Ice-axes were hardly necessary, as we had chosen a fairly easy route on the right-hand rim, and we were basking on the summit in our shirt sleeves at eleven a.m. It was a calm day of clear sunshine. After a descent by the other bounding ridge of the corrie we returned to Larachantivore for lunch, shouldered our packs and bade our kind hosts good-bye.

The walk before us was about twelve miles to Letterewe on the north shore of Loch Maree, but the route lay over two passes of about 1,700-foot altitude with a drop between to 500 feet. For quality of scenery it was one of the finest walks that I have ever done. Approaching the first summit we wound up a narrow glen on a good track, crossed a ridge and a wide stretch of moorland with a lochan here and there and were intrigued by the appearance of new ranges of mountains opening up in the south-east. But the grandest prospect came later.

The way led down a narrow, steep glen. Rounding a corner we gazed down on the waters of the Fionn Loch, a wonderful pattern of interlacing wavelets of burnished gold in the early evening sunshine. The upper part of the Fionn Loch is separated by a narrow isthmus from an inner lochan almost surrounded by savage crags. This Dubh Loch is a true mountain tarn. Above and behind is the long rocky flank of Ben Lair (2,817 ft), two and a half miles of cliff overlooking Gleann Tulacha, with the red sandstone crags of Slioch (3,260 ft), appearing over it on the left. Still more to the left was the dome of A'Mhaighdean (3,060 ft, the Maiden), another remote mountain with attractive possibilities for rock climbing. As we kept swinging downwards to our right we were impressed by the steep cliff of Torr na h'Iolaire (the eagle's cliff) just above us. The view opened out westward along the Fionn Loch and disclosed the bold, precipitous face of Beinn Airidh Charr (2,593 ft), above the southern shore of the loch. A camp at the head of Fionn Loch would be a veritable paradise for the enthusiastic rock climber, for I do not know of any other corner in the Scottish Highlands with so much opportunity for exploration in grand and imposing surroundings.

It was not the climbing opportunities but the contrast, the grandeur and the beauty of the scene that held me spellbound. Such visions are, not infrequently, granted to the hill wanderer who penetrates into the secret places of nature at break or close of day. If he is in accord with his surroundings he is enabled to accept the revelation and, for a time, to sense something above and beyond it. Of the sum total of such fragmentary experiences something at least is integrated with the personality and never lost. Such moments may come on hard and difficult mountaineering exploits. Sometimes they serve to cheer and encourage when the chances of success, or even of survival, seem heavily loaded against one, but at other times, such as the one presently described, all is peace and transcendent beauty. An older friend, who did not climb but who fished the moorland lochs of the North West, once expressed it to me thus: "The sense of beauty is so overpowering as to make one feel almost afraid." Surely here is part, at least, of the answer to the question: "Why do men climb mountains?" and the reply cannot be either made or understood unless the golden memories return on the instant, and, even so, the words are totally inadequate, whether written or spoken. All I can say is that I know of no region where such experiences are less uncommon than in the mountainous area around Loch Maree, especially at the season of spring when mountains, lochs, woodlands, sky and cloud have all renewed their youth.

Roberts and I crossed the causeway of stones between the Fionn and Dubh Lochs and slowly climbed the path for over a thousand feet to our last pass for the day. Darkness had fallen when we reached Letterewe on the northern shore of Loch Maree, but the keeper very kindly ferried us over to the hotel on the other side; the perfect ending to a strenuous day, as the boat threaded its way between the islets in the light of the full moon.

It is hard to decide which is the finest mountain in the district. The honours are evenly divided between Beinn Eighe and Liathach. The first is conspicuous as one approaches Kinlochewe from the east. The eastern end of the long range has peaks capped with greyish white quartzite, giving it a distinguished appearance, but offering long slopes of toilsome screes to the climber. The grandest feature of Beinn Eighe is the Coire Mhic Fhearchair which separates the two western summits, Ruadh Stac Mor (3,309 ft) the highest top, and Sail Mhor (3,217 ft). This is one of the most impressive corries in Scotland with its lonely lochan backed by symmetrical masses of cliff. We approached it by a long path up Glen Grudie from Loch Maree. Where the path ends a short, rough climb leads to the lip of the corrie. A floor of Torridon sandstone slabs rims the loch. On the left are long scree slopes descending from Ruadh Stac Mor, an easy way of gaining the main summit of Beinn Eighe. On the right are the great sandstone cliffs beneath the summit of Sail Mhor, with no feasible route of ascent, except a wide, straight gully opening out just below the rim of the upper corrie. This is Morrison's Gully, a good route for descending when filled with snow, but there is a small pitch near the bottom, so that careless glissaders should take warning.

Straight across, on the far side of the lochan from the line of approach, are three great buttresses of rock, sweeping up through 1,000 feet to the rounded summit of Coinneach Mhor. They have all been climbed, the left-hand one being the easiest. The lower rocks are of Torridon Red and very difficult, but the larger, upper portions are of Cambrian quartzite, a more amenable rock, very sound and offering good holds. The junction line between the two rises at a moderate angle from left to right.

Roberts and I went for the northern or left-hand buttress

and we thoroughly enjoyed ourselves. We had quite enough on our hands, considering the amount of snow and ice covering the lower ledges, and I must confess that we did not climb the sandstone directly, but traversed along from the left into the gully between the northern and central buttresses. Some distance higher we traversed out of the gully on to our buttress, and the excellent jointing of the quartzite enabled us to climb almost straight to the summit. The rock was delightfully steep and exposed, interesting throughout but never very difficult.

The day finished with a joyful traverse of ridges and peaks, with a series of glissades and an easy descent to Kinlochewe. My last day of that holiday was a sort of continuation of my southward progress across the mountains, starting from Glen Torridon and crossing over Sgorr Ruadh (3,142 ft) and Fuar Tholl (2,968 ft), with a steep descent to Coire Lair leading to Achnashellach railway station, in time for the evening train for Inverness. The upper moorland between these two mountains is the most rough and desolate country I have ever seen. It is the country of the great thrust-plane movements, when whole mountains were crumpled up and thrust bodily for several miles in an approximately north-westerly direction over the under-lying strata. There is a little hill, Sgurr Dubh (2,566 ft), to the south of Glen Torridon, which I visited with my wife in 1946, and which shows a complexity that must surely derive from this distant epoch of great disturbance. Our route was fairly direct. We started on Torridon Red, climbed many terraced escarpments of quartzite, ascended a steep cliff of Torridon Red to the first summit, crossed a small dip and finished by a gradual rise of little over 100 feet of quartzite to the true summit.

My first experience of Liathach was again at Easter time. Four of us were in the northern Coire na Caime. L. St C. Bartholomew and I were bent on doing a rock climb, and it promptly began to rain with some degree of persistence. I don't think we climbed anything of importance, but we enjoyed ourselves on the rough Torridon sandstone, until the slabs conducted trickles and streamlets of water down our sleeves and through other gaps in our defences. So we called it a day and climbed rapidly, by easy slopes, to the main ridge, where, by pure chance, we met our friends descending from Spidean a' Choire Leith, the highest summit. The problem was to effect a descent to Glen Torridon in the mist. At first everything went very well, by a series of glissades, suspiciously well I should say. Then we got below the quartzite and were faced by tiers of

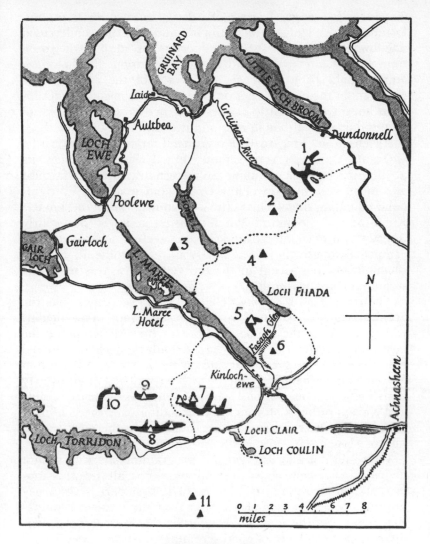

WESTER ROSS
MOUNTAINS

	height in feet				height in feet
1	An Teallach . . 3,483		7	Beinn Eighe . . 3,309
2	Beinn Dearg Mor . 2,974		8	Liathach . . . 3,456
3	Beinn Airidh a' Charr . 2,593		9	Beinn Dearg . . 2,995
4	A'Mhaighdean . . 3,060		10	Alligin . . . 3,232
5	Slioch . . . 3,260		11	Sgorr Ruadh . . 3,142
6	Beinn Mhuinidh . . 2,231			

Torridon Red crags. These took a long time to negotiate, but, fortunately, we had several hours in hand. We then understood why Liathach presents such an imposing appearance when seen from Loch Clair at the head of Glen Torridon. Bartholomew and I could liken ourselves to several of the early Alpine explorers in the classical period when it was considered meritorious to traverse a little-known pass across a high range of mountains, even although no summit was actually climbed!

At length, in June 1946, I revisited Liathach with my wife. Coire na Caime is very remote, but I wished to view its possibilities for rock climbing. So we penetrated to the farthest and most westerly arm of the corrie, and made for its right-hand bounding ridge. This is the well-known, northern Pinnacle Ridge of the mountain. We attacked the lower nose fairly directly and encountered at least one section where we were compelled to use the rope. This was really difficult, but the remainder of the ascent to the top of the nose was moderate scrambling and no more.

The ridge itself is wholly delightful and exceedingly like the granite ridges of Arran. I remember one gap, in particular, which resembles the famous one on A'Chir. After topping the last pinnacle, Meall Dearg, we crossed a little neck and the red rock gave place to grey quartzite on the last rise to the top of Mullach an Rathain (3,358 ft), which we reached at four-thirty p.m. The view was glorious, with the Outer Isles clearly visible and a mass of black storm-clouds brooding over the Cuillin of Skye. Everywhere else, from the Teallachs in the north to the hills of Monar and Affric in the east, all was clear and sunny.

We could not afford to cut our programme short on such a delightful afternoon, so we decided to traverse all the other tops of Liathach on the return journey. The first part is very easy until one comes to the narrow ridge over the Fasarinen pinnacles. That was the most enjoyable part. There are no serious difficulties, but plenty of good scrambling. At any rate, we did not require to use our rope. For those unskilled in any kind of rock climbing it is always possible to descend a little on the Torridon side and use a sheep track in order to avoid the difficulties.

Beyond the Fasarinen the Torridon sandstone finally gives place to angular blocks of quartzite, making the eastern half of the ridge much more toilsome. A longish ascent took us to Spidean a' Choire Leith (3,456 ft), the main summit. At seven p.m. we were on the last, eastern top, Stuc a' Choire Dhuibh

Bhig. The descent gave us no difficulty, as we had traced our
course in the forenoon when we were ascending the track which
runs up the Choire Dhuibh Mhoir from the Torridon road to
the gap between Liathach and Beinn Eighe. This is the most
useful line of approach, both for Liathach and for the cliffs of
Coire Mhic Fhearchair on Beinn Eighe. The combination of the
Northern Pinnacles with all the other tops of Liathach makes a
long day, but it is a grand expedition, full of interest and
variety.

Even if one does not wish to climb rocks this north-western
region, with its fascinating variety of scenery, holds much more
of interest for the hill walker if he learns the key to the
architecture of its mountains. The geological structure, in rough
outline, is not difficult to grasp. In only a few cases is it legibly
engraved on the face of a mountain so that a single informed
glance can take it in. The view of Suilven from the north, near
Suileag, is perhaps the clearest of such pictures. The foundation
of the mountain is a rough plateau of ancient Lewisian gneiss.
Most of the rough desolation of the north-western moors owes
its origin to the eroded and pitted surface of this hard rock, and
the result is a marshy, ill-drained landscape studded with many
lochans, where glacial action has carved them out or left
moraines to dam them back.

Above the gneiss the main bulk of Suilven consists of wall-
like crags of red Torridon sandstone, a hard rock which is often
of conglomerate type. The bedding is nearly horizontal and
never, at any rate, inclined steeply. It is difficult rock to climb
with its vertical cliffs and horizontal terraces. There are many
overhangs and the holds are usually rounded and not in-cut. It
is the great precipices of Torridon Red that characterize the
scenery of the North West. They are everywhere spectacular,
on Beinn Bhan of Applecross, Coire na Caime of Liathach, An
Teallach, the Coigach hills, Suilven and Quinag.

On most of these hills there is a covering stratum of Cambrian
quartzite. On Beinn Eighe and Liathach it weathers into sharp,
angular blocks and scree, very toilsome for the hill walker. At
many places, however, there are quartzite crags of perfectly
sound rock which give very good climbing.

This succession of rocks is subject to many irregularities,
owing to the violent earth movements which have subsequently
contorted the strata and thrust huge masses bodily across the
lower rocks for distances as great as ten miles. To the south-
east are mountains more akin to the main masses of the central

Highlands, built up from varieties of younger schists. There is occasionally some good climbing to be had on this rock, but there is apt to be hardly any middle way between the easy and the impossible. Schists seldom give rise to bold mountain forms, but occasionally produce impressive corries occupied by dark lochans and walled around by screes and crags.

Only one other formation need be mentioned, the Durness limestone. A narrow strip of this separates the Torridon rocks from the schists and gives rise to underground streams and "swallets" near Inchnadamph on Loch Assynt and to caves near Durness. The limestone crags near Inchnadamph are of no interest to rock climbers.

The coast-line of the region is both rugged and beautiful most of the way from Loch Carron to Cape Wrath. On a sunny day with a fresh westerly wind and quick-moving clouds I know of no more beautiful stretch of coast than Gruinard Bay, with its white, sandy beaches and rocky coves, a background of little hills and the blue Atlantic with an island foreground and the distant pale blue outline of Lewis and Harris. At almost all seasons the splendid variety of colouring has attracted artists— colouring of sea coast, of lochs studded with wooded islets, of mountain vistas seen through groves of ancient woodland, and everywhere the procession of shapely clouds drifting in from the Atlantic. The western end of Fionn Loch is rather bare and desolate, but Horatio MacCulloch, who painted the scene, describes his first view as "a splendid mirror set in a fretted frame of Alpine scenery".

Many pictures have been made of Loch Maree and its islands. There we have a mental background of ancient history, folklore and the superstition which still abounds in the country-side. On the Isle Maree bull sacrifices continued until the year 1678 as a cure for insanity. The Isle had been, for many years, the dwelling place of Saint Maelrubha, a disciple of St Columba. A draught of Loch Maree water was deemed a cure for almost any disease.

Belief in witches and fairies was very common. When Hugh Miller visited Loch Maree in 1823, he was told of a woman who had spent a year with the fairies. As late as 1840 the pious inhabitants of Aultbea set out to suppress a "water kelpie" which had been seen on a loch in the Greenstone peninsula. The loch is still called the Loch of the Beast. At North Erradale, near Gairloch, is a sea cave, Uamh an Oir (the cave of gold), where, long ago, twelve men headed by a piper marched in to seek for gold, wandering for miles in the cavern, so that the music of the pipes could be heard at a village many miles away. Neither piper nor men were seen again: it was supposed that they had "forgot to turn". Many superstitions, such as the power of the evil eye, usually exerted nowadays on cows or sheep, are still believed despite the strict disciplinary influence of the church. Indeed, I have heard it hinted that a certain cross-eyed old woman could turn herself into a hare when it suited her purpose, and resume her own form when she wished! The average tourist will hear very little of such matters. The people do not talk of such things to strangers.

XVI

ROCK CLIMBING IN THE NORTH WEST

Gneiss

THE LEWISIAN GNEISS, as the oldest and undermost rock formation, seldom appears in the form of crags on the higher parts of the mountains, but, where it does, it offers very good climbing. In western Harris there are many great crags and headlands of gneiss, the most impressive being Strone Ulladale which has furnished a grand climb of over 800 feet. There are several gneiss crags near Dundonnell which I have not visited, but they are reported to give good climbing.

When spending one or two off-days at Gruinard Bay my wife and I enjoyed delightful climbing on two small crags of gneiss which can be cordially recommended for their technical interest. One is a little 500-foot hill called Carn na h'Aire close to the bridge over the Gruinard River. Several routes are possible, but the outstanding feature is a huge, steep slab. The hill makes a splendid view-point. The other is close above the road about one and a half miles north, overlooking the sea beyond Gruinard House. This offered three climbs of about 200 feet in height, one of which was almost severe. The rock is delightfully steep and sound with very small holds. More difficult routes are awaiting attention and there are also easy ones.

The most attractive area for climbing on gneiss is at the head of Fionn Loch and above Dubh Loch, just beyond. Not much has been attempted on the long cliff of Beinn Lair, and nothing so far on A'Mhaighdean or Craig an Dubh Loch. Most attractive of all is the north face of Beinn Airidh a' Charr (2,593 ft), rising between Fionn Loch and Loch Maree. Two ex-Presidents of the Scottish Mountaineering Club, W. N. Ling and G. T. Glover, enjoyed some wonderful climbing on these cliffs in the years 1909 and 1910, but, since then, the place has been unjustifiably neglected.

A lofty pinnacle of rock juts out from the main mass and is known locally as Martha's Peak. Martha was a shepherdess who chose to climb the rocks in order to seek some errant members of her flock. Accounts of her misfortune vary somewhat. Probably she was really in search of goats. In any case, she sat down to admire the view and improved the time by winding thread on to a distaff, which slipped out of her hands and fell down the cliff. In the attempt to recover the distaff she, too, fell over and was killed.

Jack Burt, Malcolm Matheson and I had a grand day on Beinn Airidh a' Charr, when staying at Kinlochewe during Easter week 1928. I don't think we knew of the legend, but the weather was perfect and there was 1,200 feet of interesting climbing for us on good, dry rock, as grand and steep as we could desire. On the lower part we spent a good deal of time on difficult slabs, but above them the rock was more broken up, so that we were soon on the top of the lower cliff, where a short level stretch led us to the foot of the next wall. As we rose, the view downward and westward across Fionn Loch to Gruinard Bay was wide and beautiful.

The middle tier gave us continuous hard climbing, up steep rocks with good but small holds. Then again came an easy stretch to the foot of the last wall of rock beneath the summit. A scree-filled gully had to be crossed first of all before we grappled with a very steep, 200-foot rock rib which led directly to the summit. Just below the top a sensational traverse had to be made across the face to the right—a thrilling finish. A few yards beyond the top of the cliff was the summit cairn. We had taken a little over three hours for the climb.

I well remember the return by boat across Loch Maree from Letterewe. A choppy sea was running, owing to the fresh east wind sweeping along the full extent of the loch. All was forgotten in the glory of the sunset, which tinged the summit of Slioch a vivid pink. The combination of crimson snow, orange sky and blue water, contrasted with the silver birches, green firs and the russet of the bracken, is one that cannot be excelled in any of the great mountain ranges of the world. Every season has its own colour contrasts, but Loch Maree is never dull, even in late summer when much Highland scenery becomes almost commonplace.

Torridon Red Sandstone

Now we come to the great, mural precipices of Torridon "Red", the most characteristic and spectacular features of the mountain scenery of the North West. These great cliffs offer the most uncompromising challenge to the rock climber, which it is hard for the expert to resist and usually harder still to meet with success. He has really no valid excuse for refusing to make the attempt. It is true that the crags resemble gigantic walls of masonry, but the walls are broken by ledges and clefts. The sandstone weathers to form rounded edges with few, if any, outstanding spikes for belays: but the rock is both firm and rough, splendidly rough in most places, with a conglomerate structure and numerous firmly embedded fragments of quartz and gneiss. It is very hard to solve a definite problem or to strike the golden mean between the easy and the impossible, but patient exploration has yielded and will continue to offer rewards.

Suilven has been already mentioned, with its main mass of Torridon "Red" cliffs rising from a base of Lewisian gneiss. The western peak, Caisteal Liath, or the Grey Castle (2,400 ft), presents its craggy front to Lochinver and the western sea. It is not easily accessible, but I think that Nancy Forsyth and I chose the most attractive line of approach on an isolated fine day in the poor weather of August 1942. Leaving our cycles at Inveruplan (between Loch Assynt and Lochinver) we walked over the hill to Canisp Lodge, crossed the river and a good deal of marshy ground, emerging finally upon the bare, undulating moorland with the huge dome of the Grey Castle about two miles ahead. As the long ridge of Suilven runs from east to west we were approaching the mountain end-on and, whenever we looked up, saw only the graceful, tapering dome of our peak with its 600-foot wall of cliff. We had plenty of leisure to examine the rocks and decide on our line of advance. The southern view was also delightful, over a loch-speckled moorland to the sharp outlines of Cul Beag, Ben More Coigach and Stack Polly; the ridge of the latter as sharp and serrated as a cock's comb. West of these was a glimpse of Skye with the faint outline of the Cuillin over Gruinard Bay. Behind us were the distant hills of the Outer Hebrides.

In the early afternoon we were at the base of the lowest tier of rock, a pleasant hundred feet or so of slab climbing taking us to the main terrace which crosses the whole face below the middle, vertical wall of rock. We knew that the easy way was by a shallow gully at the southern corner of the terrace, a route which was grassy in its lower part and loose higher up. The central sweep of cliff was not only vertical but overhanging at many places. So we edged along towards the north-west corner, beyond which we should be on the flank of the Suilven ridge and less likely to discover any continuously interesting route.

An indentation in the cliff offered us a starting point for our climb, although it was neither gully nor chimney, but a steep scoop with a very steep rib of rock on the left. I started with difficulty in the groove and managed to transfer on to the rib. The holds were few and poor, but I was able to climb up to the right on to a ledge directly above the start. After some prospecting along a ledge I climbed another ten feet to a secure stance and brought my second up this 60-foot pitch. We were now on a horizontal ledge which we traversed for about thirty feet to the right. The worst overhang was beneath us, but the face above was little short of vertical, with numerous, narrow, shelving ledges, no in-cut holds and no belays. It was typical climbing on Torridon Red sandstone. I remember a severe mantelshelf problem followed by thirty feet straight up to another ledge.

The climbing was of the most airy and exhilarating variety, with backward and downward glances over the loch-spangled moorland and the blue waters of the Minch. One feels especially favoured if progress is made at all, although there are usually a variety of possible starting places as one glides along the narrow, horizontal bands either to the left or to the right. The cliffs of the Grey Castle are more amenable than the "Red" walls of the western buttress of Coire Mhic Fhearchair or those of the corries of Beinn Bhan of Applecross, where one may be unable to distinguish any ledges at all for many hundreds of feet.

As we progressed we were gradually forced obliquely upwards towards the centre of the cliff. We halted on a comfortable stance at the top of a wall. Here we prospected a ledge leading back to our left, but it petered out at a corner of the cliff. Nancy now took the lead, moving to the right, finding the key to the final section. Steep, interesting rocks led us straight up for over 150 feet to the end of all our difficulties, with a hard 10-foot crack near the finish, as a parting gesture of goodwill. Then we unroped and climbed up easy boulders to the summit of the mountain. The serious climbing had occupied us for three hours.

We traversed the summit ridge to the eastern top, finding it easy and grassy for the most part. A dry stone dyke actually crosses the ridge about the middle. Only at the far end did we enjoy a little more rock climbing. The small, eastern top mentioned in the Guide Book is really a small tooth on the descending ridge from the most easterly of the main tops, which are quite distinct and of about the same height when the mountain is viewed from the direction of Suileag. The hill walker can easily gain the centre of the summit ridge by one or other of several grassy gullies, either from north or south. The gullies are easy enough, but great care should be exercised when descending, on account of loose stones. We ourselves descended a loose, northerly gully and soon gained a good track which led us to the little bothy of Suileag, from which a track continues to Little Assynt on the main road. It was a delightful evening and we turned round many times to contemplate the warm, friendly, colouring of our peak in the rays of the declining sun. Suilven is one of the grand, little mountains of Scotland.

I have not enjoyed any more climbing on Torridon Red in the Coigach and Assynt districts, but Stack Polly offers many delightful and interesting problems. Quinag has a historic and difficult route, the Barrel Buttress, and the Coigach peaks are but little explored. The Coire na Caime of Liathach has been mentioned elsewhere. It has many formidable buttresses of cliff, but it is not easy to pursue a well-defined route. At the end of June 1947 my wife and I enjoyed a very difficult climb on a steep buttress which terminates on the main ridge of Liathach on the next subsidiary top to the east of Mullach an Rathain. At one or two places we were forced to discard boots and proceed in stocking soles. The climb went in three sections, not just directly following each other, of 130, 200 and 210 feet respectively, the standard varying considerably from moderate to severe. Careful choice of route is essential if sporting difficulty and continuity are to be achieved, without landing in an *impasse*.

The southern limit of the Torridon Red is in the Applecross peninsula on the cliffs of Beinn Bhan and Sgurr na Caorach. One of the most delightful discoveries of Professor Norman Collie was the terminal pinnacle or eastern buttress of Sgurr na Caorach (2,539 ft). It is quite easy to reach from the Applecross road, a mile or two beyond Kishorn Bridge. With careful route finding the climbing is not specially difficult, starting in the gully which separates A'Chioch (the pinnacle) from the upper ridge. Even after climbing the pinnacle there is much more to be done as one follows the ridge over several humps, with intervening deep depressions, to the top of the mountain. In June 1947 my wife and I had a grand, sporting climb on A'Chioch, in the course of which we straightened out the routes of our predecessors, the issue remaining in suspense for a considerable time. We learned enough to whet our appetite for another bout with these grand crags on some future occasion. They demand a technique peculiar to themselves, and exact such a measure of respect that I usually carry a *piton* with me, even although I have not yet been compelled to use it, either as a last hope of victory or a safeguard in defeat.

Cambrian Quartzite

This uppermost member of the Torridon family of rocks is more often execrated than commended. It is generally encountered as an objectionable covering of grey, angular scree, of all sizes, above the red sandstone, making the passage of the ridges exceedingly toilsome and the ascent of steep slopes even worse in summer conditions. Those who have traversed the north-eastern tops of Liathach and Beinn Eighe will hardly believe that any good thing can ever come out of the Cambrian quartzite.

In Coire Mhic Fhearchair of Beinn Eighe the state of affairs is very different. Quartzite forms the main part of the three great buttresses and is exceedingly steep, sound rock. The ascent of the northern, or left-hand buttress has already been described. In August 1946 my wife and I tackled the southern one. It was raining and the lower tier of Torridon Red cliff, with no positive but all rounded holds, and running all over with trickles of water, was altogether too desperate and formidable an adventure for us. I knew that George Bower's party had climbed it in dry conditions, using rubbers, in July 1919. They had found the "Red" part a severe climb. We compromised by working our way up the gully to the right and traversing on to the buttress by a ledge which enabled us to ease our consciences, to some extent, by climbing the uppermost 150 feet of the sandstone to a broad terrace at the foot of the quartzite cliff.

The rain now abated, having achieved its malign objective, and permitted us to enjoy ourselves. At first the climbing was easy, but, later on, the cliff became a good deal steeper as we neared the terminal tower. The rock was sound, with square-cut holds, and I remember a splendid 100-foot pitch which was very steep indeed. Then we gained an upper terrace below the vertical, final crag. The left wall was smooth and unclimbable, with a curious, square-sectioned, horizontal arm of rock protruding over the top of a vertical chimney, like a big gun from the battlements of a fortress. If we could reach the "gun" we knew that there was little difficulty above it.

A traverse to the right was easy, but did not, at first sight, offer a key to the fortress, although we passed by and rejected one chimney, as it did not appear to go high enough. Farther round I ascended another for over forty feet, traversed out to the left on steep slabs and climbed up the remainder of the face so long as there were any holds at all. Only ten feet of smooth wall remained to be climbed. We had to retreat. Another attempt, in the line of the original chimney, was no more successful. It almost appeared as if we should be beaten after all. I may say that I had not read Bower's account of his ascent, although I knew that the buttress had been climbed.

Something drastic had to be done. We retreated along the terrace until we reached the foot of the chimney which we had rejected. The outcome was both surprising and a trifle disappointing. The chimney was easy. It was unnecessary to pursue its upper continuation, which was steep, narrow, holdless and nearly vertical. I traversed out to the left on to good, steep slabs. There I discovered two things: the gun was just below the terrace on which I stood and another convenient chimney split the face, leading to the top of the buttress. That was the dramatic solution to the problem. From Bower's account I conclude that he found it at once, and was also somewhat dissatisfied that the finish was tamer than it had any right to be.

For the rock climber who uses Kinlochewe as his base there is a whole range of quartzite cliffs along the south-western and western faces of Beinn Mhuinidh (2,217 ft), the hill on the northern side of the main valley extending between the glen leading to the Heights of Kinlochewe and Glen Bianasdail which separates it from Slioch to the north-west. The earliest climb on this face goes up to the left of a conspicuous waterfall, visible for miles from the main road west of Kinlochewe. The others are on a band of cliff more to the north-west and starting from a conspicuous terrace which girdles the steep face of the hill. This part of Beinn Mhuinidh is called the Bonaidh Don. Our most enjoyable route went straight up the cliff from the terrace, where it has just turned the corner northwards above the Fasagh glen. This gave an exceedingly steep and continuous climb of 400 feet on sound rock, with a standard which is almost severe on the final 80-foot wall.

There are many more problems on this excellent wall of cliff. We ourselves found another good route near Fasagh Corner, and two more near the waterfall. It is a grand place for spending an easy day, or even a pleasant afternoon and evening. I have not found space to mention the Torridon Red buttress of Ben Hope (3,040 ft), the most northerly Munro of Scotland, the schistose crags above Lochan Coire Ghrannda on Beinn Dearg of Ross, where we enjoyed a delightful slab climb of 500 feet with a severe finish, or many another little-known rocky peak in this fascinating region, but the reader may rest assured that there is still a great opportunity and reward for the single-minded mountain lover.

APPENDICES
ON TECHNIQUE

Note

The whole objective of this book, as the author stated in
its original prologue, was "to conduct the reader along a
progress in mountaineering, by encouraging him to start
on the nearest hill, to climb our British hills in all seasons
and weathers and by all manner of routes: to begin by the
easy ways and, at a later stage, by more difficult routes
over rocks, snow and ice", to lead, eventually, to the Alps
and beyond. By omitting the early instructional chapters
and the Alpine ending we have perhaps lost something of
the book's flow but, as the techniques have altered so
considerably, what Bell wrote is now of historical rather
than practical interest. However, there is a deal of personal narrative and general hill philosophy in these chapters and a selection of passages is given here. If some of
the methods have changed, the game remains the same;
and were Bell alive and active today he would be in the
thick of it, learning and widening his experience. We too
can gain by taking heed of the wisdom of a past master.

H.B.

HILL WALKING

IT SEEMED OBVIOUS to an older generation that getting to the top of a hill or mountain under one's own power meant climbing, or even mountaineering in the case of a really big hill. Nowadays mountaineering has a definite technique. On the large scale it usually involves difficult passages over snow and ice or over rocks. In Britain, where we have no large mountains, the experts have made the most of our hills, and have devised difficult ways up the rock gullies and faces. Especially in England, among the *élite*, climbing is synonymous with rock climbing and everything else is hill walking. Let us leave it at that, whilst inclining towards the broader meaning of the word. What seems perfectly certain is that the art of walking over rough, steep and difficult country is the only possible foundation for any kind of true mountaineering, and that its importance is increased and not diminished as we proceed from the lower hills to the greatest mountains of the world. This art should be well and truly learned on the easier and lower hills as a necessary stage in the education of the mountaineer. Moreover, it is surprising how one continues to improve, even after years of experience. This is one factor which makes the enthusiasm for mountaineering such a life-long treasure and delight. Speed belongs to youth, and many sports must be abandoned on that account in early middle age, but the hill climber improves his skill, preserves his fitness and learns to economize energy to such good purpose that he may still pursue his craft until long past the age of three score years and ten.

It has often been said truly that on the higher British hills, and especially in Scotland, conditions may become wintry on almost any day of the year; so the hill climber, even in summer, must be prepared for cold winds, heavy rain and sleet, or even snowfall, as well as for finding the way in mist, cloud or storm.

The equipment and technique which are the minimum essentials are well described in other books. Here I give a brief account of several expeditions involving no special difficulties. It is by means of such expeditions, and plenty of them, that one learns hill sense, and does so much better and more naturally than by starting out with the more exciting and gymnastic problems of rock climbing. Far more mountain accidents are the outcome of a lack of hill sense than of the inability to cope with difficult technical problems of rock or snow, which ordinary hill sense would have enabled the party to recognize and avoid.

Finding the Way

When visibility is good, finding the way over mountains is not difficult, for a route can be selected by the exercise of common sense and deduction from past experience over that part which is seen, whereas the descent over the far side of the mountain, which is not seen, can be facilitated by the study of the map, or, at the worst, one can return by the same or part of the same route. Three things are therefore advisable: the habit of observing and memorizing mountain form and the prominent features of a landscape, a general knowledge of the characteristic mountain and valley configuration of the district and the ability to read maps, whilst realizing their shortcomings in matters of minor detail.

It is assumed that we are trying to find the easiest way, avoiding the passage over difficult ground or precipitous rocks. The best way to learn about the form and structure of hills and mountains is to select several of the smaller hills which are known to be easy; not too high, yet not without some steep and rocky sections which can provide a spice of interest and difficulty for the expedition. One should make a study of such hills, climb them from different sides on days of settled weather, at first returning by the route of ascent, and later traversing the hill and descending by another way which had been previously examined from below or, better still, ascended. Thus one learns much about the structure of a hill or group of hills.

One will learn to observe, and will gain something like the experience of the earliest Alpine guides, who knew their own hills intimately from having gone over them many times when hunting the *chamois* or exploring the rocks in search of valuable crystals and precious stones. These men were limited in their knowledge and outlook, but outstanding in hill-sense. Many of them became excellent, all-round mountaineers when they continued to climb with good amateurs who, better educated than themselves, could apply more scientific methods to the problems of orientation, weather and snow-craft. In these first expeditions one should rely on natural observation. At the end of the day the map should be used in order to elucidate obscure points, resolve difficulties and explain mistakes. Mountaineering is like other sports. One learns by mistakes, and it is better that these should be made in good weather and on easy ground, where the only penalty is some additional fatigue and loss of time. I have followed this plan from the beginning and have often reverted to it, purely for the delight of exploration, when I have found myself among homeland mountains with which I was not familiar. There were failures, but they were more than repaid by the lessons I learned. On the other hand, it must be admitted that some people never seem to acquire this "bump of locality". They ought to do both planning and execution with the constant help of guide book, map and compass, from start to finish.

My earliest explorations were mostly on a group of three minor hills in Fifeshire, the pleasant and isolated range of the Lomond Hills—East Lomond 1,471 feet, West Lomond 1,713 feet and Bishop Hill 1,492 feet. To the north the ground falls steeply to the low valley of the Howe of Fife, the southern slopes being much more gentle. There are drops of 500 and 800 feet respectively between the hills, and wide expanses of upper moorland. The views are wide and satisfying: across the Firth of Forth to the south-east and a whole semi-circle of Highland hills to the north. I have crossed the hills alone in all seasons and weathers. On the somewhat featureless plateau of the Bishop Hill I have occasionally been at fault in a heavy mist when there was no wind to indicate direction. It is surprising, however, to what extent a sub-conscious sense of locality acts as a guide. I never once descended the southern side instead of the northern. I have seen the waning moon rising from the North Sea after midnight, close by the Isle of May lighthouse, and have picked out the snowy peaks of the Grampians, from Ben Vorlich to Ben Lawers, Schiehallion and Ben-y-Gloe, by the light of a February full moon from a vantage point close by the summit cairn of the West Lomond. These early ventures not only gave me hill-sense, for the West Lomond possesses some sizeable tiers of vertical, dolerite cliff on which I made my first attempts at rock-climbing, but also a growing desire to make a closer acquaintance with that boundless range of the Grampian summits to the north. Since these earlier days I have become equally familiar with the higher, more extensive but less shapely Ochil Hills to the east of Stirling, which again stand up as a frontier chain between the industrial plains and the northern mountains of Scotland.

Many of my earlier expeditions on larger mountains were carried out alone, before I had entered the ranks of the mountaineering fraternity, before I possessed a compass and when I had only the most elementary type of cycling map to indicate the locality of the mountain and its height. They were days of settled good weather. I cycled fifty-five miles before ascending Schiehallion and returned the same day. I was caught aloft by swirling cloud on Ben More (Perthshire), but could not see that there would be any difficulty in returning by the same eastern ridge to my starting point and bicycle, by the Glen Dochart road. The ascent of Ben Macdhui by the Glen Derry track and Loch Etchachan gave me inspiring views across the Larig to the great corries of Braeriach and Cairn Toul. My first visit to Ben Nevis was by the pony track, at the age of sixteen, but was none the less exciting for all that. My base was at Newtonmore in Speyside. I left by bicycle at six a.m., and once or twice I nearly turned back on account of the strong west wind which faced me throughout the 47-mile run to Fort William. But a little food works wonders. It took me exactly two and a quarter hours to climb the Ben by track from Achintee in Glen Nevis. In those days there was still a wooden hotel on the summit. Part of the way I talked to the pony-driver who escorted the supplies to the hotel. There was mist between 2,500 and 3,500 feet, but the top was perfectly clear, calm and sunny. I shall never forget that wonderful view, with the Glencoe hills (then unknown to me) and the twin Paps of Jura gleaming like dull gold beyond a shimmering sea.

Several years later I explored all the higher mountains of North Wales alone, enjoying myself on the perilous narrows of Crib Goch and the Gribin Ridge of Snowdon. On the summits of the Glyders I was in cloud and nearly descended towards Pen-y-gwrd, but I recovered my bearings in time and completed the day's sight-seeing by descending to Llyn Idwal after an inspiring peep down the Devil's Kitchen. Abraham's *British Mountain Climbs* was leading me on towards the more exciting phases of the sport, but these random, early experiences did not make me a devil's advocate for solitary climbing. The practice has serious drawbacks and even more obvious dangers. Nowadays, there are far more opportunities for joining an inexpensive climbing club, or for graduating into such from friendships contracted whilst touring round Youth Hostels in mountain districts. Yet, when all is considered, it is a good thing to go alone on the mountains at times, even although it is advisable to confine such expeditions to lesser and easier hills. When we are alone the mountains can speak to us so much more intimately. Even a single companion may, to some extent, form a barrier—even a friend like-minded with ourselves.

Orientation in Mist or Storm

When we come up against real mountaineering difficulties in bad weather conditions, the all-important thing is to know our location before entering the mist, and to be careful, by compass steering, noting landmarks and, if necessary, by "dead reckoning" not to lose that knowledge. It is useless to steer for a very distant objective in difficult mountain country. The direct route, although the shortest in space, may not be practicable as regards time, effort or difficulty. Suppose we are on a ridge which may be joined by side ridges. We are aiming at a more or less distant mountain top where there is a cairn that can be identified. The ridge proceeds straight for a mile, descends, then bends at an angle to the right and rises again. There is no straight line on the ridge from our present position to our objective. What we do is to lay down a course on the first straight section. In order to find out when to change our course, we can either estimate the probable time we shall take to cover the mile and reach the dip or saddle, or we can actually count the estimated number of paces to that point, preserving direction meanwhile and, of course, knowing the average length of our pace. This is called proceeding by "dead reckoning". On difficult ridges it is often necessary and can be very accurate. The late Mr J. A. Parker, of Aberdeen, civil engineer by profession, who climbed all the 3,000-foot peaks of Scotland, besides many mountains in the Alps and elsewhere, often employed this method with uncanny accuracy in very difficult weather conditions on Scottish mountains. It is worth learning and trying out in bad weather on a hill we know, or think that we know.

The same procedure should be followed on ridges where there are forks or side ridges at various points. Estimate the distance to the fork, following a bearing. Then take another bearing and proceed to the next landmark. A difficulty often occurs in such country. One finds oneself on an apparent ridge which ends in a cliff. Then one must go back to the fork and try again. Many accidents and benightments have resulted from delay in facing such a situation, and from proceeding on what is rightly suspected to be the wrong course, just because no one takes the initiative and insists on a halt for reconsidering the position. On a really narrow, twisting ridge the compass cannot help, nor can it always discriminate between two possible ridges at a fork. Local knowledge can, however, be amplified by the evidence of the compass.

Summing up the position, the following points are the most important if one is caught by mist or storm in unknown and, to a lesser extent, in known mountain country:

1. Locate position on the map before losing sight of surroundings.

2. Accurate bearings, direction keeping and distance estimation. Pacing is better than timing for the latter.

3. If a party is involved in mist it is best to keep the steersman with the compass in the rear, so that he can keep the party in line and check up the direction frequently. However, each man should have a compass, and the leader should also use his own.

4. Always consult the compass at a halt, or at a cairn or mountain top. As all ridges, even when they are smooth and hump-backed, radiate from the summit, it is of the highest importance to take accurate bearings when leaving such a point. Always mark the line of approach before halting. A map may not always help with narrow, twisting ridges, but accurate bearings do help in the long run.

5. The compass is nearly always a reliable guide on Scottish hills, except in a few cases where magnetic rocks vitiate its readings, for instance, on the Cuillin gabbro of Skye or Ben More in Mull.

6. Narrow ridges limit possibility of error. It is at the broad stretches of ridge and the wide *cols* or saddles between gently sloping plateau mountains that difficulty is greatest. Be accurate in such regions.

7. Do not contour slopes in a mist. One loses direction and may, sooner or later, be forced to climb up again to the ridge crest. One can wander endlessly around the upper slopes of a corrie in mist, and also encounter difficult ground.

8. Mist exaggerates heights, depths and obstacles. Do not retreat without a close-up attempt to proceed, if you know the course is right.

9. If a ridge peters out in a cliff it is probably a "false" ridge. Go back to the last forking point. This is quicker and safer than attempting to continue.

10. There are two other aids to location and steering. The first is a pocket aneroid barometer. This can be very useful in mist for determining, in collaboration with the map, when a top or *col* has been reached. Over short distances and small differences of height a good instrument is fairly accurate. The other aid is wind direction. On open ridges and plateaux the direction of the wind is usually fairly constant for reasonable periods of time. On saddles between mountains, wind direction is of no value whatever as a guide. The hill contours modify it completely. In funnels and corries, and often on narrow ridges where there are cliffs and irregularities, wind direction is equally unreliable.

Some Useful Hints

1. WARMTH. It is almost as bad to be overheated as to be chilled, and climbing is warm work. Better start off without too much clothing and carry spares in a rucksack. One soon warms up, and it is a bad plan to halt whenever anyone wishes to discard clothing. When a halt is made for food one should, especially in cool or windy weather, put on spare clothing at once and take it off after the meal, when one has gone far enough to warm up again. Digestion, in its early stages, takes away the heat from the skin: it absorbs bodily energy rather than supplying any.

2. FOOD AND HALTS. It is a very good plan to train oneself to go without food for long periods, but a very bad one to start this training on a long expedition. If conditions become cold and stormy, food helps the morale of the party enormously. There are times when unexpected difficulties crop up along with the storm or blizzard, making a halt for food almost impossible. Then it may be a question of struggling on, so as to get clear of difficulties before nightfall. This is what tests the staying power of a party, and brings out the value of being able to do without frequent feeding. Even then, a little food, such as chocolate or dried fruit, may be kept ready to hand. Always keep a small reserve of food in a dry corner of the rucksack. It may as well be dry, as there is plenty of water on the hills! I have never found that alcohol was worth carrying, least of all in a dilute form, as an emergency reserve. Sugary foods are the best kind of reserve, but I do not think there are any general rules applicable to everyone. Personally, I dislike sugary foods in normal life, but feel the benefit of such immediately in conditions of hunger, fatigue and cold. When much energy is consumed, as in climbing, the work is done by the oxidation of

carbohydrates, and the easiest way to carry them is in the form of bread, in as dry a form as possible. Other foods are chiefly useful for affording variety and palatability. For untrained men the other foods may be more essential. Rapid convertibility into energy is not necessary for a properly trained individual. The habit of using such foods is likely to be a disadvantage on really hard expeditions.

3. PLANNING AND TIMING THE EXPEDITION. Good preliminary staff work, with a clear knowledge of the objective and study of maps, is essential. The best rule for timing an expedition is Naismith's formula, originated by W. W. Naismith, the founder of the Scottish Mountaineering Club. He knew what he was talking about, as one of his exploits in the company of Gilbert Thomson, his friend and collaborator in the starting of the S.M.C. will show. They set off from Dalwhinnie, having arrived by the midnight train from Perth. They were bound for the Easter Meet of the Club, which was being held at Inveroran, Argyllshire, on the old Glencoe road. They reached their destination in the evening of the same day in good-going order, having climbed Ben Alder and traversed Rannoch Moor. Their achievement is best appreciated by studying the map and noting the roughness and undulation of the ground. Naismith's rule is to allow one hour for every three miles on the flat and an extra hour for every 1,500 feet climbed.

When applying the rule in practice the time for halts should be added, and a generous allowance made for any strong, adverse wind, and in winter for snow and bad ground generally. It is better to have plenty of time in hand and to make an earlier start than is really necessary. Most distances are under-estimated from the map, and mistakes in finding the way can consume a lot of time.

4. CONDUCT OF PARTY. There should be no rushing at the hill. The pace should be comfortable for the slowest member of the party. Shorter steps are best when climbing, especially on uneven ground. Accurate placing of the feet is very important, on a rough, loose slope especially. Keep the foot as level as possible and save energy. A good pace will usually enable everyone to breathe through the nose and not with open mouth. This does not dry up the body so much nor accentuate thirst on a hot day. If conditions are difficult, and if possible at all times, the party should keep together. If a party splits up, each fragment should know the programme, route and destination of the others. In the event of a mishap it saves a lot of trouble if a search party has to go out later on.

If a party is overtaken by nightfall in cold and wet conditions some sort of shelter should be sought. Even although it proves inadequate, provided that it does protect to some extent from wind and rain, it is safer to stay there rather than venture down an unknown mountain face in darkness. If there is enough spare clothing and the party is in good health and training it is less dangerous (if dangerous at all) to remain there, moving arms and legs as much as possible during the night so as to keep the circulation going. Wind is the worst enemy and cold rain may be as bad. In summer and autumn a night's exposure on British hills is usually neither fearsome nor dangerous, especially if one has a reserve of food.

Accidents

To accidents involving mechanical injuries must be added those where a party or its members lose their way and, in consequence, suffer from exposure to cold and storm. The risk can always be reduced to minor proportions by observing the precautions advocated in this section, by careful training and all-round experience. The risks and inconvenience to a search party may be minimized if every party leaves information regarding its route, objective and destination before setting out on an expedition. Another rule which should always be observed is not to split up the party until all dangerous ground is left behind and the way back to civilization is safe and well marked. When the party must be split up, each fraction should know the destination and route of the others. If these rules are followed, the labour of a search party, if at all necessary, will be greatly simplified.

Now suppose that one member of the party is injured. Perhaps he thinks he can walk to safety and shelter. If there is any doubt as to his condition it is best to summon help. If possible, one member of the party should remain with the injured man, but this may not be possible (a) if there are only two, or (b) if there are three, but the route of descent is difficult or dangerous. Then the injured man must be left in a safe place, with as much shelter as can be arranged and with all available spare clothing and some food. Warmth and shelter are most important, because most mechanical injuries involve some degree of shock, and chilling is then particularly dangerous.

Only elementary first-aid should be applied by unskilled persons. This would include (1) stopping bleeding and cleaning and sterilizing open wounds, (2) immobilizing broken limbs, so

that movement can do no damage and pain is minimized, and
(3) applying warmth. Stimulants, such as alcohol, are generally
harmful. Sugary foods are best, if possible supplied in a hot
condition.

If other parties can be contacted it is essential to know the
conventionally accepted signals and answers. The distress
signal is made by whistle, waving flag or flashing light—six
signals at intervals during one minute, one-minute's interval
and then a repetition. The reply is similar, using only three
signals (blasts, waves or flashes) instead of six.

Conclusion

I shall conclude with a brief account of the sort of mistakes that
are liable to occur when traversing easy mountains. On New
Year's Day, 1935, Dr Myles, C. M. Allan, D. C. MacDonald
and I set out to climb Ben Alder, having left a car at the eastern
corner of Loch Pattack. The streams were in spate and we were
unable to cross a main feeder of the loch until we had gone far
enough upstream to the fork where two equal streams joined to
form it. We then decided to ascend the sharp little peak called
Lancet Edge and to leave the main top of Ben Alder for another
occasion. It was a pleasant, mild, sunny day, so mild that I
went up the narrow ridge stripped to the waist. We lunched on
the summit at 2.50 p.m. Allan thought we ought to return by
the same way, but Myles wished to go on to the summit of Geal
Charn (3,688 ft). This was in cloud and snow-covered. We
reached it at four p.m.

We descended by an easy ridge into a narrow glen on the
north-east side, where the map had led us to expect a path.
Unfortunately, it was beginning to get dark and our only torch
had a battery very near exhaustion. We knew our general
direction, but I shall not weary the reader with our flounderings
over endless peat hags as we struggled towards a faint, low gap
in the hills to the east. Having crossed it we struck a faint track
which gradually improved. Far ahead was a pale, grey blur
which we hailed as Loch Pattack. But the car was on the far
side of the loch, and both incoming and outgoing streams were
unfordable! The map, faintly illuminated by the orange glow of
the dying torch, showed a bridge two miles lower down over
the river Pattack. On we trudged in mist, rain and gloom,
missing the path twice on account of two-way forks and having
to retrace our steps. At length, when we felt sure that we had
covered much more than the two miles, we cut straight across

the right and found the road on our side of the river. Weary and sodden, we regained the car at eight p.m. We had failed by neglecting at least two vital considerations, probably because we were over-confident regarding the easy nature of the ground.

In early September 1941 I spent a week-end at Aviemore. Monday was a good day of strong, fresh, west wind and scudding cloud. I parted from my sister on the lower reaches of the Larig Ghru track, intending to climb Cairngorm and to meet her on my return journey on the Lurcher's Crag. She had map, compass and watch: I trusted to hill-sense. I enjoyed the bracing walk across the moors, crossing the northern corries of Cairngorm until I breasted the final slopes beyond Coire an't Sneachda. Then I passed up into the cloud and the full force of the wind. I lunched by the summit cairn (4,084 ft). I intended to catch the 5.30 p.m. train south from Aviemore, the depressing alternative being a midnight train and hours of weary waiting at Perth. The correct thing to do was to return by the way I had come. I should soon have been beneath the cloud level with no further difficulties.

But I thought I might as well try to cross the high plateau over Cairn Lochan to the Lurcher's Crag. It was good going and I did find the top of Cairn Lochan. My direction guide was the wind and the declivity on my right. The wind is never very constant on high mountains, owing to the contours of the ground. In this case, as I discovered later on, the wind veered towards the south. Beyond Cairn Lochan I found a track, marked at rare intervals by a series of stone men. There is so little up and down in this region that it is hard to decide where one is really going. I had not been in these parts for nearly twenty years. Then I came upon a wide, mossy hollow with a stream issuing from a spring in the moss. For the moment the place seemed vaguely familiar, but I could not recall the association. Then it recurred to me. I was convinced that I was at the source of the Feith Buidhe, a stream which ultimately plunges down to Loch Avon. I suspected that I was making for the top of Ben Macdhui.

At any rate I acted on this supposition, swung to the right, crossed a gentle ridge and began to descend a steep, rough slope, broken by occasional small crags. At length the mist thinned out. Beneath me were two small lochans, which I soon recognized as the Pools of Dee. When I got down to them I felt pretty certain that I had lost my train in any case, so I stripped and plunged into the dark, icy water for a swim. After a yard or two the bottom fell away quite suddenly, just as if I had stepped off the edge of a wall. This is not an uncommon feature of the mountain lakes in the Cairngorm region. Then I turned northwards, crossed the wilderness of boulders at the head of the Larig Ghru Pass, 2,733 feet above sea level, and soon met a party who were ascending from the north.

They told me it was a quarter to four. I had still a sporting chance. I trotted and ran all the way to the crossroad to Loch an Eilein, beyond the iron footbridge put up by the Cairngorm Club, and found my sister awaiting me in a car at five o'clock. No one could be more surprised than I was at catching that train. It is a distance of five and a half miles from the top of the Larig to the footbridge. I had a good thirst when the train got to Perth. Things do not always end so pleasantly when one wanders about in the mist, without map or compass, on the summit plateaux of the Cairngorms.

Let me add one more word of advice to the younger mountain-eers, straight from my own experience. Do not imagine that hill-walking requires no technique. It requires much more than you imagine, and you will continue to learn all sorts of odd, useful things for many years. Do not try to take a short cut to the greater thrills of severe rock climbing. Hill walking is true mountaineering, however the hard-bitten rock-climber may regard it. Walking is the head and corner stone of all mountain climbing, whether we are dealing with the little 1,000-foot hill near our homes or taking part in an assault on an unclimbed 20,000-foot giant of the Himalaya. In certain kinds of weather and atmospheric lighting the one can look almost as beautiful and impressive as the other.

ROCK CLIMBING

Scope and Training

ROCK CLIMBING IS an integral part of mountaineering, but it is only a part. Mountaineering on the larger scale involves difficult questions of exploration and transport of supplies before the main climbing problems are even reached. Great mountains are usually covered with accumulations of snow and ice, particularly on their higher slopes. The bigger the mountain the more necessary to choose the easiest way of ascent, and the more likely that a route will be selected over glaciers, snow slopes and snow-covered ridges, with a minimum of difficult rock. Consideration must also be given to the all-important factors of time, weather, wind, cold and a rarefied atmosphere. Any rock climbing must be done fairly quickly and should not be too difficult or strenuous. These considerations apply in a greater or lesser degree to the ascents of all big peaks in the Alps, Caucasus, Rockies or Himalaya. In the Alps the approaches are well known, marked by paths to a considerable height, and there are many high huts, conveniently situated so as to shorten the final ascent and enable more time to be spent on severe technical difficulties Even in the Alps, however, severe rock climbs are unusual on the bigger peaks.

On British hills difficulty must make up for the lack of height, if the sporting possibilities of our lower mountains are to be exploited to the fullest extent. It may be assumed that many readers of this book aspire to mountaineering in the High Alps as one of their objectives. For them, training in British rock climbing has considerable value. The earliest British mountaineers learned their rock climbing from Alpine guides. It was not specially difficult rock climbing in those far-off days. There is no longer any excuse whatever for British climbers going to the Alps without an all-round training in this branch of mountaineering.

There is evidently a need for two different sorts of training in rock climbing. The kind that will fit a man for dealing with the ordinary problems of rock-craft on the bigger mountains is more important from the mountaineering point of view. This would lay the greatest emphasis on the ability to move quickly and safely over moderately difficult rocks, sound or unsound, wet or dry or patchy with snow and ice, throughout a long and strenuous expedition which necessitates a certain amount of route finding, with little guidance from other parties or printed directions. Such a course of training, involving both ascent and descent, is indispensable for work on the big Alpine peaks, and is the primary objective of this section. It can easily be achieved on British hills, but the Scottish mountains, on account of their greater number, height and variety of rock structure, are better adapted for this purpose than the more difficult and standardized routes in Lakeland and North Wales.

This is not a matter of difficulty or exposure; English rock climbing cannot be excelled anywhere in those respects. There is far more moderately difficult rock available in Scotland, so that long days can be spent on traverses over a great extent of climbable rock, demanding rapid and rhythmic movement of the whole party for many hours at a stretch, including many ascents and descents. During winter and spring months Scotland can offer on its higher mountains a typically Alpine alternation of snow, ice and rock, which is seldom available in England and never on the same scale.

This kind of training possesses certain other advantages from the aspect of safety. It is well known that accidents occur, very frequently, on the easier places, especially during the descent after a party has completed a difficult climb. The nervous tension is relaxed and succeeded by a reaction of comparative carelessness when there are still minor difficulties to be faced. On a difficult rock climb certain safety measures are always adopted.

Only one man moves at a time, and the rope which links the party together as one unit is firmly anchored to the rock. There is a tendency to accept these static devices as a complete guarantee of safety in themselves, with the after-effect of an unwarranted carelessness when the rope has been taken off and each member of the party moves off by himself. What is required is habitual awareness at all times on the mountains, developed in every member of the party and not only in the leader. This is best acquired on long expeditions where the degree of difficulty, never too great, varies continually. Where there is danger or difficulty for the weakest member of the party the whole party should be roped, but all moving together unless the difficulty is considerable. It will not be necessary to anchor the rope, in general, for the rope will only be required for checking a momentary slip and never an actual fall. It is by such training that a party will work together as a single team and acquire dynamic rather than static security. The real factor of safety will lie in the habitual awareness and response to difficulty on the part of each member. Like other habits, that of dynamic awareness and security will not be easily lost when the rope is taken off or when its use is no longer necessary.

Rock climbing is also an independent sport in its own right, quite apart from getting to the top of the mountain. As such, it is a valuable training for all forms of difficult mountaineering and makes full use of the sporting possibilities of our smaller British mountains. It trains a man to co-ordinate eye and limb, to observe and weigh up a situation and come to a decision. It trains him to know and examine himself and to know, as A. F. Mummery says, "that the fingers of one hand can still be trusted with the lives of a party, and that the lower limbs are free from all trace of knee-dissolving fear." But it is much wiser to learn how to move safely over complicated hill country and over long stretches of moderately difficult rock first of all, without taking a short cut to the greater thrills of the more severe climbs.

Types of Rock Climbing Problems

Rock climbing routes, as a rule, should follow some properly defined natural line and must be neither too easy nor impossibly difficult. On great mountains, such as the Alps, it may be a difficult matter to reach the summit by any route whatever, and especially if the intention is to follow a particular ridge or face of the mountain. We must then select the easiest route on that ridge or face and surmount any difficulties we meet. On British mountains there is always an easy way, unless in severe conditions of weather or snow and ice, so the climber sets himself the problem of getting up the cliff within narrowly defined limits.

Even so, he is often following a line of structural weakness, a sort of breach in the natural defences of the crag. There are many such features available. One cannot climb a smooth, vertical face of rock. The angle must slope back to some extent. There must be terraces or ledges for occasional resting places. There must be miniature ledges or cracks in the face, to be used as footholds or handholds.

In the early days, climbing routes followed two types of rock feature as a rule: ridges and gullies. The first projects from the face and the second cuts back into it, both lying at an easier gradient than the face itself, even although each may have occasional steps or vertical sections. Such steep sections are known as *pitches*. Climbing routes described in guide books are usually split up into a succession of pitches, not necessarily all natural ones. The next development was to attack still narrower rifts, known as *chimneys*, which could usually be bridged between back and foot or back and knee. If these became too narrow, admitting only a foot or a hand, they were still useful as lines of ascent and known as *cracks*. In chimneys and cracks support could be obtained by friction and jamming against the retaining walls. The climbing was often very strenuous, but balance was not always so important as strength and endurance.

At a later stage of development it was discovered that lateral support was not essential, but that an improved balance would enable one to climb near-vertical walls with tiny holds and steep slabs with hardly any holds at all. This was not done so much by strenuous arm pulling, but rather by neat foot-work, good balance and accurate co-ordination of eye and limb. The result was the discovery and execution of many new and exceptionally difficult rock climbing routes on crag faces which the older climbers had only favoured with a glance before pronouncing them to be impossible. Let us review the different sorts of rock climbing problems. The novice will have his preferences, but should try and gain some degree of proficiency at all of them. On many of the greatest and longest climbs, British and Alpine, one may encounter all or most of these types in a single day's climbing on one mountain.

Arêtes or *Ridges* of any length and difficulty are not common in Britain. Most of them, having stood the rough and tumble of ages of geological denudation, are of fairly sound rock. They are the natural routes between peaks. The best known and most attractive ridges, only difficult for short stretches at a time, are to be found on the Cuillin Hills of the Isle of Skye, and are of very sound rock. Other examples of the horizontal type are the Aonach Eagach in Glencoe, the A'Chir in Arran and the Crib Goch ridge of Snowdon. Steep lateral ridges, abutting against a mountain face, are commoner and afford very good climbing. Sometimes they are called buttresses and partake of both architectural habits. A buttress has often a narrow ridge on part of its upward sweep, generally near the top. The Amphitheatre Buttress of Craig yr Ysfa (North Wales) and the knife edge of Scafell Pinnacle (Cumberland) are instances of this. There are many in Scotland, such as the Tower and Observatory Ridges on Ben Nevis, the Crowberry Ridge in Glencoe, the upper part of Rosa Pinnacle in Arran, and the Eagle Ridge of Lochnagar. The latter has several long, steep, narrow and difficult sections and is probably the finest example of a steep and difficult British ridge. Wind can be a serious menace on an exposed ridge.

Ridges are often blocked by steep, or vertical sided gaps, steep walls, and towers known as *gendarmes* to the climbing fraternity. Contrary to civilian traffic regulations the best plan is to attack the policeman boldly and climb over him—unless there happens to be a clear way round on either side. It is seldom wise to recoil from such difficulties, for a traverse below the obstacle often lures one on to a very unsound rock, on to smooth slabs or round a corner on a narrow ledge which frequently thins out to vanishing point over a vertical cliff. Another great advantage of sticking to the crest of a ridge is that there are nearly always good projecting rocks available for holds, or as hitches and secure anchors for the climbing rope.

Gullies are natural lines of weakness on a cliff face. The average gradient is usually less than that of the face itself. But there are compensating disadvantages, for the rock has usually been hollowed out because it is less resistant and, consequently, less sound than that of the surrounding walls. Much loose rock remains in the bed of the gully. It is, therefore, a bad plan for two parties, or even one large party, to be climbing in a gully at the same time, for the upper members, however careful they may try to be, are likely to drop stones on the people below. Even a small party of two or three ought to keep close together. Pitches occur in gullies where a boss of rock has resisted the weathering agencies and stands up as a wall, or where a great block, with or without a few smaller ones, has jammed at the narrow part and serves as the roof of a cave. As gullies are natural watercourses such caves are often wet, with slippery, moss-covered walls. They present difficult problems. Sometimes one wall can be climbed with foot and handholds until one is high enough to get an arm across the top and pull up on the edge of this boulder, called the *chockstone* (although this word is mainly applied to blocks in chimneys which are usually much narrower). Then a mighty heave and wriggle will land the climber on the roof.

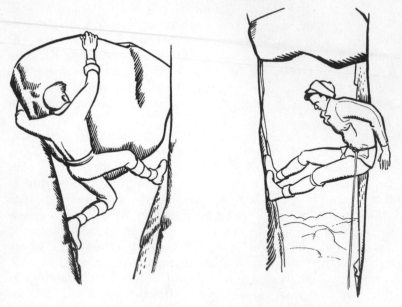

Surmounting a Chockstone   Backing Up

Gully climbing was a very early development in English rock climbing. On Scafell, Deep Ghyll and Moss Ghyll; on Pillar, Walker's Gully; and in Wales, the Great Gully of Craig yr Ysfa were climbed. It is not to be thought, on that account, that gully climbing is inferior or out of date. The three longest Scottish gullies, the Waterpipe in Skye, the Chasm of Buachaille Etive and the Clachaig Gully in Glencoe, are all splendid climbs. The rock is not very good in the Waterpipe, but the Chasm offers all types of pitches of increasing difficulty in a long day's climbing, and the rock is sound. The Ben Nevis gullies, which are high up on a north-east face and snow-filled for many months, have much decayed and unsound rock and are not to be recommended as rock climbs.

Chimneys are much narrower and steeper than gullies. They often overhang altogether in places, but may, nevertheless, offer practicable means of ascending vertical steps on a face, or even on a ridge. Where there are adequate holds on the back or side walls, and if the chimney is wide enough, the method of climbing is straightforward, either facing in or sideways. In other cases one must wriggle upwards between the walls with back on one wall and knees or feet on the other. In very wide chimneys the necessary span must be between feet and hands. Such procedure is known as "backing up", in general. Energy can be saved by using the palms of the hands behind the hips as a help in lifting the body. It is important to rest wherever possible, as it may be necessary to economize energy for a final strenuous effort in the nature of an arm pull, where the chimney is closed at the top by an overhanging chockstone. Chimney climbing can be very tiring work.

The following are good rules which are worth observing at all times:

1. Use all available holds on the walls, and use them for resting places.

2. Don't get too far inside a chimney, especially if it narrows at the top. One has less freedom of movement and the apparent, additional safety is more than counterbalanced by a strained position. Positive holds on the walls cannot be properly used in a narrow space.

3. Always economize energy and keep a reserve for the final movements which may be very strenuous. Keep enough energy for a safe retreat, if necessary.

4. Make sure about the final holds, e.g. behind the chockstone, before making any irreversible move towards them.

5. Climb chimneys with the feet and body muscles, and as little as possible by pulling up with the arms to high handholds.

Chimneys and cracks on faces are normally of fairly sound rock, although this depends entirely on the prevailing rock structure. They are not so often wet, and usually provide belays for the rope. In many cases the leader can anchor himself firmly by wedging across the chimney. Even although these places may overhang, the in-cut nature of the holds makes them less dangerous than difficult and strenuous.

Cracks and Corners. A crack is simply a very narrow version of a chimney. Sometimes both feet and arms can be used. In narrow cracks only one arm and perhaps a toe can be inserted, while the other foot finds a few minute holds on the outside face. Sometimes the hand or fist can be inserted in a crack as a wedging hold for steadying purposes, or even for taking part of the weight of the body while raising a foot. Crack climbing can be very strenuous. The "Lay-back" is a useful but exhausting method of climbing steep cracks with a sharp edge, when they split the angle of an open corner. The climber grips the edge, using feet or knees against the smooth rock face. Considerable pressure is often necessary and the position is tiring to hold. As

The Lay-back
*Climbing Corner and
use of Thread Belay*

in climbing a vertical steeple-jack's ladder, the arms must be kept straight so as not to tire them out prematurely.

Open corners on vertical rock can be exceedingly strenuous and difficult. Both in cracks and corners the utmost use must be made of any kind of foothold, even when only the toes can be inserted at an unnatural angle. Hands should only be used for preserving balance and not so much for lifting. Both hands can sometimes be inserted side by side in a vertical crack, pulling against each other on opposite sides, but only for short distances.

One final aid may be occasionally useful in a crack of varying width. This is to carry up a suitable stone which can be wedged in a crack as an *artificial chockstone*. That is a last resort for solving an intractable problem. I have known of a case where it had been inserted and had come loose on a future occasion when used by another party. Test them always.

Slabs. Steep, smooth slabs offer difficult problems. Any roughness, protuberances or cracks are a great boon. It is here that rubbers and stocking soles are particularly useful. Just as on steep snow and ice one should remember that the danger is not one of falling backward but of slipping forward and downward.

The best posture is the nearest to the upright, using foot friction, arms outstretched with fingers caressing the rugosities of the rock, so as to preserve the balance and maintain the maximum friction. One must not cling to the slab or lie along it. When the rock is rough it is amazing how steep slabs can be climbed. The upper part of the south-west route on Pillar and Mallory's Slab on Sron na Ciche (Skye) are examples. The Long Climb (already described) on Ben Nevis gives grand practice on steep, smooth slabs (see diagram, p.98).

Face Climbing. Many of the foregoing types of problem occur as incidents on a steep, face climb. The crucial difficulties arise where it is necessary to effect a lodgment on an overhanging sill or ledge. Climbers often talk of overhangs where the face is still on the right side of being vertical. So much imaginative vision must be allowed in the description of a new, severe climb! Nevertheless, short, slightly overhanging walls of rock are actually climbed. Everything depends on what sort of hand-holds are available on the ledge above. If these are positive and in-cut the labour of pulling up with the arms is so much lighter. If they are not in-cut the utmost use must be made of friction against the palms of the hands. In the case of an overhang, the important principles are as follows: (1) Make the most of any footholds, however rudimentary. (2) Learn to step up high on one foot whilst preserving the balance. (3) Reconnoitre all the holds, plan the necessary moves and rest before starting off. (4) Don't try and pull up with one arm unless you are exceptionally strong. (5) Once you have started don't hesitate, but proceed rhythmically and quickly until you are in safety. (6) Be well anchored by your second whilst moving.

If you can climb up securely to a position of equal height, or slightly above the overhang, a few feet on either side of it, this may be the best way of reaching it by a traversing move. Such a move may be irreversible, meaning that you are likely to fall off if you don't succeed. It is, therefore, all the more necessary that it should be carefully planned and exactly executed. The final crossing may be effected by a hand traverse with the whole weight of the body hanging from the fingers. This type of gymnastic problem is best practised on a suitable boulder where there is no danger. It is often very useful on a difficult rock climb.

Many of the hardest British rock climbs are face climbs. They do not, on that account, call for the greatest strength and endurance. Good balance, good planning and hold selection and rhythmic movement count far more than rush tactics and pulling strength.

Traverses link upward movements, avoiding overhanging sections of cliffs. Here again, good balance and rhythm are essential. All movements on a traverse ought to be reversible. The art of interchanging the position of the feet is indispensable. Ledges have a habit of petering out when explored round corners on a cliff. One must be able to retreat at all times.

Combined Tactics is a method for assisting the leader from below by other members of the party, so as to enable him to overcome a specially difficult problem. So long as difficulty overcome is not succeeded by greater difficulty unforeseen or actual danger in the manoeuvre, the method is often justified by results. In that respect it bears a distant relationship to the practice of jumping for holds! The procedure is justifiable, if (1) the leader is competent and reliable, (2) those below have a perfectly sound stance and anchorage, and (3) it is reasonably certain, so far as one can see, that if the leader is so assisted he will be able to get up the pitch, and will not find himself in just as difficult a position afterwards. The third condition means that the immediate difficulty appears to be the only bar to success or a safe retreat later on. My own experience of combined tactics is scanty but justified by success. On the Knife Edge Arête in the Amphitheatre on the west face of Aonach Dubh, Colin Allan pushed me up so far that he was still taking a good deal of my weight on his outstretched left hand when I finally got good, pulling holds on a smooth scoop of rock. But Colin was exceptionally strong and I was a lightweight. I was once the victim when offering a shoulder to a friend who fell off. Luckily, it was only on a biggish practice boulder.

Descent

On British hills, where there is always an easy way down, we tend to neglect the technique of descending difficult rocks: on Alpine rock peaks there is usually no easy way and we may be forced to descend them. Even if we do not climb outside of Britain we may be faced with the same problem if we get stuck during an attempt on a new route, or if we are forced to retreat from a difficult position by the onset of bad weather or by a minor accident. If we have mastered the technique of descent, which is simply a matter of training and experience, we can retreat with confidence and in safety. Many accidents have been caused by incompetence and neglect, so far as this branch of climbing is concerned. The terrors of descending difficult rocks are partly imaginary and will disappear with practice. Some kinds of pitches are actually easier to descend than to climb up. This is often true of chimneys.

Wherever the difficulties are not too great one should face outwards. In so doing one does not feel as secure as when facing the rock and clinging to handholds. In the latter position, however, the extra security is static and often strained in character. When facing outwards one can see the next move, plan ahead and move continuously. That is dynamic security. The hands should be kept as low as possible. On more difficult rocks it is often possible to move downwards from a sideways position, getting the best of both worlds, so to speak. This may be very good for chimneys. Walls and face climbs are most difficult to descend, but the sideways position is helpful, and it is usually not too difficult to change the feet and face the other way when necessary. One should learn this useful art when climbing up, for it is no more difficult when descending. Neat footwork is especially useful on the descent.

Unless one is highly competent it is unwise to descend difficult rocks which one has not previously ascended, at least once. It may appear simple in the guide book, but one cannot expect to be able to identify and make use of all the small holds on a rock face during a descent unless one knows the feel of the climb beforehand from actual experience. Comparatively short sections of vertical cliff may present insuperable difficulties for a first descent and may yet be easily climbed by utilizing one or two undercut fingerholds, or a combination of a very small foothold and a press-handhold just beneath a slight overhang. One solution of the difficulty is to lower a man on the rope, let him climb up again and persuade him to lower the others and finally climb down himself with the aid of his new-found knowledge. This is not guide-book knowledge, but acquired skill and tactile memory: it resides in the balance, finger tips and soles of the feet. The physiologists sometimes call it the *proprioceptive* sense, a sense of the relation of the parts of the body to each other, which is essential to balanced movement.

It is unnecessary to consider the problems of descent in detail. The motions of ascent are reversed; the maximum use must be made of friction. If motion is kept under control by friction, gravity becomes an ally, and descent can be made an almost continuous succession of short moves, where no overhangs require to be negotiated. Thus, it is usually not difficult to descend steep slabs, as it is always possible to slide down the last few inches or more to a hold. Where there is any loose rock on a face great care should be exercised by everyone during the descent. The rope may dislodge stones on to the lower members of the party.

Security measures are practically the same for descending as for climbing, but the leader goes down last without assistance from the rope. The most experienced of the others will go first as pathfinder, under the direction of the leader if necessary. If a pitch is too difficult for the leader to climb down without assistance he must descend on the doubled rope. This *Roping Down* (or "Abseiling") should be learnt by all climbers. It is very much used in the Alps as a time-saver on long rock climbs. In the Chamonix district, for instance, the usual method of traversing the Grand and Petit Dru involves a long series of descents on the doubled rope, with convenient, fixed iron rings where necessary. Harold Raeburn, one of the pioneers of guideless climbing in the Alps, says in his book, *Mountaineering Art*, that roping down is unnecessary on this traverse. I cannot speak from experience about the Drus, but have found many other fixed rings on Alpine rock peaks where roping down was not really necessary. It is only needed for emergencies in British climbing, but the method, being simple and easily learnt, ought to be known and occasionally practised by all rock climbers.

However, roping down is a very dubious policy in descending an unknown face of rock, unless one is satisfied that there is only one impossible pitch and that the rest of the descent is feasible. If there are no natural belays it may be necessary to insert a *piton* into a crack in the rock, from which to suspend the rope loop. If there is only a short, awkward section the others can easily be lowered by the leader, who can often hang the doubled climbing rope over the belay, without unroping himself, and so descend past the difficulty, using both hands to hold the doubled rope. Practise the art of roping down on easy places to begin with, where there is no great drop. You will not then be alarmed if you spin on the rope whilst hanging freely.

Kinds of Rock

The climber should aim at getting experience of many different kinds of rock. The standard routes on Lakeland crags, and generally, but not always, on Welsh crags, are on very sound rock. The Cuillin of Skye are composed of a very rough and sound, tertiary lava called gabbro, so sound as to inculcate bad habits of stretching up and trusting to arm pulls, but dykes of trap rock occur in many places which are not nearly as sound. Ben Nevis offers excellent porphyrite in many places, but unsound trap rock in others. Glencoe offers a similar variety. Granites vary a good deal. On Rosa Pinnacle, in Arran, the rock is magnificent and rough, but elsewhere the granite is not nearly so good. Cairngorm and Lochnagar granite weathers badly into rounded holds, and grows a patina of lichen which becomes slimy and difficult in wet weather. The great mass of the Scottish Highlands is composed of metamorphic schist which, when it forms bold cliffs, offers very few holds and even fewer belays. Schistose cliffs are usually either easy or impossibly difficult. They tend to develop overhangs and thin horizontal ledges. In the north-west of Scotland, little known but very interesting climbing can be obtained on any of three superimposed geological formations: the oldest of British rocks, Lewisian gneiss, at the bottom; a rough, red Torridon sandstone above it and Cambrian quartzite on top. The Torridon sandstone forms great walls of cliff, very like tiers of masonry. It is the most difficult of all good, British climbing rock, usually perfectly firm, but offering only rounded holds and hardly any belays.

What determines the suitability of rock for climbing purposes is not so much the chemical composition but the texture and jointing, and especially the lie of the bedding planes. For easy climbing these planes should slope downwards towards the mountain and away from the climber. He thus climbs over their sharp edges without great difficulty, even though the general inclination of the face is very steep. The opposite kind of slope resembles that of the roof tiles of a house and offers much more difficulty with a lower gradient. All rocks, even igneous ones, have some system of three dimensional joint planes, not necessarily at right angles to each other. Some interest in the geological structure of mountains and a natural gift for observing these details will stand a climber in good stead if he is looking out for new rock routes in unknown mountain country.

SNOW AND ICE CLIMBING

SNOWFALL ON THE higher hills, not a mere sprinkling but sufficient to offer difficulties to the climber, can be met at most times of the year except for about three or four months in summer. Serious snow difficulties are unusual before December, and there may be none at New Year. All except north faces and corries may be nearly clear by the end of March. That is unusual, but it all depends on the winter's weather. At the other extreme there may be brief storms and blizzards at the height of summer, so that reserves of clothing are necessary at all times.

Many types of snow surface are encountered on Scottish hills—deep, powder snow; the same covered with light, breakable crust; deep, wet snow; half compacted snow where steps can be made by kicking with the toes; very hard snow, on which the boot makes no impression; and all varieties of ice, varying from hard-frozen material which still retains air space to the dense, solid, black, brittle ice, formed directly from water trickling over rocks and freezing as it flows. This is the hardest type. As it is also brittle the art of cutting steps in it with the ice-axe is both a strenuous and a skilled occupation. An intermediate stage, still retaining some air-space, is tough, glutinous and awkward to cut. Such tough snow-ice appears to be formed in a moist climate.

Even when steps can be kicked up a snow slope it is advisable that every member of the party should carry an ice-axe. For severe winter climbing on steep ice and icy rock it is a great help to carry an additional short axe.

Snow Slopes

The correct way to climb difficult snow and ice can be learned on steep, open snow slopes, but not too steep to begin with. Open snow slopes do not, in general, lie at an angle exceeding forty-eight degrees. It is wrong to take the novice, as a subordinate member of a roped party, on very difficult winter climbs. He may become timid and adopt a posture of clinging to the slope. Climbing steep snow or ice is rather like climbing a steeple-jack's ladder. The jack does not cling to the ladder with bent arms—a fatiguing and ill-balanced posture. Instead of that he keeps his arms straight and walks up erect, hanging slightly outwards, but with little strain on the arms, which slide along the trams. No illustration is an exact parallel. The points to note are balance and mobility.

On steep snow and ice one may slip *downwards*: when one falls it takes place *upwards* against the slope. The slip is what one must guard against, and there is only one reliable method. Keep the arms, considered as extended by means of the ice-axe, without strain, at all times ready to correct any momentary lack of balance or the beginnings of a slip. That is all they have to do. Keep the centre of gravity above the base line joining the feet. It is a small but sufficient base, from which all movements must be made. This demands an erect position, with as little bending at knees or hips as may be absolutely necessary to preserve flexibility. This rule holds good, as far as possible, for any kind of climbing on snow and ice, whether one is ascending, traversing, descending or glissading. Avoid all tendency, from fear or misplaced caution, to lean inwards towards the slope. The proper use of the ice-axe, apart from cutting steps or belaying a moving member, is as a steadying arm or lightly used prop against the slope above one—not as a prop below or a tie above. This avoids tension or cramp of the muscles, and makes for flexibility, alertness and security. It is best learned on short slopes, not too steep at first, where unroped practice is safe if there is a good run-out of soft snow below, should one chance to slip. In positions of greater difficulty the ice-axe may be used properly as a tie with the pick secured above, but if erect, balanced movement is already habitual, the harder problems become much easier.

Open snow slopes can usually be climbed by kicking steps into them. The ladder of steps should go straight up the slope, as a rule, and the interval between steps should not be too great for the shortest man of the party. When the snow becomes harder the need for cutting steps can still be avoided by zig-zagging and kicking sideways. If there is any tendency to slip, the ice-axe should be driven in slightly above one, using the spike as a steady against the slope. Additional security and a resting place can be obtained by cutting an extra large step, or "soup plate", at the corners of the zig-zag.

As the slope steepens the party will be roped together, as for

rock climbing, but all moving together, each man carrying a
single loop of rope in the hand and watching the man in front,
but not impeding or jerking his movements. Each man keeps
his axe ready to fix in the snow, for use as a belay for the rope
in the unlikely event of a slip. This is the only practicable
method on long snow slopes, which are occasionally encountered in Scotland and frequently in the Alps. It saves vital time
and makes for alertness and team work in the party. For
belaying in snow the axe is thrust in deeply, somewhat above
the climber, vertically downwards, and the rope is passed round
the shaft at snow level. If the slope is extremely steep the axe
shaft should be somewhat between the vertical and a line at
right angles to the slope. The use of the body belay and the
practice of tying on to the belay axe with a knot are both
unnecessary and inadvisable.

A different situation arises if the snow is in bad condition,
either dry, loose and powdery or wet and slushy. The surface
layer does not then adhere properly to an underlying, hard,
frozen layer, and there may be a danger of the top layer peeling
off the underlayer, taking the party with it in a snow slide or
avalanche. Only experience will show when the danger exists.
It is common in the Alps and less likely in Scotland. Avoid such
slopes, if possible. As a rule, they are found only in steep gullies,
but they may occur as open, steep slopes, especially when a
partial thaw follows a heavy snowfall. They may only occur in
patches. When they must be climbed, security precautions
should be taken. The leader, belayed by the rest of the party on
sound snow, proceeds alone, removes loose snow and cuts steps
into the firm layer underneath. He then brings up the other
members, one at a time, from a secure, basin-like stance, with
the rope secured over a well-sunk ice-axe. This takes a lot of
time. It is often possible for the leader to proceed by kicking for
twenty to thirty steps before digging out his security stance. It
all depends on the conditions. Always, the belaying axe should
be deeply driven into firm snow, and the rope to the others
should pass over the shaft at ground level, so as to exert as little
leverage on it as possible.

Gullies
Great difficulties are unlikely to be met on an open snow slope,
but it is well to be prepared. Snow-ice can lie at much steeper
angles in a gully. Then the leader must cut steps all the way. It
may be quicker to cut a ladder straight up, but the cutting

position is easier for a zig-zag staircase. There are two further advantages. The chips from the steps will not constantly bombard the other members of the party. The zig-zag ladder will be much easier to descend, if a retreat is forced upon the party by unforeseen circumstances. In easy snow-ice one or two slashes with the adze will cut a good step; in really tough snow-ice many blows of the pick may be required. Seize the axe with both hands; do not swing it too far back; try to use the weapon in a balanced and rhythmic manner, so that the weight of the axe and the blow fall at the right moment. Step-cutting may then be continued for long periods without muscular fatigue. A slight sway of the body, always in balance, will ease the work of arms and wrists. Only long, continued practice can make perfection. It all follows from an erect, balanced posture and rhythmic movement. The completed step should have a slight inward and downward slope, not too much or the steps may break away under the following members.

It takes a long time to learn to judge the different condition of the snow in varied situations and types of weather. It varies a good deal inside the same gully. There is often a hard channel in the centre, especially in late winter and spring. That is where masses of avalanche snow have slid down. It is often better to keep to one side and secure occasional anchorage by means of holds on the rocky walls, where possible. The altitude has a considerable effect, for the upper sections of the Nevis gullies are usually much harder than those on lower mountains. Where the angle is not severe and the snow is soft the weight of the climber will often compact it satisfactorily, even though he sinks in up to the knees.

Then it is quite a good plan to wriggle straight up the gully, making use of the maximum of body friction, and using arms and legs almost in the way that a swimmer does. Of course, the ice-axe must be thrust in deeply above the climber for security. The knees are very useful, although progress is rather a cold business. There is often a thin, top crust on the snow. No general rule can be given as to the safety of such snow slopes. Only experience and the compacting of the snow under pressure can serve as a guide. The expert will not be slow to give heed to any warning signs. Scottish snow is much safer in this respect than Alpine snow, but the safety does not last indefinitely when there is a heavy thaw, especially in spring time.

At the top of the gully there is often a great eave of overhanging cornice which may be very difficult to negotiate.

Surmounting a Cornice,
compare photograph of
Braeriach

Gullies which are known to have cornices should be avoided by beginners; and such gullies should always be avoided when there is a thaw, as large slices of the cornice must, sooner or later, break off and fall down the gully. Some Ben Nevis cornices may be as much as thirty feet high with an overhang exceeding ten feet. It will be appreciated that the fall of a substantial part of such a cornice would sweep a party of climbers down the gully with it, not necessarily burying them, but very probably knocking them about severely, with possibly fatal results.

On most Scottish mountains there is some sort of a funnel at the top of a gully, and the cornice does not overhang all the way round, leaving, perhaps, only a short, vertical wall of snow at one corner. That is the place to seek an exit. Always get the rest of the party well secured just below the cornice. There is often a hollow lip underneath which affords secure anchorage in hard, old snow. The leader can then tackle the wall. He will need both hand- and foot-holds, and may have to borrow someone's ice-axe to drive in horizontally, as an extra hold or step. The short, slater's hammer type of auxiliary axe is very useful. Climbing up the wall is then a matter of cutting holds for hands and feet and taking no undue risks. A certain amount of snow may require to be hacked away so as to make the angle easier near the top. The important thing is that the leader should be perfectly secured by the others, as cornices can always break away in slices.

A fatal error is for the leader to tackle the cornice at the end of a long run-out of rope. If he falls off he will have acquired considerable momentum when he shoots past the rest of the party, and the shock on the rope, when it tightens, may drag them all from their stances and pull out the belays. Something of this sort seems to have occurred in April 1933, on the Castle of Ben Nevis, to two English climbers of the front rank, the leader being badly injured and his second killed, as there were steep rocks some distance below.

On a few occasions cornices have been overcome by tunnelling operations. That may take many hours of hard work. On one occasion, at least, the party retreated and returned next day, when they completed the tunnel—hardly a practicable method for everyday use! Never risk an attempt to tunnel through a cornice unless you are certain that it is composed of old, compacted snow and that the weather is good and frosty. Such an attempt on a Ben Nevis cornice in the spring of 1949 resulted in the break-away of a huge slice, the party being swept down a steep gully with one fatal injury and another lesser casualty to its members.

Ridges

Snow-covered ridges offer exhilarating, sporting and variegated routes. Ridges which are narrow and difficult as summer rock climbs are usually still more difficult, and often impossibly so, in hard, winter conditions. The chief difficulties can be discussed under three headings: a thin film of ice on the rocks, known as *verglas* in the Alps; ice or icy crust on the crest or flanks of the ridge; cornices projecting from the ridge on either or both sides. Double cornices are exceedingly uncommon on Scottish ridges.

Very little need be said about *verglas*. It is an exceedingly dangerous condition, as the film is too thin for steps to be cut in it, and usually consists of dense, black ice. It is found when ridges have been strippeed of snow by a thaw wind, wetted with rain and refrozen. Steep rocks and ridges are best avoided under such conditions. If the rocks are only partially iced and are mainly covered with snow-ice, well frozen to the rock, careful climbing and strict security measures, using rock belays, are essential.

On very narrow ridges, like the Cuillin in Skye, the crest may be a mass of ice, where there are *gendarmes* or rock towers which are usually climbed over in summer. The only alternative is then to descend and traverse the flank of the ridge. This may involve a lot of difficult step cutting in ice before the crest can be regained. In difficult spring conditions this is commonly found on the ridges of Ben Nevis. The rocks are often thickly encased in frost crystals, which must be cut away before holds and belays can be excavated. Such conditions can make the Tower and Observatory Ridges of Nevis exceedingly difficult and exciting expeditions, suitable only for a team of experts.

Cornices are a problem only on very narrow ridges such as the Cuillin, Aonach Eagach and a few places on other mountains. Double cornices are said to have been found on the Aonach Eagach (Glencoe), but I have not experienced them there myself. Wherever there is reason to suspect the existence of a cornice the party must keep well back from the corniced edge. They may have to get off the crest altogether and traverse below it on the other side. The important thing to remember is that, if the cornice does break away, the line of fracture may be as far back as where the line of the steep snow slope below the cornice, when produced upwards, would cut the top snow surface. That may be some distance behind the overhanging edge. The safe procedure is always to anchor one member of the party in an absolutely secure position while the others are moving. Scottish snow is tough, except under conditions of a spring thaw, but precautions ought to be taken. If someone does fall through the cornice unexpectedly it may be necessary for the next person on the rope to jump down the other side of the ridge in order to save him.

Steep ridges can also be difficult after a considerable fall of dry, powder snow, which has not adhered to the old snow or rock beneath. Knowledge of the summer rock structure will be a good guide as to whether this powder snow is likely to slide off or not, but proper belaying measures are always essential in such places. A typical case is the Eastern Traverse round the Great Tower on Ben Nevis. Snow builds up in winter above some lower ledges until it lies against the upper cliff at a very steep and terrifying angle. Unless the snow is powdery and uncompacted it is, however, usually safe. The ledges form a good, incut base.

Traversing easy ridges under snow conditions is splendid practice for acquiring good snow technique. The party may not require to be roped at all. In most other cases, where the use of rope is advisable, the party can still move all together, and proper security measures can be taken, just as for narrow ridges on rocks. Sometimes rock holds can be used, but usually the ice-axe can find a lodgment between the rocks.

Steep Ice

Ridges and gullies vary considerably in gradient and are liable to contain vertical steps. If there is a sufficient stretch of gully at a gentle angle below the steep pitch, a winter snowfall may fill up the pocket completely until no pitch remains. For this reason No. 2 Gully on Ben Nevis offers a good, difficult winter climb, with no severe section or much alteration in gradient throughout, although it has one severe pitch in summer, when free of snow. Gullies can be more difficult in early winter, before there has been enough snowfall, for the same reason. Steep pitches on ridges are seldom or never marked in this way by accumulations of snow. There is too much wind. That is why ridges are usually much more difficult in snow conditions. The difficulty is at a maximum when the ridge has been partially cleared of snow by a thaw, followed by a spell of frosty weather. Conditions are even worse if a dry snowfall covers the icy surface.

All sorts of intermediate conditions are found according to the prevalent type of winter. It is therefore an essential part of winter climbing technique in Scotland to learn how to deal with steep ice. A common and very beautiful condition is encountered when all the rocks are heavily plastered with fog or frost crystals. This condition is more awesome than menacing, for the crystals are often easily detachable, leaving clean rock holds underneath. Fog crystals grow by vapour condensation on cold rocks, building up against the flow of the prevailing wind. They are normal on Scottish mountains in winter and may attain to huge dimensions.

Let us consider a steep ice pitch in a gully. The angle may not be far short of vertical. Hard snow-ice can lie in Scottish gullies at angles up to fifty-five degrees or so. I have verified this on different mountains with a clinometer.* The clear ice may lie at any angle, as it has been built up after a thaw by a trickle of water. Every safeguard is necessary when climbing steep ice, as there is seldom enough depth to get a satisfactory belay, even with the pick of the axe. The best plan is to bring up the rest of the party to the highest good anchorage where the axes can be deeply fixed for a secure belay. They should all reinforce each other, so that, if the leader falls and pulls out or breaks one ice-axe, the others will hold. A body belay can be used, but it offers no advantage as compared with the direct belay over the axe. The leader will find that the short axe is exceedingly useful. It gives him a secure hold with one axe whilst he is cutting holds, often above his head, with the other.

Cutting up steep ice is a very slow business. Steps and holds must be well fashioned and well spaced at very short intervals. The position is trying, and the leader may have to retire more than once for a rest, or the lead be changed. Blows of the axe have little force above the head of the leader, and ice is often brittle. Rhythm and balance are keys to success. If the pitch is a long one—over twenty feet—ice *pitons* could be inserted for security. I have found that nine- to twelve-inch lengths of half-inch (outside diameter) steel conduit tube, such as is used for enclosing electric wiring, buffed sharp at one end, make excellent pegs for the purpose. They can be driven well in at a suitable angle, not too far off the vertical, and the rope can be slipped through a removable ring hanging on the peg. If one is very particular it is easy to drill a couple of holes opposite each other near the blunt end of the tube, through which a stout cross-wire can be fitted to prevent the ring sliding upwards and off the peg when the rope suffers a jerk. Such things are easy to carry and to replace.

A long run-out of rope may be necessary for climbing an ice-fall of this nature in a gully. The leader must finish the pitch and arrive at a secure anchorage with a good belay, either on rock or in deep, secure snow-ice, before bringing on the other

* *Snow Angles.* Zero Gully, Ben Nevis, April 1936. Below great ice-pitch 40° rising to 47°. Upper part below an ice-pitch, uniformly 56° for a long way. Final section under summit 51°. Centre post of Coire Ardair 42° low down, 48° below the basin underneath great pitch, 55° at foot of ice wall, over 70° on the wall. No one has yet climbed this wall (March 1948).

members of the party. If the side walls of the gully are coated with frost crystals it is worth while to cut them away, wherever there is any prospect of discovering a crack which might serve as a belay for an ice-axe. Knowledge of the gully in summer conditions can be very useful. A leader negotiating an ice pitch must be sure of his holds and must think out his movements in advance. If he trusts entirely to one hold at any one time he cannot hope to correct a slip by grabbing something else. I have known an ice wall of fifteen feet in height which took over an hour to climb, and another case where a traverse across thirty feet of ice wall occupied nearly an hour and a half.

The same type of problem is encountered on vertical steps of a ridge, except that one is likely to be able to make more use of rock belays. One may also start up a snow slope which gradually steepens to ice, below a wall of cliff which one must circumvent. The final stage below the cliff is often broken up by outcrops of rock. The utmost use should be made of these for stances or belays. Fairly steep rocks may become coated with snow, partly thawed and refrozen, so as to yield a surface up which one may cut steps. It is a fascinating problem to convert known summer rock routes into practicable, if severe, winter climbs.

It is extremely difficult for a solitary climber to check a slip on hard ice. It can only be done by immediate action. Throw yourself on your face, with pick of axe biting vertically into the ice, with all your weight on it. If the pick is sharp and it can be maintained in position you have a chance of stopping. Try it out first on a safe slope, or with someone else holding you at a rope's end.

Descent

Every climber should learn how to descend steep snow, and occasionally to descend short ice pitches which have already been ascended by the party. The general plan of descent is much the same as for difficult rocks. The expert descends last and his second in command acts as pathfinder, with the additional duty of seeing that any novice in the party secures himself at each stance, if the party is moving one at a time. The pathfinder must test the condition of the snow as he goes. There will be no question of persisting in a way of descent if there is any doubt about the security of the snow. This cannot, in all cases, be judged from above, and it is not sufficient to throw a stone into a gully in order to see whether it will start a snow slide or not. Less experienced parties, on this account, should either descend by the way they came up, or choose a way which is known to be safe from former experience. The first of these is the most educative plan. It is the best way to learn how to descend steep snow.

The steps used for the ascent can be utilized for the descent. If there is time available it is even better to cut a fresh staircase downwards. Every ambitious climber must learn to cut steps downhill. This involves a difficult balance and, in general, one-handed cutting. More blows will be required per step, as the force expended is less. It is usually necessary to cut downwards in a zig-zag, and it is well to cut an extra large stance at each corner. The last man must descend very carefully. It is always best to face outwards for the descent. With a zig-zag staircase it is at least possible to face sideways. Security measures are the same as for climbing up. Only in the case of a steep ice pitch would it be advisable for the last man to drive in a peg and descend with the safeguard of the rope from above, or by means of the doubled rope, using an extra length of line for the purpose. On ice pitches the party would have to face in if using the steps constructed for the ascent, or double rope down from a peg in other cases. Such descents are only for a united team of experts. Common prudence would forbid them altogether unless the section below the ice pitch was known to be straightforward.

On a long slope of snow-ice the labour and time taken over a descent, if no steps are available, can be greatly curtailed by lowering all but the last man on the rope for short stretches, and anchoring the members securely below. Then the last man descends as safely as possible by short steps, digging in his toes and securing himself continually with the pick of his axe struck into the slope above. If the danger of a slip is less, the whole roped party can descend continuously in this way, as there is sure to be at least one pick securely fixed at all times. This applies to an experienced party and not to novices. It is not advisable if the hard slope ends lower down above a cliff. Experience, alone, will show what method is permissible, and that is why the actual descent of steep snow-ice is so necessary a part of an all-round technique.

Glissading

If the snow slope is not steep, is in good condition and has a perfectly gentle and easy run-out lower down, glissading (or

Standing Glissade   Sitting Glissade; Braking

sliding) is the quickest and most enjoyable mode of descent. It is absolutely necessary that the final run-out should either be perfectly visible or known to be easy, as control may be lost during a fast glissade. If one glissades down a gully there should be no ice pitches, or one should be absolutely certain of being able to stop before reaching one. Neither should there be any ice-hardened avalanche runnels, where one would lose control. If the snow is too hard frozen no glissade ought to be attempted at all.

The standing glissade is far the best and easiest to control in good snow. The position is erect, with flexibility at the knees, in order to preserve balance when the surface is uneven and the speed varies accordingly. One foot has a slight lead, taking more of the weight, but the feet are kept fairly close together. Pace is regulated by digging in the heels for slowing up and pointing the toes downward to accelerate. The axe is not a prop for leaning on. It is used for steering, and as an emergency brake. Change of direction can usually be effected by the feet, and by altering the distribution of weight between them. Furrowed snow is difficult. Lean back slightly and use the axe a little more. Be very careful in gullies, especially if they narrow at any point, for there may be hard snow-ice at the narrows. If control is lost at such a place the climber may be flung helplessly on his back.

Sitting glissades may be possible when the snow is not good

enough for a standing glissade. If the snow piles up underneath, a sideways roll will get you started again. Do not use the axe pick as a brake. Grip the shaft by the head with one hand and a bit lower down with the other. Press the spike backwards and downwards into the snow for steering or braking. Arch the body upwards between heels and axe for maximum braking power. If control is lost there is still some hope of regaining it if one turns face down and tries to brake with the full weight pressing the pick of the axe into the snow, but not too abruptly, or the axe may be wrenched sideways or lost altogether. That is one reason why axe shafts are made oval in section.

Experience of glissading on one mountain and during one season is valuable for technique, but does not give all-round knowledge of possible Scottish snow conditions on other mountains or after a different kind of winter. The only safe plan is to keep the speed within control at all times. I learned this myself, with a few bruises and more good fortune, after a good many years of climbing. Roped glissading by a party is seldom satisfactory.

Remember that it is possible to start a snow slide or minor avalanche in a gully by glissading, where a slow, step-wise descent would be quite safe. The only good advice, in such a mishap, is to try and keep on the surface of the descending mass of snow. Adopting a swimming position is said to be best, but I have no personal experience of riding Scottish avalanches. If there is a gentle run-out the avalanche will come to rest of itself, but it may be much compressed and refrozen. I know of no Scottish records of climbers being buried in such cases, but I should imagine, from certain huge mounds of avalanche debris below certain gullies, that the risk is there. Dry, powder snow is not a serious hazard in Scotland. It is the wet snow avalanches, with or without falling cornices, during a heavy spring thaw, that are the real danger. Avoid gullies at such times.

Some Alpine climbers assert that Scottish avalanches are innocuous. They can be referred to the story of the "Loss of Gaick", when five persons were killed by an avalanche in January 1800. This avalanche came down a steep hillside during the night and destroyed the hut in which the men were sleeping. Accidents are not uncommon, however, and four people were carried down by an avalanche on an open hillside near Braemar, in January 1948.

INDEX